SOUNDS IN SPACE,
SOUNDS IN TIME

SOUNDS IN SPACE, SOUNDS IN TIME

Projects in Listening, Improvising and Composing

by Richard Vella

with additional topics by Andy Arthurs

First published in 2000 as
Musical Environments, A Manual for Listening, Improvising and Composing
by Currency Press Pty Limited
PO Box 2287, Strawberry Hills NSW 2012 Australia
enquiries@currency.com.au
www.currency.com.au

This edition published in 2003 by
Boosey & Hawkes Music Publishers Limited
295 Regent Street, London W1B 2JH
www.boosey.com

Book design and layout by Alzbeta Totova
Cover design by Lynette Williamson

CONTENTS

THE PROOF IS IN THE LISTENING

What is creative music? First of all, it is a way of saying things which are personal to the individual. It also implies the freedom to explore chosen materials... It is essentially an experimental situation.

John Paynter and Peter Aston*

1 WHO IS IT FOR?

In an age when musical experiences and musical traditions are so diverse, a challenge for the music educator has been to develop musical thinking and understanding applicable to differing musical styles and contexts. *Sounds in Space, Sounds in Time* discusses and explores music and sound in terms of spatial models, while acknowledging musical and cultural diversity.

Sounds in Space, Sounds in Time is a secondary and tertiary level resource for class use. It emphasises improvisation, listening and composition as a way of developing both the creative and conceptual skills needed for music-making and understanding relationships between sounds. The book does not rely on an assumed knowledge or a required level of musical competency. Due to its non-specialist approach, students and lay readers from almost any walk of life, *including both professional and amateur musicians*, will find this book useful, as will music teachers working in other fields such as primary and instrumental music. Many of the concepts discussed in these pages have relevance beyond composers, musicians and teachers; for example sound designers, architects, sound mixers, sound producers, film makers and screenwriters.[†]

2 HOW THIS BOOK WORKS

Sounds in Space, Sounds in Time is a manual for creative music-making via improvisation, listening and composition. The creative music-making and listening exercises are organised around themes of sound and texture.

Part 1 of the book examines different applications of sounds in space. We listen to the environment, explore making sounds in space, appreciate the migration of sounds around geographical space, experience the sensations of register shift, delve into the nature of sounds in enclosed space, such as a violin's resonating chamber; and explore the sounds that can be made at different locations on an instrument, the body or a piece of material.

---

[*] John Paynter and Peter Aston, *Sound and Silence: Classroom Projects in Creative Music*, Cambridge: Cambridge University Press, 1970 p.7.

[†] *Sounds in Space, Sounds in Time* is the result of a general music education course (delivered between 1992 and 1996) which was housed within the School of Mathematics, Physics, Computing and Electronics at Macquarie University in Sydney. The course was open to anyone wishing to study music at tertiary level and included students from the humanities, economics and science streams. It relied on listening and improvisation as a means of understanding musical concepts and generating material.

There are large number of books existing on creative music education. The books significant to *Sounds in Space, Sounds in Time* are acknowledged in the text of this introduction.

Part 2 examines sounds in time. Here music is discussed in terms of abstract perceptual models based on texture in which the placement of sounds within each model requires different listening strategies. These are analogous with the way individuals and communities express their relationships with each other and their environments. In a sense, Part 1 deals with sounds in the physical space whereas Part 2 is more abstract, dealing with types of musical spaces. Part 3 deals with approaches and techniques commonnly used in composition.

Structurally *Sounds in Space, Sounds in Time* consists of seven modules, each module containing three chapters. Each chapter introduces new concepts, activities, improvisations, listening examples and a discography for further listening. The listening lists provide a valuable resource to which teachers may add their own examples. While it is possible to use the improvisation exercises separately, they and the composition exercises are linked to the listening programme. Their purpose is to develop musical intuition, literacy and sensibility.

Throughout the book Special Topics, written either by Andy Arthurs or myself, provide historical contexts, terminology, musical facts, items of interest and more specialised technical knowledge. Readers are invited to dip into these independently of the course structure.

STRUCTURE OF THE BOOK

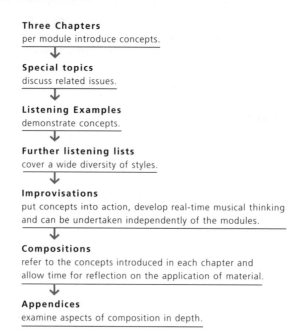

Three Chapters
per module introduce concepts.

Special topics
discuss related issues.

Listening Examples
demonstrate concepts.

Further listening lists
cover a wide diversity of styles.

Improvisations
put concepts into action, develop real-time musical thinking
and can be undertaken independently of the modules.

Compositions
refer to the concepts introduced in each chapter and
allow time for reflection on the application of material.

Appendices
examine aspects of composition in depth.

A course based on this book should allocate at least a one-hour class session per chapter. Ideally, an independent improvisatory programme would run simultaneously with these listening and composition exercises, and so construct a sophisticated course on creative musical thinking. However, if this is not possible, the teacher could break the programme into sections alternating between clusters of improvisation sessions in which the improvisation exercises at the end of each chapter are included, and classes based on the modules.

3 THE ROLE OF COMPOSITION AND IMPROVISATION

This book has been conceived from a composer's point of view – fundamentally a sensory approach to the creation and ordering of sounds. As soon as sounds are placed next to each other, the listener automatically invents relationships between the sound events and therefore meaning. *Sounds in Space, Sounds in Time* does not provide rules for composing; but it equips the student to discover processes needed to implement and develop ideas. The composition projects at the end of each module enable the listener to devise and implement larger structures based on the concepts introduced in each module.

The process of composition can be summed up as design, implementation, testing and revision. It is fundamentally intuitive and often non-sequential; usually composers are unable to tell what order a creative process has taken until it is over. There are no rules for composition: the choice of one sound following another is often discretionary. The creative process involves a set of skills such as pattern recognition, analysis, conceptualisation, experimentation, categorisation, variation and selection. All these require different ways of thinking, a finely tuned judgement of when to act analytically, intuitively or randomly, and even time to unravel one's own creative process.

While the compositions at the end of each module allow the student to address a specific musical problem over a period of time, the improvisation exercises explore spontaneous approaches to musical thinking.* By exploring musical concepts in real time, the user should develop a sense of musical thinking based on doing. The 'doing' informs the 'thinking' and the 'thinking' informs the 'doing'. Learning intensifies when the student actively engages with the material.

Anything can be used as a basis for improvisation because the process is as important to improvisation as the outcome. The starting point could be a tune or a chord progression, or other stimuli such as speaking, singing or laughing; or even tapping a table or bouncing a ball! A more detailed discussion of improvisation is given in Improv Break: Teaching Strategies for Improvisation (page 99).

4 THE LISTENING EXAMPLES

In *Sounds in Space, Sounds in Time* no preference is given to any particular musical style. Musical examples have been selected from pop, rock, blues, jazz, contemporary, medieval, world musics, classical and folksong repertoires.

The important work of ethnomusicologists has shown that one type of music cannot be explained in terms of another.[†] Each musical tradition has its own benchmarks, language and cultural references. For example, an Aboriginal song, performed as part of a special rite, would have a completely different meaning for the participants in the ceremony from a non-Aboriginal person listening to a recording. The song to the Aboriginal people might be highly symbolic with particular relevance to location, mythology and their relationship to the world. The listener with the recording might not be aware of these references and would most likely listen to the music through a different set of references based on his or her own experiences. The gap that exists between different musical cultures is a problem that can only begin to be addressed by studying and performing the music

* An important discussion on attributes of musical thinking can be found in Howard Gardner's book, *Frames of the Mind: The Theory of Multiple Intelligences,* New York: Basic Books, c. 1985.
† See *The Anthropology of Music*, Allan P. Merriam, Illinois: Northwestern University Press, 1964, Ch.1.

of other people's cultures. While this book does not attempt to bridge these cross-cultural gaps, it proposes generic listening strategies that involve the perception of patterns and structures. The composition, improvisation and listening exercises form the basis for the development of musical thinking and perception via texture. The student is thus equipped to transfer these perceptions into his or her own work.

5 TEXTURE, TIME, SPACE AND MUSICAL PERCEPTION

In *Sounds in Space, Sounds in Time* texture is discussed in terms of time and space, and the relationship between these two is fundamental to the book's strategy. Music is a temporal art and requires time to be understood. Akin to this is the spatial dimension of music. Space does not have to be visual: there are also sensory, acoustic and emotional spaces. Sounds exist in time and their relationship to each other can either be homogenous, meaning perceived as belonging to the same time-space continuum, or heterogeneous, perceived as involving more than one time-space continuum. A musical texture is a sonic environment. As in any environment, a unique combination of forces, elements and parameters are held in a delicate balance, and a noticeable change to any one may affect the whole environment. This book explores musical textures in terms of time and space.

The perception of texture and musical events falls within the domain of music cognition, a complex field of study that draws together the two disciplines of music and psychology.[*] Cognition is largely concerned with the way that the listener perceives musical structures, differentiates and organises sonic information, remembers, predicts and rejects musical events, internalises larger formal structures, and creates relationships between sounds. The concepts used in *Sounds in Space, Sounds in Time*, common to books on music cognition and perception, include the discussion of textures as hierarchical or non-hierarchical environments; the use of perceptual terms such as listening, focus and streaming; foreground, middleground and background layering; temporal processes such as repetition, closure and succession; transformation and abstract processes such as recontexualisation and generic pattern recognition.[†]

6 PRECEDENTS

Of course no book is written in isolation and many writings on creative music education exist. While *Sounds in Space, Sounds in Time* was originally written from my perspective as a composer, it will be apparent that it has synthesised various theoretical approaches, consciously or unconsciously, into this stand-alone manual. Three important predecessors are *Sound and Silence* by the English educators and composers John Paynter and Peter Aston; and *Ear Cleaning* and *Composer in the Classroom* by the Canadian educator and composer R. Murray Schafer.[‡] Crucial to their work is the notion that musical composition and/or improvisation provides a valuable insight into understanding musical structure.

---

[*] An excellent collection of essays on music cognition can be found in 'Music and Psychology: A Mutual Regard', Stephen McAdams (issue editor) in *Contemporary Music Review*, Vol 2, Part 1, London: Harwood Academic Publishers, 1987.

[†] A more detailed discussion on some of these concepts can be read in Mary Louise Serafine, *Music as Cognition: The Development of Thought in Sound*, New York: Columbia University Press, 1998, Ch.3.

[‡] John Paynter and Peter Aston, *Sound and Silence: Classroom Projects in Creative Music*, Cambridge: Cambridge University Press, 1970; R. Murray Schafer, *Ear Cleaning: Notes for an Experimental Music Course*, Ontario: BMI Canada Ltd, 1967; R. Murray Schafer, *Composer in the Classroom*, Toronto: BMI 1965.

Two important influences in the areas of music perception and texture were *The Art of Listening: Developing Musical Perception* by Jeanne Shapiro Bamberger and Howard Brofsky and *Sound Structure in Music* by Robert Erickson.* *The Art of Listening* provided some important concepts for the discussion of listening strategies in Module 6.

Other philosophies and theories which have informed this book can be found in the pioneering work of Emile Jaques-Dalcroze, and Karl Orff in their use of improvisation;† the concept of hierarchical layers found in the theories of the German theorist Heinrich Schenker; and the musical aesthetics of the American composer John Cage.

A word must be said about the Australian context. There have been many successful education programmes in creative music-making in schools over the past 30 years. A look through the various journals published since 1969 such as the Australian Journal for Music Education (AJME), Australian Society for Music Education (ASME) and the Australian Association for Research in Music Education (AARME) conference proceedings show many examples of creative uses of improvisation and composition in the classroom. Many Australian composers in the 1970s used improvisation and composition as a basis for music education. These included Don Kay (Tasmanian Conservatorium of Music), David Ahern (Sydney College of Arts), Martin Wesley-Smith (Sydney Conservatorium of Music), Malcolm Fox (Elder Conservatorium of Music, Adelaide).

Finally, three further acknowledgements must be made: *Music Now: A Discovery Course for Secondary Students*, Geoffrey R. D'Ombrain, Melbourne, Cassell Australia, 1969; the pioneering work of the Music Department of La Trobe University (1975-99) and the Melbourne State College of Education (1969-82), both in Victoria.

---

* Jeanne Shapiro Bamberger and Howard Brofsky, *The Art of Listening: Developing Musical Perception*, 3rd edn, New York: Harper and Row, 1975; Robert Erickson, *Sound Structure in Music*, Berkeley and Los Angeles, California: University of California Press, 1975.

† A summary of the work of these pioneers can be found in Beth Landis and Polly Carder, *The Eclectic Curriculum in American Music Education: Contributions of Dalcroze, Kodály and Orff*, Beth Landis and Polly Carder (eds), Virginia: Music Educators National Conference, 1972.

7 ACKNOWLEDGMENTS

I would like to thank Boosey & Hawkes Music Publishers, especially Sara-Lois Cunningham; Katharine Brisbane, Harriet Parsons, Victoria Chance from Currency Press; ABC Radio: Lorna Lander; ABC Classics: Robyn Ravelich and The Listening Room; Queensland University of Technology (QUT): Professor Andy Arthurs, Jason Zadkovich; The Ten Tenors; The Elision Ensemble: Daryl Buckley.

I would also like to thank the composers and artists who allowed me to use excerpts from their music and work: Andy Arthurs, Ros Bandt, Brigid Burke, Phillip Chambon, Jim Denley, Jon Drummond, Monique Eichperger, John Encarnaçao, Andreé Greenwell, Robert Iolini, Herb Jercher, Elena Katz-Chernin, Graeme Leak, Liza Lim, Rainer Linz, Manrae, Raffaele Marcellino, Trevor Pearce, Edward Primrose, Alistair Riddell, Rik Rue, Greg Schiemer, Amanda Stewart, Greg White, Jason Zadkovich.

Finally, a very special thank you is given to the composers Jon Drummond, Greg White, John Encarnaçao and Adrian Luca who helped me teach and test the ideas of this book at Macquarie University in Sydney.

EDITOR'S NOTE

Sounds in Space, Sounds in Time refers to a large range of music from different periods, cultures and genres. We have attempted as far as possible to treat all the references uniformly as follows:

- The titles of musical compositions such as symphonies, concerto, operas and cantatas are given with maximal capitalisation
  For example: Mozart's Sonata in C, K545

- Those with specific non-musical titles are italicised
  For example: *The Flying Dutchman.* John Cage's *4'33"*

- Popular titles stemming from the composer are therefore italicised
  For example: Beethoven's *Pastoral Symphony*

- Popular titles which do not stem from the composer are put in quotation marks
  For example: Haydn's 'Surprise' Symphony

- Parts of works are also put in quotation marks
  For example: 'Sinous' from Rik Rue's *Water Works*

- Songs are put in quotation marks
  For example: 'This Old Man'

- Record albums are italicised
  For example: *Are You Experienced?*

In the case of works which are not songs but distinctly belong to a particular compilation, the track is treated as a part of a larger work, the album collection, and therefore put in quotation marks. For example: 'Revolution No. 9'.

- Recordings given in the Further Listening lists are presented in the following order: artist, title of the piece, album title, followed by the record label and year in brackets. For example: Ros Bandt, 'Cymbal and Water', *Improvisations in Acoustic Chambers* (Move 1979).

PART 1
SOUNDS IN SPACE

TUNING THE EARS

The world around us is full of sounds to which we decide to listen or not.
Listening skills like many other skills require development and refining.
Module 1 discusses various approaches to listening, our expectations of music
and different aspects of the music-making process.

CHAPTER 1	What is Music?
Key concepts or themes	Defining music
Special Topics	1 The Futurists' Future
	2 Two Big Noises: Beethoven and Hendrix
Improvisations	

CHAPTER 2	Who's Asking?
Key concepts or themes	The listening process
Special Topics	1 Film Sound Tracks
	2 Sound or Music?
Improvisations	

CHAPTER 3	Tuning the Ears
Key concepts or themes	Types of listening
Special Topics	1 Sound and Silence
	2 4'33" by John Cage (1952)
	3 Sound Walks
Improvisations	

Composition Project 1

1 WHAT IS MUSIC?

> If one group accepts the sound of the wind in the trees as music and another does not, or if one group accepts the croaking of frogs and the other denies it as music, it is evident that the concepts of what music is or is not must differ widely.
>
> Alan P. Merriam[1]

1 MUSIC IS... (FIRST VERSE)

Music is part of our everyday lives. You can hear it in shopping malls, on the radio, in the car, in restaurants and lifts, at a concert, coming out of a window while walking down the street. We talk about music, sing it, listen to it and play it. Very rarely do we actually ask, 'What is music and what do we mean by music?'

The *Macquarie Dictionary*, published in Australia, gives seven definitions for music:

> 1 an art of organising sound in significant forms to express ideas and emotions through the elements of rhythm, melody, harmony and colour. 2 the tones or sounds employed, occurring in a single line (melody) or multiple lines (harmony). 3 musical work or compositions for singing or playing. 4 the written or printed score of a musical composition. 5 such scores collectively. 6 any sweet, pleasing or harmonious sounds or sound: the music of waves. 7 the appreciation of or responsiveness to musical sounds or harmonies.

Each of these definitions describes an aspect of music but none of them defines the whole. It is an approach much like the story of the blind men defining an elephant by touch. The first describes the 'art' of music and offers a narrow interpretation of composing limited to four elements: rhythm, melody, colour and harmony; the second describes its materials: tones and sounds in one of two forms: simultaneously (harmony) or in progression (melody); the third describes it in a potential form, as the 'work' removed from the context of generated sound; the fourth and fifth, the score and the repertoire, describe the visual representation of this potential sound in the form of notation; and the sixth limits music to a particular quality of sound. The seventh at least faces up to the challenge of defining what music really is, but its answer – which boils down to 'you'll know it when you hear it' – is the least helpful definition of them all.

Do any of these definitions adequately describe Alistair Riddell's *Black Moon Assails*?

Listening Example 1: *Black Moon Assails*, Alistair Riddell (1985)
This musical example utilises a computer linked to an old piano sound board.

Perhaps the terms 'sweetness', 'harmonious' or 'pleasing' from definition 6 are not relevant here. Definition 3 may seem appropriate but, who is doing the activity: the computer, the musician or both? The composer, Alistair Riddell, writes about *Black Moon Assails*:

> This improvisation, performed through the interaction between a microcomputer and the remnant of an acoustic piano, explores the resonant characteristics of the instrument and its 24 wound bass strings.[2]

We need more definitions or another way of thinking about this activity of music. The quotation by Alistair Riddell informs us that his musical composition is a result of a series of actions either human or non-human (the computer).

2 CAN I QUOTE YOU ON THAT?

The following descriptions show the diverse use of the word 'music'.[3] What is each speaker trying to say? Is the quotation telling you about music, what it can do or something else? Decide what each one is saying, with reference to the context, background and motivation of the writer. Can you group the quotations into categories?

1 Music is the medicine of a troubled mind. Walter Haddon

2 *Music is well said to be the speech of angels. Thomas Carlyle*

3 Music hath charms to sooth a savage breast. William Congreve

4 *You just pick a chord, go twang, and you've got music. Sid Vicious*

5 Music is a safe kind of high. Jimi Hendrix

6 *If music be the food of love, play on. William Shakespeare.*

7 If the word 'music' is sacred and reserved for eighteenth and nineteenth-century instruments, we can substitute a more meaningful term: organisation of sound. John Cage

8 *All music is nothing more than a succession of impulses that converge towards a definite point of repose. Igor Stravinsky*

9 Music is the arithmetic of sound as optics is the geometry of light. Claude Debussy

10 *Music is a sublime art precisely because, unable to imitate reality, it rises above ordinary nature into an ideal world, and with celestial harmony moves the earthly passions. Gioacchino Rossini*

11 Music tells no truths. P.J. Bailey

12 *A distinguished philosopher spoke of architecture as frozen music, and his assertion caused many to shake their heads. We believe this really beautiful idea could not be better reintroduced than by calling architecture silent music. Johann Wolfgang von Goethe*

13 A piece of music is simply a chink of time you are simply paying attention to with your ears. Barney Sanford Childs

14 *A method of employing the mind without the labour of thinking at all. Samuel Johnson*

15 Music is a kind of counting performed by the mind without knowing what it is counting Gothfried Leibniz

16 *Mathematics is music for the mind; music is mathematics for the soul. Anonymous*

17 Music is a complex of activities, ideas and objects that are patterned into culturally meaningful sounds recognised to exist on a level different from secular communication. Anonymous

18 *Music is the incorporeal entrance into the higher world of knowledge which comprehends mankind but which mankind cannot comprehend. Ludwig van Beethoven*

19 Music never expresses the phenomenon, but only the inner nature, the in-itself of all phenomena, the will itself. Arthur Schopenhauer

20 *Music is your own experience, your thoughts, your wisdom. If you don't live it, it won't come out of your horn. Charlie Parker*

21 Music is ... well I know it's better than working in Ford's. Ian Dury

22 *Music is an organisation of sounds which is intended to be listened to. R. Murray Shafer*

23 Music – that no one knows what it is – and the less he knows what it is, the nearer it is to music. Charles Ives

Some of these quotations tell you about our expectations of music, others about its structure or the experience of music. For example, number 1 positions music in a therapeutic context whereas number 8 adopts a functional view, reducing it to a series of sounds in time. It is very easy to fall into the trap of making generalisations based on one's own experiences and to forget that someone else may have a completely different response. The lesson to learn is that it is important not to make all music fit one's own definition, but rather find a definition for, or understand the context of, the music one is listening to.

Activity 1
Using only the quotations from section two, create a conversation between two or three people representing different points of view.

Listening Example 2: *The Sink*, Graeme Leak (1992)
All the sounds in this example are derived from kitchen implements, such as a sink, a running tap, a frying pan and a container of rice. They have been combined to create an exciting rhythmic machine.

3 SUMMARY
Sometimes it is necessary to search deeper to understand a piece of music. One has to piece together information or delve into its history. This helps to avoid value judgements or positioning music in too narrow a set of definitions. In the next chapter, the intriguing question of music and its meaning is developed further.

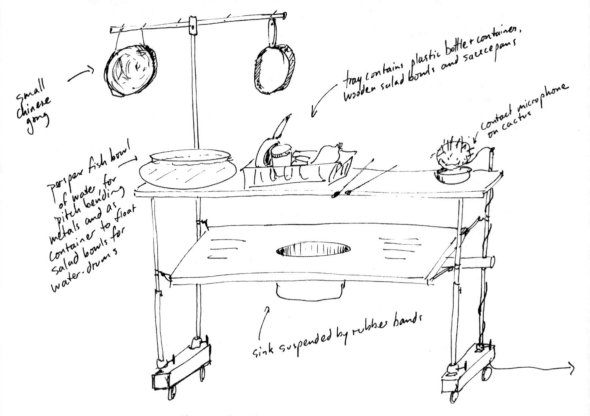

Figure 1: The Sink, *Graeme Leak's portable percussion unit.*

Special Topic 1
The Futurists' Future
Listen ... The Music of Life is All Around Us.

Music is not immune to social and political upheavals. The Industrial Revolution was no exception. During this period the ordered classical world of Haydn and Mozart, who mostly composed for aristocratic patrons, gave way to the more egalitarian music of Berlioz and Beethoven. Musically, the structure of tonality was also breaking down. But in no sense did it fully reflect the noise and dirt of industry, nor the human condition in which most people found themselves. It took another hundred years for that to happen.

The world is often a brutal place and bruitisme *was a movement in the early twentieth century which embraced the realism of sound. The ideas of the Futurists were encapsulated by Francesco Pratella (1880-1955) in his 'The Manifesto of Futurist Musicians' (1910). However it was Luigi Russolo (1885-1947) a Futurist painter who saw a 'great renovation of music through the Art of Noises' which would 'present the soul of the crowd, of great factories, of the railways, of the transatlantic liners, of the battleships, of the automobiles and aeroplanes'.[4] To add to the great central themes of the musical poem, the domain of the machine and the victorious kingdom of electricity, he also envisaged an orchestra of sirens, whistles, machine guns etc. The Art of Noise, a group who formed in the 1980s, was inspired by Russolo and applied the Futurist aesthetic to the popular music arena. Since then the ideas of the Futurist composers have taken a more central role. Another pioneer of noise as music, was Edgard Varèse, whose creative life spanned the twentieth century.* Ionisation *(1930-33) is notable for its use of anvils, sirens, chains and an enormous percussion section. He also wrote 'electroacoustic' scores, such as* Déserts *(1949-54) which mixed recorded sounds with acoustic instruments.*

Noise has always been an essential part of music, its anti-melodic or harmonic component, the percussion section. But the noise of a snare drum, for instance, was essentially there to supply the rhythmic element of the music. The Futurists and later evolutions of their music, in such styles as musique concrète, *made noise an integral part of the sound.*

Musique concrète came about as a result of the invention of audio recording. It suddenly made possible the manipulation of ordinary sounds through elongation, compression, pitch shifting, reversing, filtering, modulation and editing. Sounds were taken out of their everyday context and given new relevance. The intention was to make something out-of-the-ordinary out of the ordinary. Redefining the relationships between sounds also partly freed listeners from their original responses to them. The juxtaposition of sounds became one of the aesthetic foci (post-modernism's 'recontextualising'). Gesang der Jünglinge *(1955), an early 'acousmatic' piece on tape by Karlheinz Stockhausen, is an example. Eleven years later came 'Revolution No. 9' by the Beatles and 33 years later, techno.*

With the introduction of digital samplers, MIDI controllers and digital signal processors, real-time noise and sound-making (and their manipulation) have come of age. We have all become much more familiar with the sound of electronic music, thanks initially to film scores. The expanding opportunities for interaction between real-time performance, improvisation and electronic music have allowed us to throw away the strict division between pre-programmed or pre-recorded and spontaneous performance. Techno has broadened the appeal of acousmatic music, creating a new, widespread listening paradigm shift.

And in the future we shall see more new developments, much centring around new technology, particularly in the digital arts of the computer. New forms and structures will no doubt address the interactivity of this medium, new aesthetic values emerge, and over time may become accepted. There will be pioneers and followers, but the opportunities for artists will be too great to ignore. And who knows, soon we may be able to bypass the ears all together and direct music straight to the brain. A.A.

4 QUESTIONS

1 What are some of the ways people describe music?

2 Does music require a musical instrument in order to be called music?

3 Can you name a piece of music which uses sounds not played by musical instruments?

4 Does music need to have a melody?

5 Can you name a piece of music which does not have a melody?

6 Can you name two pieces of music which seem to be completely different from each other?

FURTHER LISTENING

- *Australia: Aboriginal Music, Musics and Musicians of the World Series,* (UNESCO 1992).
- *Austral Voices: For Telegraph Wires, Tuning Forks, Computer-Driven Piano, Psaltery, Whirly, Cello, Synthesizer and Ruined Piano* (New Albion 1990).
- The Beatles, 'Revolution No. 9', *The Beatles: The White Album* (Apple 1966).
- Beethoven, Piano Sonata *(Pathétique)*, Opus 13, No. 8 (1797-8).
- Jimi Hendrix, *Are You Experienced?* (Track 1967).
- Peter Jenkin, *A Day in the Life of a Clarinet* (Tall Poppies 1996).
- King Crimson, Thrakattack, (Discipline 1996). ‡
- Alistair Riddell, *The Computer Controlled Piano* (1982-87)

  http://www.alphalink.com.au/~amr/ccp-hist/.
- Karlheinz Stockhausen, *Gesang der Jünglinge* (1955-56).
- Edgard Varèse, *Ionisation* (1930-33).
- Edgard Varèse, *Déserts* (1949-54).
- *New Music for Electronic and Recorded Media* (Arch 1977).

Special Topic 2
Two Big Noises: Beethoven and Hendrix

When people don't have a word for a sound or find a piece of music irritating they often use the word 'noise'. Noise can be defined simply as unwanted sound: sound that doesn't fit in a particular context. The sound of a truck drowning out my CD player is one example of noise. Hearing music that is foreign to our experience or unfamiliar is like experiencing noise and sometimes it also sounds threatening. Two big noise-makers from the past are Ludwig van Beethoven (1770-1827) and Jimi Hendrix (1942-70). Both these musicians sent shock waves through their musical worlds. Beethoven's use of different levels of loudness is said to have led many piano teachers to forbid their students from playing the Sonata (Pathétique), Op. 13 No. 8 (1797-8), for the sake of their health. Today the Pathétique is a test piece for entry into many conservatoria. Similarly the range of sounds and techniques Jimi Hendrix introduced changed the course of guitar playing. The Jimi Hendrix sound uses distortion, feedback and recording techniques previously associated with electronic noise. R.V.

IMPROVISATIONS

These exercises are intended to develop musical thinking. It may help to record them on tape. The teacher should consult the approaches outlined in Improv Break: Teaching Strategies for Improvisation (page 99).

Start and finish the session with a free or structured improvisation:

1 Use an object that can be struck, rubbed, hit, scraped or scratched to explore all its possible sounds. Try all the surfaces. Listen to the difference between using your knuckles, the palm of your hand, a stick or your finger-tips.

2 Improvise a short solo using these found sounds. Don't think about what sound to make next; listen to the sound you are making now. If you are listening, you will always know what to do next.

3 Play or sing a short solo as fast as possible. Then do another one and another. Were there similarities? If so, do a slower one and make it as different as possible.

4 Explore the whole range of your voice including moans, buzzes, hums, screams, vowels and consonants, squeaks and whistles, nasal, chest, head, throat and salival sounds.

5 Improvise a series of short solos using found sounds, your voice or a musical instrument. If you hear patterns or repetitions, try something different: if you hear yourself repeatedly articulating short statements or gestures, try long ones. If you hear yourself making the same type of sound, try one that is completely unrelated.

2 WHO'S ASKING?

In Akan society, if someone scraped mud off a bottle with the lid of a cigarette tin, he would produce noise as a by-product. If he performed this act of scraping in the performance of ahyewa music, the sound, though similar, would have a different meaning. It would be purposeful in a musical sense.   J.H. Kwabena Nketia[5]

1 MUSIC IS... (SECOND VERSE)

As we listen to sounds, we allocate meanings to them. We need to do this for them to make sense. However, a sound might have a completely different meaning to two different people. This is why context and our relationship to the sound event are important. The process of listening has three aspects:

    1 the music itself,

    2 its context and

    3 its meaning.

The music itself includes all its auditory qualities; its context is defined by where or how the music is positioned in relation to the listener and its purpose: listening to music through a pair of headphones, for example, is a very different experience from hearing it in the concert hall; and the meaning of the music is determined by who is listening and the cultural experiences and associations of the audience.

Consider this: do you think your national anthem would have the same meaning to each of the following listeners?

    1 a tribe from a remote region who have never had any contact with your country,

    2 a group of soldiers during World War Two,

    3 you, when you were in junior school.

Conversely, do you think this music would have the same meaning for these listeners many years later? The complexity of meanings embedded in music and their relevance to different social groups is summed up by Alan P. Merriam in *The Anthropology of Music*. He argues that a universal music – one that can be understood and appreciated by any group of people in any culture – is unachievable because every cultural group assigns its own meanings and associations to the way sounds are used and heard.

2 MUSIC IS... (THIRD VERSE)

When music is viewed in these terms, one can begin to appreciate just how complex it can be. Its definition needs to take into account variables ranging from the cultural conditioning and expectations of the participants, the social function of the music and its familiarity to the listener, to the physiological factors that affect how we listen.

Sometimes the concerns that affect composing are not crucial to listening or performing. Compare it with a car race. Is watching the race the same for the spectator as the driver? The driver requires different skills from the spectator. And does the driver need to know the same things as the designer of the car?

Although the three activities of composition, performance and listening require skills and listening faculties, they are interdependant as well: musicians do play their own compositions.

The options open to composers are limitless. One might concentrate on perfecting a sound that only lasts a couple of seconds; another might be more concerned with the technical limitations of instruments or the problems of a particular sound combination; a third could set up structures purely so as to hear new sounds or combinations of sounds.

The performer's concerns tend to be physical: how to achieve a certain sound with the body. Physical limitations will determine the overall strategy for the music. In performance, detail, such as finger technique or embouchure, gives way to the interpretation of the piece, just as in everyday speech we become oblivious to the articulation of each word in favour of the larger structures such as phrases and sentences.

The listener has the luxury of taking everything in, free of the pressures of time in performance. Listeners can focus on detail or the large sound structures, making connections by free association. They can transcend time, bringing the past forward or the present into a new understanding.

The difference between composing, performing and listening was summed up in a comment by the American composer John Cage:

> Composing's one thing, performing's another, listening's a third. What can they have to do with one another?[6]

3 SUMMARY

Developing composition and performance skills can take a long time but listening skills can be learned quite quickly. In this chapter it has been shown that the meaning of the music depends on the expectations and associations of the listener. The next chapter, 'Tuning the Ears', focuses on developing structural listening and analytical skills. Instead of asking 'What does the music mean?', we concentrate on how we perceive the parts of the music to function. This is called analytical or structural listening.

Special Topic 1

Film Soundtracks
Film soundtracks can often blur the boundaries between music and sound. In some soundtracks the music and sound effects are quite distinct from one another—think of the use of orchestral music and sound effects in Lord of the Rings *for the battle and fight scenes for instance. However, in recent years, many soundtracks combine music and sound to form a more unified texture. In these soundtracks it can be meaningless to ask when the music begins and the sound ends.*

Listening Example 3: The End, Manrae (2002)
In Listening Example 3, all sounds have been carefully placed to form a total musical and auditory event. The song begins with thunder and rain sounds followed by a car windscreen wiper. Cars speed by in the wet weather and we hear a mobile phone being dialled. All these events indicate a rainy day or night and someone, inside a car, dialling a mobile. The repetition of the windscreen wipers becomes a rhythmic layer over which a bass guitar and bass recorder begin playing. The entry of the voice unifies all these events and it is now all heard together as part of a song.

Special Topic 2
Sound or Music?

In prehistory there was sound and a perceived absence of sound called silence. Women, men and particularly children and babies discovered, explored and made sounds with their mouths, throats and bodies. Drones, groans, utterances, shouts and claps would have become forms of sonic expression in communication, play and ritual.

As cultures shifted from aural to literary cultures, it became possible to write down sounds and pass them on intact from generation to generation. Over the past 1,000 years the representation of music with symbols has become an important factor in formalising and preserving music. Ironically, as a result, in some areas of authority the idea grew up that music that could not be written down was inferior. Consequently, freedom and experimentation in sound-making was often discouraged in the academies and conservatoires of earlier times.

In the twentieth century things have loosened up again thanks to the emergence of new ways of communicating sound, such as radio, television and other electronic media. We have become a more oral and aural society again – less dependent on books and writing with all their limitations. Recording has enabled us to archive sounds that were untranscribable in traditional notation. How, for instance, could the sound of a steam train have been recorded for future generations who had never experienced the real thing? And yet this sound alone has inspired hundreds of songs, ballads and sound pieces.

The twentieth century has heard a vast array of sounds included in music-making. One important addition was distortion which transforms an original sound by adding noise to it. One example is acoustic feedback which is caused by sound emanating from a public address (PA) system returning into the microphone at a louder level than the original so that a sound loop develops that increases rather than decays. Some modern sound pieces use this phenomenon in a controlled way to distort traditional aural perceptions. In the world of rock music Jimi Hendrix built his 'sound' around fantastic aural pictures created with the electric guitar and feedback.

More recently, as technology has accelerated, many new methods of recording sound have emerged. During the 1980s and 90s, the ubiquitous digital 'sound sampler' made its presence felt in popular recordings. Using a sampler, snatches of audio can be played and manipulated, in much the same way as a traditional instrument would have played and shaped the sound in a previous century.

So do we cease referring to 'music' and instead only to 'sound', or do we open our ears and minds to include in our definition of music all the sounds that the natural, mechanical, human and electronic world can offer?   *A.A.*

4 QUESTIONS

1 What are the three aspects of listening?

2 What is the difference between them?

3 Can you name a piece of music which has a different meaning for different audiences?

4 What are the differences between composing, performing and listening?

FURTHER LISTENING

- The Art of Noise, *Who's Afraid of the Art of Noise!* (Island 1986).
- *Austral Voices: For Telegraph Wires, Tuning Forks, Computer-Driven Piano, Psaltery, Whirly, Cello, Synthesizer and Ruined Piano* (New Albion 1990).
- John Cage, *Piano Concerto for Prepared Piano and Orchestra* (1958).
- Deep Forest, 'Sweet Lullaby', *Deep Forest* (Epic 1992).
- Krzysztof Penderecki, *Threnody for the Victims of Hiroshima* (1960).
- Malcolm McLaren, 'Madame Butterfly', *Fans* (Island 1984).
- Terry Riley, *In C* (1964).

IMPROVISATIONS

Start and finish the session with a free or structured improvisation.

1 Watch television with the volume turned down while listening to FM radio. Change the radio stations at random: what is the relationship between the sounds and the images created? Do the opposite: randomly change the television channels while keeping the FM radio station constant. How is this different?

2 Play a solo improvisation to an audience. Ask each listener what he or she thought was the meaning of the work. Discuss your own interpretation. Was it different from or similar to the audience's?

3 Group activity: Give a group of four performers a set of six cards each. Each person should have the same set of directions:

sing a nursery rhyme

make a noise

speak naturally

yell or scream

hum

sing a melody.

Ask the performers to shuffle their cards and perform the sounds in whatever order they appear in their decks. Start together and keep going for at least five minutes. The rest of the class should listen to the overall sound. What happens when the sounds are heard simultaneously? Does the 'meaning' of any sound change when it is heard with other sounds?

3 TUNING THE EARS

Sounds came to me through the darkness: the cries of the wind, the whisper of the trees, the voices of nature, animal sounds, the hooting of an owl.

John Fire Lame Deer[7]

In Chapters 1 and 2 it became clear just how involved a discussion on music can be. To gain a better understanding it is useful to begin by analysing the sound, construction and organisation of a piece of music within a particular context. This is called analytical listening. Holistic listening, on the other hand, involves listening to the overall sound of music with little attention to detail or structure. It must be stressed that all listening is subjective and that there is no such thing as pure objective listening. In spite of its name, all analytical listening is necessarily subjective because it starts with each listener's unique interpretation of the sound source. Furthermore, two people listening to the same sound from opposite sides of a room will hear the sound physically in different ways. This is why context is so important.

1 LISTENING AS SURVIVAL

> Breaking the silence
> Of an ancient pond
> A frog jumps into water –
> Plop.   Bashō (1644-?)[8]

There are many ways of listening to sounds and we should never underestimate our listening powers. Our survival depends upon it, as this haiku by Bashō demonstrates. Contemplating his environment, still and safe, the poet is alerted by the intrusion of a new sound. In an instant his ears determine whether it is one of danger or safety. Later he recalls the sound a frog made jumping into water and, in appreciation, he recreates it onomatopoetically: plop.

Compare the different listening strategies in the following situations:

1 It is late at night and you are alone in a house. All of a sudden you hear a crash of glass nearby followed by footsteps. Your ears prick up. You wait for a new sound to find out if you are in danger.

2 The telephone rings. You automatically pick up the receiver without thinking about the sound.

3 The telephone rings again; it is a close friend whose voice you instantly recognise.

4 You are at a party. The music is very loud and someone is talking to you. In order to understand what she is saying, you have to screen out all the surrounding sounds.

5 You are at a party telling a joke, inventing different voices for each of the characters in the story.

Listening event 1 is a highly focussed type of listening. In these situations we are actively differentiating sounds and their quality. Are the footsteps getting closer or faster? Was the broken glass in my house or nearby?

Listening event 2 is a stimulus and response event. We are conditioned to react to the sound of the telephone as if someone wants to speak to us. Although we hear the telephone ringing, we actually don't listen to the sound but rather to what it means: someone calling.

In listening event 3, we recall the subtle inflections and details of all our friends' voices and can readily recognise each of them without any introduction.

In listening event 4, in order to hear what is said we must actively screen out all unwanted sounds. This is the opposite to listening event 1, in which all sounds are heard with equal intensity.

In listening event 5, we choose which aspects of the voice quality to imitate so that the audience understands the story.

2 WATER MUSIC

Each of the following examples treats water in a distinctive way. Some use it to represent location, others as an important element of the composition. Listen to each example, carefully asking yourself: what are the roles of the water sounds and how are they used differently here from the other examples?

Listening Example 4: M'saddar, anonymous (thirteenth century)

How do you hear the role of the fountain in this example? Would you consider it one of the instruments or is it irrelevant to the instrumentation? Does it have a function in the creation of atmosphere or location? Does it provide another layer of musical accompaniment like a drone sound? Would the piece 'mean' the same without it? Do you think this combination of instruments with water is successful? Why?

Listening Example 5: 'Cymbal and Water', Ros Bandt (1979)

In this piece, the composer improvises on a metal cymbal inside a large reverberant water tank. Do you hear the water sounds in the same way as in the previous example? How is it similar and how is it different? Do you hear any interaction between the water drops and cymbal sounds or are they independent?

Listening Example 6: Water Dreams, Paul Dresher (1985)

In this example, the composer has combined water sounds from several different sources: drips, rain, pipe water, waves, lakes and rivers. Over the top of these sounds he has mixed in synthesised and acoustic sounds. Is the differentiation between the water sounds and the instrumental sounds as clear as in 'Cymbal and Water'? How do you interpret the synthesised sounds that are distinctly not water sounds? Do you hear the instrumental sounds as complementary or independent? What would happen to the piece if the water sounds or the synthesised sounds were taken out? Would it be the same piece? Do you think certain sounds have particular functions in the music: emotive, rhythmic, textural or signifying location?

In all the examples so far, the compositions have combined instruments with water sounds, but in each case their relationship has been different. Because of the individuality of the sounds used, the components and their relationship to the overall composition have not been too difficult to understand. Location and literal representation have been important – but they have not been the only components necessary in the listening process.

In the following two examples, both make reference to a river: the title of Listening Example 7, *Vltava*, is the name of a river whereas Listening Example 8, 'Sinous', uses a river as its sound source. The treatment of the subject is quite distinct in each example. How does this affect the way you listen?

Listening Example 7: *Vltava*, Bedrich Smetana (1874)

The composer has generated this instrumental work through a metaphor of the river based on his memories of the place. What aspects of the river has he explored to evoke the concept of 'river'? Clearly the instruments do not incorporate water. Is the listening process different from *Water Dreams*? If so, how is it different?

The composer has created something quite distinct from the other examples: instead of *presenting* the water sounds, he has used the instruments to *represent* these sounds. What was the composer listening to within the river's sound that has enabled him to communicate this idea to other people? How has the music become symbolic of the river and its many facets? Do you think it important to know the reference to the river to understand the music? Can you 'understand' the music without reference to the river?

Listening Example 8: 'Sinous', Rik Rue (1985)

What do you hear in this example? Can you hear any changes in the sound? Can you sing the change? Can you hear different layers of sound and their speeds? Can you hear different parts? If so, how would you describe them? Are they high, low, do they change, are they just occasionally low? After hearing this example, are you better able to describe the ways the composer of *Vltava* has created the metaphor of the river? Are you aware of your listening strategies changing now? Sometimes you might be listening to a river, other times you might become more absorbed in the internal construction of the sounds themselves.

Activity 1

1 If you have a tape recorder, record a few sounds from your house that you find interesting. Hold the microphone as close as possible to the source. It could be something very soft, such as a finger touching a table top or a tap running gently. Play the sound back. Do you hear it differently now?

2 Use your tape recorder to construct a journal of sounds you find interesting. Record the sounds so that each one is immediately followed by another: listening to your sound journal should be like looking through a photograph album.

Activity 2

Choose a location and listen to all the sounds present. The longer you listen, the more detail you will hear. Keep a journal of the sounds you hear. Go back to the same location another time. Are the sounds the same? Is anything different?

3 SUMMARY

The questions accompanying the listening examples in 'Water Music' were designed to develop your analytical listening skills. An important part of analytical listening is determining the function of one sound in relation to others in a particular context. This necessitates separating the sounds into different groups, types, categories, actions or qualities. For example, we may group them as fast or slow, soft or loud, harsh or gentle. Once all the types of sounds have been identified, it is possible to construct a model of how all these sound events relate to each other. This type of detective work is very valuable, providing important insights not just into how the music works but how we think it works and why. And like any good detective story, the better the question the better your understanding of the event. However, just as the question 'what is music' depends on who is asking, the answers analytical listening provides depend on who is listening. Ten different people could easily produce ten different interpretations of the same sound or music. It is not a question of who is right. Rather, analytical listening enables you first to distinguish details and then to relate them to each other. The more detail you can distinguish, the more complex patterns you can create and the deeper your understanding of the whole.

4 QUESTIONS

1 What are the different listening strategies we use in daily life?
2 Can a piece of music consist of only sounds?
3 Can you name two music examples which use sound in completely different ways?
4 Can you list and describe the sounds you are hearing now?
5 How are water sounds used differently in Listening Examples 4, 5, 6 and 8?
6 How does Listening Example 7, *Vltava*, refer to a river?

Special Topic 1
Sound and Silence
'Hello darkness my old friend, I've come to talk with you again'. **Simon and Garfunkel**

Sometimes the loudest sounds are the most silent of all – the distant roar of the city, waves on a beach or even formula rock or classical music played over and over on the radio. Silence is often a lack of changing sounds rather than the absence of sound. How often have you thought you were sitting somewhere silent until an air conditioner was turned off?

Was the dropping of the atomic bomb at Hiroshima a sound or a deep silence? The conductor Leonard Bernstein said that death was the overriding theme of music in the twentieth century. Ours is an era in which humans, for the first time, have the means of silencing the planet with weapons of mass destruction. Certainly artists of all disciplines have been moved by this weighty topic.

In this century we have also come to fear real silence as a threat. Shopping malls, elevators and airports, radio and television constantly substitute mind-altering noise to make good the gaps between sounds.

Does it fill the void or is it another form of silence itself? Is it like blocking our ears with our fingers and humming loudly?

Opposites are defined by each other, solids are defined by empty space and happiness by the knowledge of what it is to be sad. So it is with sound and silence. In a symphony many instruments are silent for long periods. Silence is used in music or a pause in speech as a dramatic effect, a dynamic – just as stillness is a powerful element of dance.

No one has made more conscious use of silence than John Cage. In his landmark work 4'33" (1952) an instrumentalist sits poised to play (any instrument), but never actually starts. The piece lasts four minutes and 33 seconds. You may wish to sit for this length of time and imagine the result. Listen...

Did you hear absolute silence? Of course not; unless you live in outer space, it is impossible. And this is the paradox. Take time to listen to the sounds around you: air noises, distant cars and planes, muffled voices, people breathing. Even if all these sounds were eliminated and you were sitting in a soundproofed anechoic room (an echoless room) you would still hear the sound of your blood circulating around your body. John Cage's piece has caused problems for radio broadcasters as many transmitters automatically shut down after an extended period of silence.

Real silence is only possible where energy and life itself are extinct.   *A.A.*

Special Topic 2
4'33" by John Cage (1952)

4'33" for any soloist or group of instrumentalists by the American composer John Cage (1912-92) is a landmark of twentieth-century musical aesthetics. The score has three movements, each with the instruction tacet (remain silent) and a period of time. The total of the three movements equals four minutes and thirty-three seconds. The musician or musicians enter, open their scores, prepare to play but do nothing. At the end of each movement, they adjust their seats before proceeding on to the next movement. The work caused a sensation when it was premièred. Instead of asking the audience to listen to the music as an object of reproduction, 4'33" acts like a framing device for all the sounds that fill the concert hall: people breathing and coughing, the rustle of programs, embarrassed laughter and passing cars. 4'33" questions the word 'music' by demanding that the listener abandon the strategy of screening out sounds and listen instead to all sounds as musical events and with equal intensity, not just those specified by the composer or musician.   R.V.

Special Topic 3
Sound Walks

The Canadian composer, R. Murray Schafer, devised the sound walk.[9] In this activity a map is drawn up which follows a listening path. Instead of looking for visual landmarks, such as monuments and historic places, the walker is presented with a map which introduces aural landmarks, be they human, industrial or natural. In a sense the sound walk is a composition in which the composer decides which sounds the listener is to attend to. The walk can take ten minutes or an hour. The map directions provide the details.

For example:
1 Walk down the main street to the shopping centre.
2 Stop next to the fountain on the corner.
3 Walk through the tunnel.
4 Turn right into the park and stand near the children's playground.   R.V.

FURTHER LISTENING

- Ros Bandt, 'Cymbal and Water', Improvisations in Acoustic Chambers (Move 1979).
- John Cage, Cartridge Music (1960).
- Paul Dresher, Water Dreams on Another Coast: New Works From the West (Music and Arts 1985).
- Olivier Messiaen, Quartet for the End of Time (1941).
- Rik Rue, 'Sinous', Water Works (Pedestrian Tapes 1985).*
- Karlheinz Stockhausen, Hymnen (1966-67).

IMPROVISATIONS

Start and finish the session with a free or structured improvisation.

1 Use words to describe a sound: it could be a door slam, a tap dripping or a car driving by. Try to copy the sound with your voice. What part of the sound have you copied? All of it or a particular part of it? Once you have mastered the sound, explore variations.

2 Take a piece of newspaper and slowly tear it into strips. Listen for the changes in the sound when you tear faster or slower.

3 Explore sounds made by actions usually associated with daily life. For example, dragging a chair across the floor, bouncing a ball on different surfaces or scraping different surfaces.

COMPOSITION PROJECT 1

The purpose of this exercise is to home in on your musical thinking. Record all the improvisations on a tape recorder.

Do an improvisation that lasts no more than a minute. You can use any instrument, including percussion or your voice. As soon as you finish one, start another. Continue until you have at least twenty on tape or until you feel you have completely run out of ideas.

Play back the tape. Do you find that:

1 Each solo is refining ideas from the previous one? This is a type of real-time perfection of an idea.

2 Each solo is completely different from the last? This suggests that you have a broad repertoire of material to go through before the patterns of your musical thinking will begin to show themselves.

3 Each solo is basically the same as the last one? Players tend to repeat patterns and processes of which they are unaware. Becoming aware of them will probably change the way you play next time.

If you feel you have exhausted your resources, go back and listen to each solo. Listen for similarities and differences in the way you articulated sounds, approached your instrument, used particular types of notes or sound combinations, applied speed and emotional qualities. Once you have made these observations, try something completely different – not just a variation on the original sound. For example, you may have noticed that each solo was always using the middle range of your instrument. A different approach might be to play only in the high and low ranges. Another observation might have been that you always used short soft sounds, so try using long loud sounds or a combination of long soft sounds with short loud sounds. There are infinite variations. This way you are developing your repertoire of possibilities. After exploring these variations, try another series of solos. Again, listen to the tape afterwards and observe your approach. Does this series use similar patterns or has it broadened out to include a wider range of events?

Continue this process over a period of days or weeks, and listen to the ways your musical vocabulary broadens.

THE VIBRATING SOUND

As we become more aware of the different types of sounds in our environment, we need to have a language to describe them. This module introduces a method of inquiry into the nature of sound and its basic anatomy.

CHAPTER 4 **The Sound of Music and the Music of Sound**

Key concepts or themes Describing sounds and music

Special Topics 1 Getting an Earful
2 Audio Recording
3 Sound Texts and Poetry

Improvisations

CHAPTER 5 **The Basic Parameters of Sound**

Key concepts or themes Loudness, register, duration, sound envelopes and timbre

Special Topics 1 Close, Far Away and Sounds Moving in Space

Improvisations

CHAPTER 6 **The Vibrating Sound**

Key concepts or themes Vibrations, frequency, natural frequency, amplitude, resonance and the harmonic series

Special Topics 1 Frequency, Pitch, Tuning and Scales
2 Amplification
3 The Rumble of Thunder
4 Upper Harmonics and Their Vibrations

Improvisations

Composition Project 2

4 THE SOUND OF MUSIC AND
THE MUSIC OF SOUND

Now I will do nothing but listen ... I hear all sounds running together, combined, fused or following, sounds of the city and sounds out of the city, sounds of the day and night...

Walt Whitman[10]

1 THE EARS HEAR – THE BRAIN LISTENS

While our tastes, preferences and experiences make a distinction between music, noise and sound, our eardrums do not. All sounds are received indiscriminately. Our eardrums are designed to pick up everything. Every sound event, whether it be music or noise, is heard because it radiates vibrations. Hit a gong or bell and you can feel the metal shudder with vibrations. In order for an event to be heard, it must produce repeating vibrations that disturb the air particles in the atmosphere. If there are no air particles, as in a vacuum, no sound is produced. The repeated disturbance of the air particles creates sound waves that radiate in all directions. These sound waves are similar to the expanding waves created when a pebble is dropped into water. The greater the distance from the sound source, the weaker the wave's power. Our eardrums respond to these sound waves in the same way as microphones, translating the vibrations into electrical signals which are then sent to the brain for decoding.

Because our ears are indiscriminate receptors, we have to actively make decisions about what we want to hear. Some of these were discussed in 'Listening as Survival' in the previous chapter. In order to make sense of the chaos of information streaming into our ears, we have to differentiate, decode, make relationships and group all the incoming sounds as useful, useless, meaningful and meaningless. Listening to music is a highly specialised form of categorisation, but it still requires these same skills of separation and categorisation. When we listen to a piece of music, we create meaning or sense by perceiving or constructing relationships between sounds. We establish hierarchies, focus on interesting details and ignore some events.

This is precisely what happened in the examples given in Water Music in Chapter 3. The musical examples used water sounds in completely different ways. In order to reconcile the water sounds with the instrumental sounds, the listener had to find relationships. Some of the pieces demonstrated listening in which water sounds and instrumental sounds were treated equally. In others, one took precedence over the other. The important issue was the way the sounds combined with each other.

2 QUESTIONS TO ASK A PIECE OF MUSIC

Is it high?
Is it low?
Is it in the middle?
Is it soft?
Is it loud?
Are there two?
Are there more than two?
Is it a piano?
Why isn't it?
Was it an aeroplane?
Is it a noise?
Is it music?

John Cage[11]

Asking questions leads to answers, which only leads to more questions. The questions posed by John Cage come from a lecture he gave on his musical philosophy. Using questions and quotations only, Cage interrogates and meditates upon the nature of music and the cultural expectations we place on it. This technique is similar to Socratic interrogation in which understanding is achieved through continual questioning.

The questioning process is quite simple. Each question explores all the possibilities of a particular musical concept. If something is not high, it must be low or in the middle. Defining the unknown through what is known already creates a gradual expansion of awareness. This process of finding variations, alternatives or unknown solutions is a fundamental aspect of composition and creative thinking, which is why Cage entitled his lecture 'Composition as Process'.

Another American composer, Mark Sullivan (b.1954), elaborated on Cage's text with his *Questions to Ask a Piece of Music.*

> Is it fast, slow or quickly changing in speed?
> Is one sound fast and another slow?
> Is it soft, loud, medium, or changing in loudness?
> How does the sound begin and end?
> Does it start gradually, suddenly, or something else?
> Does it fade away or end abruptly?
> Are all the sounds equally loud or can you hear some sounds further away or closer?
> Do you hear the sound's various components layered or stacked on top of each other?
> Do the various components of the sound blend or fuse together into a new unit?
> Does it swell, fall or rise?

Many of the questions posed by Cage and Sullivan make no distinction between music and sound. All sounds exist in time. Therefore, they all have a beginning, middle and end; and each sound consists of a number of smaller units which combine to produce an infinite number of possibilities. Cage and Sullivan treat music and sound as equivalent entities in shape and time. Shape and time are convenient ways of thinking about sound: they allow us to engage with sound as if it were a physical entity. When we use an onomatopoeic word, like 'bang', 'clatter' or 'whip', the word imitates the sound.

Activity 1
Say the word 'splash'. It only has one syllable – but can you hear three different components? Sp-la-sh. If you had to draw the sound of 'splash', representing the loudness and speed of each part, it could look like this:

Sounds are physical. Sometimes you could almost touch them, walk through them or throw them like a ball across the room. They are like bubbles, ephemeral and unique.

Because they exist in time, more than one can be sounding at any given moment. Our ears are highly specialised in differentiating two or more sound events at once. Sounds can occur in succession, simultaneously, mix together, overlap or erupt in a chaotic explosion.

Activity 2
If you have access to a tape recorder, record a sound with the microphone as close as possible to the sound source. It could be your finger scraping along the teeth of a comb, water dripping or a pen writing on paper. Play the sound back. Try to describe the differences you can hear between the original and the recorded sound.

Special Topic 1
Getting an Earful

The ear receives all sounds and is the auditory interface between sounds made in the physical world and their conversion into neurological impulses. The ear has three main sections called the outer, middle and inner ear. The following diagram shows the main parts of the ear.

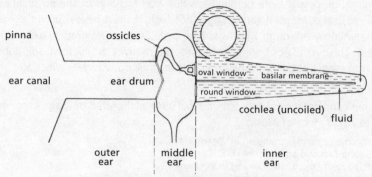

Figure 2: *The parts of the human ear.*

On reaching the external ear, sound travels down the auditory canal to the ear drum. The ear drum, like a normal drum, vibrates. These vibrations are conducted across the middle ear by the ossicles which consist of three bones called the hammer, anvil and stirrup. Passing through these bones, the vibrations pass on to the oval window, the border of the inner ear, which is a membrane sealing off the cochlea. The cochlea is filled with fluid. The vibrations from the membrane cause the fluid in the cochlea to be stimulated and transform them into waves. The fluid stimulates fine hairs on the basilar membrane of the cochlea which are connected to the nervous system. The hairs send small electrical currents to the brain which then decipher the signals as sounds.

Special Topic 2
Audio Recording
Capture Time, Chop It Up, Stick It Back Together

Writing and subsequently printing were a means to encode and capture verbal ideas and thoughts. The introduction of audio recording in the 1870s opened the door to a means of capturing sounds (emitted in time). The ramifications of this are still being felt. It played a large part in forcing us to broaden our definition of music to encompass all areas of sound. A digital computer sequencer captures the process of making sound, the actions themselves. An audio recording, on the other hand, captures the product (or result) of a sound-making process, be it a performance or a natural environment.

Audio signals can be recorded on a variety of media. Early approaches were mechanical and until the end of the 1980s, the principal method for home users to retrieve sound was through the mechanical 'record'. Magnetism (tape or hard disc) is a common way to record sound. Magnetic tape was used on a tape recorder, which was developed during World War Two. The usual materials of magnetic recording tape is rusty metal (ferric oxide) glued onto a flexible strip (often PVC). By the 1960s the Compact Cassette system started the widespread use of domestic recording. By the mid 1980s Recordable Digital Audio Tape (RDAT) was in common use. Now sound is often stored on a computer which uses magnetism to record information.

There are other methods, most notably optical, where the path of a light beam is modified to emit the waveform of the relative sound. For years this was the way most film soundtracks were stored. More recently digital recording has meant that optical storage has become

→ *increasingly popular. Using a laser light beam, very high frequency digital codes can be read and recorded. The Compact Disc and DVD use this method. Its advantage is that it is not susceptible to magnetic fields, which can partially or wholly erase the audio data.*

In non-linear, random-access computer-based recording, bites of sound can be cut, copied and pasted, just like text in a word processor. Now we can increasingly handle audio material in the same way that we think. Digital sound samplers also use this technology. They were originally devised mainly as musical instruments (such as the Fairlight CMI) but now the distinction between a sampler and a digital non-linear recording system has been blurred almost to extinction.

During the past 100 years the concept of what is authentic and what is a copy has been turned on its head. Originally a recording was a record of a live event. But now rarely is the live event considered the authentic thing. The performance has become the edited copy of the recording. The increasingly perfect copying of sound, culminating in digital 'cloning' has led to problems for the record companies of copyright infringement. This in turn leads to the question put by post-modernist theorists, 'What does "authentic" mean?'   A.A.

3 MORE QUESTIONS

Now further elaboration is possible on the questions put by Cage and Sullivan, with more questions to ask a sound.

Does it sweep up or down or stay the same?
Is it high, low, somewhere in between or a combination of all three?
Do the sounds overlap or are they distinct from each other?
Are the sounds automatically understood or do they need time to be heard completely?
Do the sounds linger, stop abruptly or end some other way?
Does it repeat?
Does it change speed?
Does it change volume?
Is it gradually or constantly changing?
Can you sing the sound or is it impossible to repeat with your voice?
Does one sound answer another or does it continue in another way?
Does one sound seem similar to another or are they completely different?
Do the sounds build on each other or gradually fade out?
Are there any pauses or silences in between sounds?
Is one sound quickly followed by another sound and even another?
If it seems heavy, dense, thick, fragile, thin, transparent, what makes it seem so?
Does it make you feel like you can walk inside or is it impenetrable?
Does it meander, tremble, shudder, repeat in changing ways?
Does it crackle? What do you mean by 'crackle'?
Is it metallic, wooden, plastic, breathy, plucking, scratching, scraping, dragging?

These questions can be used to form the basis of a musical vocabulary. They all investigate certain qualities of a sound: loudness, highness or lowness, how long its lasts, shape and 'colour' (or tone quality). The next chapter examines these qualities in more detail.

Activity 3
Return to the location you chose for the final exercise in the last chapter. Listen again to the sounds in the environment. Has your listening attention changed? Do you hear more detail than before? Write down what you hear. Compare it with what you wrote last time.

postiche

nnnnnnnnnnow
      now
      now that distance is solved
              difference resolved

      now   that you can
      now   that it isn't

              post-post p r e r
                           e f
                             o
                              r m
                                 a t i
                                     o
                                      n

              empires crumble r
                             e f
                               o
                                r
                                 m the next location

as self   the mean of generalisation in the individual's back pocket
              a reflexive net across difference a finite law within
              everything's relative in the doctrine of commodities
              post-renaiss   reconnaissance body trans
                                                     c
                                                      e n
                                                         d.
                                                          ng in a stockmart of
          re
           a lter
              i
               t y inducing abstractions cheap b
                                               an
                                                 al
                                                   it
                                                    y deducing re
                                                              duction
          for your convenience

       high above on a Plato of strategy
              an internet sky
                            channels into a privatised black hole
              a host of bob's boys r
                                    r
                                       rise
              from the ashes of socialism
              sacrificial lam whit
                                  t
                                   l
                                    e d from the consensus of mates
              born-again-bureaus meet next-to-be-business-boomers
              murd
                  ocked in a tabloid of now is a pay for the right to
              say, 'I
                    still call Aust
                                  r
                                   a
                                    l
                                     d
                                      i
                                       n
                                        g the integrated verticals of
              capitalised fate

                                                        outta here!

Figure 3: *Postiche by Amanda Stewart – refer to 'Special Topic 3'.*

4 SUMMARY

Any piece of music is made up of a series of sound events. A sound event can be anything from a clarinet note to a bird chirping or the hum of the city, someone speaking or singing, a car misfiring, an electronic ping, a slap or a dog barking. These sound events can come from any source and combine in an infinite number of ways. Sound and music converge into a celebration of listening. We should never underestimate our listening powers. Our ears can hear everything. So much information passes through our auditory system that we have to actively choose between necessary and unnecessary information. Unfortunately, if we make these decisions carelessly, we can miss the intricacy of certain sounds. Sometimes, even if we hear the complete sound, it is very difficult to describe it to someone else. Sounds, like sculptures, have shape and form. To appreciate each sound's individual shape, a common vocabulary that addresses all its qualities, like an object, is essential.

5 QUESTIONS

1 What is the difference between hearing and listening?

2 What do onomatopoeic words evoke when they are spoken?

3 Describe two completely different sounds.

FURTHER LISTENING

- Amanda Stewart, 'postiche', I/T: *Selected Poems 1980-1996* (book and CD), Sydney: Here and There Books, 1998.*
- Luciano Berio, *Sequenza III* (1966).
- Ella Fitzgerald, 'How High the Moon', *Mack the Knife* (Verve 1960).
- John Cage, *Cartridge Music* (1960).
- David Bowie, *Low* (RCA Victor 1977).
- David Bowie, *Heroes* (RCA Victor 1977).
- Laurie Anderson, *Big Science* (Warners 1982).
- Brigid Burke and Rainer Linz, *Intersect* (NMA 1997).*
- Jim Denley, *Dark Matter* (Tall Poppies 1991).
- Any rap recording exploring the voice as a rhythmic instrument.

Special Topic 3
Sound Texts and Poetry

There are many definitions of sound poetry. One of its broadest is oral literature which occurs in diverse cultures. The Australian Aboriginal oral tradition of literature, for example, could be considered a type of sound poetry. Literature uses myriad techniques to explore the sound of words, such as alliteration ('Peter Piper picked a peck of pickled peppers') and onomato-poeia ('pop', 'bang' and 'whoosh'). Some experts attribute its origins in the twentieth century to the Futurists and Dadaists. As well as exploring the sound of words, sound poets are concerned with the structure of language, words and meaning, and their metamorphosis. They often utilise performance or electronic manipulation in its delivery.

The meaning of words, inflection, the sound of speech, speech rhythm, onomatopoeia and the use of words as independent entities, either in clusters or alone, can all form part of a sound →

→ poet's repertoire. *The sonic juxtaposition of words can be playful or sensuous. Each word is exploited for its structural and semantic meaning. The juxtaposition of different words can bring forth new meanings. The German sound poet Kurt Schwitters composed a sound poem called 'UrSonata' phrasing letters and words according to a musical structure. Another of his poems,'What a b what a b what a beauty' explores the transformation of the word beauty into severed units of vowels and consonants through a process of rhythmic repetition.*

> *What a b what a b what a beauty*
> *What a b what a b what a beauty*
> *What a b what a b what a beauty*
> *What a b what a b what a a*
> *What a beauty beauty be*
> *What a beauty beauty be*
> *What a beauty beauty beauty be be be*
> *What a be what a b what a beauty*
> *What a b what a b what a a*
> *What a be be be be be*
> *What a be be be be be*
> *What a be be be be be be be be a beauty be be be*
> *What a beauty.*

The Australian poet Amanda Stewart writes poetry based on the sound of words and their structural and semantic meaning. In 'postiche', she explores the layout of words on the page, rhythm and semantics (see Figure 3 on page 42).

Listening Example 9: 'Postiche', Amanda Stewart, (1993)
Musicians also often explore the use of words to create musical structures. The vocal beat box for example, using the voice to make percussive sounds, is pure onomatopoeia.

IMPROVISATIONS

Start and finish the session with a free or structured improvisation

1 Using onomatopoeic words, like whip, bang, crackle and pop, improvise a voice solo exploring speed and loudness. Stretch your words out and cut them into smaller units.

2 Try improvisation 1 with a group of people.

3 Write a sound poem using words for yourself and a group of people:

Write the words down like a sound poem:

Sound Texts

| voice 1 | whip whip pop bang crackle jangle |
| voice 2 | whip whip crack |

Or you could present it spatially. The horizontal axis represents time in seconds.

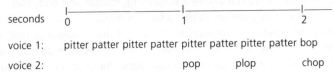

| seconds | 0 | 1 | 2 |

voice 1:   pitter patter pitter patter pitter patter pitter patter bop

voice 2:   pop   plop   chop

Figure 4: *Example of text piece written spatially.*

4 Create a repeating rhythm with words or phrases then build it up with new repeating phrases over the original pattern. For example:

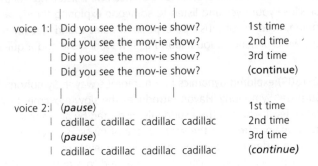

voice 1:| Did you see the mov-ie show?   1st time
       | Did you see the mov-ie show?   2nd time
       | Did you see the mov-ie show?   3rd time
       | Did you see the mov-ie show?   (continue)

voice 2:| (*pause*)   1st time
       | cadillac cadillac cadillac cadillac   2nd time
       | (*pause*)   3rd time
       | cadillac cadillac cadillac cadillac   (continue)

(The vertical lines represent the beat and the words and syllables are evenly spaced.)

Figure 5: *Example of a text piece written to a beat.*

5 THE BASIC PARAMETERS OF SOUND

A sound is high or low, soft or loud, of a certain timbre, lasts a certain length of time, and has an envelope.

John Cage[12]

The previous chapter showed how sound descriptions could be grouped by certain qualities: loudness, highness or lowness, how long its lasts, shape and 'colour' (or tone quality). The sonic terms for these qualities are loudness, register, duration, envelope and timbre.

The eardrum detects the loudness of a sound by the intensity of the vibration. It is not a matter of distance. A car alarm a hundred yards away can be louder than an alarm clock on your desk. This is because of the power level (intensity) of the alarm's sound waves. Highness or lowness refers to register. It is determined by one or a number of frequencies. The sound of a glass shattering consists of high frequencies while the hum of a powerful engine consists of low frequencies. Frequency and pitch (which is a special class of frequency) are discussed in the next chapter. The duration of a sound event can be as short as a microsecond or very long, like the sound of a waterfall. The way a sound changes in time refers to its ENVELOPE. All sound envelopes have a beginning, middle and end. The envelope could start abruptly and slowly die away, like a bell sounding; or it could build up to a tremendous volume, like cicadas in the Australian summer. Tone quality or timbre refers to the difference perceived between two sound events when register, loudness and duration are equal. The quality of a sound is determined by many things and it is this quality that makes the difference between the sound of a violin and a piano. Like fingerprints, the timbres of two sounds are never identical.

1 LOUDNESS AND DYNAMICS

Loudness in music is referred to as dynamics. There are three general levels: quiet, loud and middle. The different dynamic levels create a sense of distance and a listening 'focus'. You can experience this if you close your eyes and listen to someone exploring the dynamic levels of a table surface by tapping. In terms of music perception, a quiet sound is really no further away than a loud one but we experience a loud sound as if it were close and a quiet one as if it were more distant.

Franz Josef Haydn (1732-1809) explored dynamics in a humorous way in Symphony No. 94 (1791), known as the 'Surprise' Symphony. Haydn introduces the slow movement by establishing a quiet dynamic level which is then suddenly disrupted by an unexpectedly loud chord. Dynamics can have a major effect on the way a piece of music is perceived. Due to their design, instruments have different capacities for producing levels of loudness. A quiet sound from a trumpet might be perceived as very loud compared to a quiet sound from a flute. Consequently, balancing the dynamics of instruments so that they don't drown each other out is an important part of the composer or arranger's role.

Special Topic 1
Close, Far Away and Sounds Moving in Space
Sounds constantly change their dynamics. Our whole world is one sonic landscape in which sounds recede and approach. Our survival depends on our ability to detect sound movement. In music there are two signs for describing the change from one dynamic level to another:

Crescendo (becoming louder) is represented by the sign $<$

Decrescendo or diminuendo (becoming quieter) is represented by $>$

➤ *Many pieces of music explore the combination of these two simple sound structures.* R.V.

Listening Example 10: **Overlapping Crescendo, Richard Vella (1996)**
The overlaying of the different envelopes produces subtle waves of sound.

2 REGISTER – HIGH, LOW OR SOMEWHERE IN BETWEEN

Sounds, frequencies and pitches from any source can be divided into different registers. Register is a relative term, classified into high, middle and low. On musical instruments, registers generally belong to a physical location, i.e. a collection of fingerings or note positions. However it can also be defined simply by similarity of certain sounds. For example, singers categorise different parts of the voice in terms of chest, middle (or throat) or head register. This means that the sounds emitted from these regions have different qualities created by their vibrations (frequencies).

Activity 1
Listen to the different *qualities* of your voice as you:
1 'leap' or 'jump' from register to register.

high

middle

low

Figure 6: *Jumping from register to register.*

2 Slide from a low register to a higher register.

high

middle

low

Figure 7: *Sliding from low to middle to high.*

Listening Example 11: Demonstration of drum registers
In this example, three registers are presented by distinctive drum sounds. Low registers are played by the bass drum, middle registers by the tom-tom and high registers by the snare drum. Each register is established first before it is played against the others.

In some instruments, such as the clarinet, the different registers are very distinct whereas in others, like the guitar, the transition is smooth and even. Three Pieces for Clarinet by Igor Stravinsky dedicates each movement to a single register of the clarinet: low, middle and high.

Listening Example 12: *Cut to the Chase,* Richard Vella (1996)
Here a repeated middle-register note is punctuated with patterns and notes from the low and high registers. The work alternates between registers and gradually combines them.

Activity 2
Draw a register plan of the solo in Listening Example 12, Clarinet Solo, using lines to represent high, middle and low.

Jimi Hendrix (1942-1970) was a master of register shift and focus. His solos are extra-ordinary examples of unleashed sound using distortion, 'wah wah' effects and feedback. His solos exploit the full potential of the electric guitar and each uses a unique approach and structure. *Driving South* (1967) juxtaposes the high and low registers, represented by chord strums, before setting them into conflict. The two register extremes are gradually reconciled as the guitarist focuses on the middle range, pushing up to the high guitar registers towards the conclusion of the piece. Clearly separating the registers builds up a vocabulary of approaches belonging to each and allows the listener to take in the music's large-scale structure. Each attack recalls the previous utterance in that particular sound range. The result is a complicated layering of registers which shapes this exciting solo.

Listening Example 13: Guitar Solo played by Jason Zadkovic
This electric guitar solo utilises three registers. It begins in the middle register, followed by a higher register phase which slowly descends, concluding with a low note before the entry of the voice.

Listening Example 14: Piano Sonata Op. 31, No. 1 in G major, Ludwig van Beethoven (1802)

Beethoven was another register panel-beater. In Piano Sonata Op. 31, No. 1 in G major (1802) the right hand plays a run from the high to middle register while the left accompanies with a chord. This is followed by a gradual expansion back to the high register again. The last part of the excerpt is a closing statement in the middle to low registers. The result is a balanced structure in which, like the solos of Jimi Hendrix, each register is counterbalanced by the others.

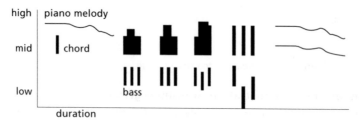

Figure 8: *Schematic representation of the registers for the opening of Beethoven's Piano Sonata Op. 31 No.1*

---

3 SOUND ENVELOPES – ATTACK, SUSTAIN, DECAY

All sounds have a beginning, middle and end which combine to form the sound envelope. Envelopes are involved in many aspects of making sound. Identifying the beginning, middle and end of a sound is essential to understanding a sound's structure. It is analytical listening which is very focussed. These 'close-ups' provide valuable insights into the detail of a sound event. The musical terms for these three parts are attack, sustain and decay. All sounds have an attack, sustain and decay sound. To understand the shape and structure of envelopes we shall discuss the dynamic envelope.

The attack of a dynamic envelope is its beginning and refers to the time it takes to establish its loudness. The sustain of the sound envelope refers to the period of time the sound remains constant. Decay refers to the decrease from this point to silence. The sound of an aeroplane approaching, passing and departing would consist of a slow attack, a momentary period of stability at maximum loudness, followed by a decay as the aeroplane moves away into the distance. An digital clock's alarm has an instantaneous attack time, a constant sustain and an instantaneous decay when it is turned off.

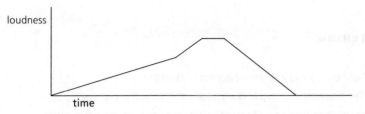

Figure 9: *The envelope (attack, sustain and decay) of an aeroplane passing overhead.*

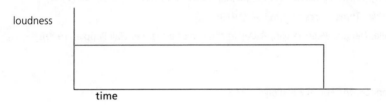

Figure 10: *The envelope (attack, sustain and decay) of a digital alarm clock turned on and off.*

4 SOUND QUALITY – TIMBRE

Timbre involves many aspects of acoustics and psychoacoustics. Some people refer to timbre as tonal quality or colour. The quality or colour of a sound depends on its register, frequency, envelope, dynamics and duration. It is a sound's timbre that gives it its individual character. The fact that you can recognise a friend's voice on the telephone is due to its particular timbre. When you mistake a voice on the phone for somebody else, it is because the two voices have similar timbres. Similarly, you would never mistake the sound of breaking glass for a piece of metal being struck. All sounds are made from the same components, but it is their combination that makes them unique. A clever orchestration or arrangement of music will utilise the similarities and differences of instrumental timbre. For the present we shall define timbre simply as *that quality of auditory sensation where a listener can judge two sounds as being different even if the two sounds have the same pitch, loudness and duration.*

Listening Example 15: Demonstration of changing instrumental timbres
In this example all the instruments play the same note. The instruments in order of entry are: flute, oboe, saxophone and trumpet. Each instrument can be distinguished from the others because of its unique timbre.

5 SUMMARY

Every sound consists of five elements: dynamics, register (high and low frequencies), duration, timbre and envelope. The combinations of these elements produces an infinite number of sound types. A sound is a constantly changing physical entity with a beginning, middle and end and can be discussed as such.

6 QUESTIONS

1 What are the basic parameters of sound?

2 What defines each of these parameters?

3 Describe the sound of a car passing by in terms of the basic parameters.

FURTHER LISTENING

Register

- Elliot Carter, Eight Etudes and a Fantasy, Piece No. 1 (1950).
- Céline Dion, 'The Power of the Dream' (Sony 1996). The vocal line explores register.
- Woody Herman, 'Golden Wedding', At the Woodchopper Ball, (ASV/Living Era 1995). The drum solo is a good example of the use of register.
- W.A. Mozart, 'Der Hölle Rache kocht in meinen Herzen' from Die Zauberflöte (1791).
- Igor Stravinsky, Three Pieces for Clarinet (1919).
- Richard Vella, 'Tango', Peter Jenkin, A Day in the Life of a Clarinet (Tall Poppies 1990).

Dynamics

- Robert Fripp, Let the Power Fall (Polydor 1981).
- Josef Haydn, first movement, Symphony No. 94 ('Surprise') (1791).
- Karlheinz Stockhausen, Kontra-Punkte (1952-53).

Register and Dynamics

- Cecil Taylor, 'Pontos Canados', One Night With Blue Note, Vol 2 (Blue Note 1985).
- Olivier Messiaen, Cantéyodjayâ (1949).
- György Ligeti, Lux Aeterna (1966).

Timbre

- Laurie Anderson, 'O Superman', Big Science (Warners 1982).
- John Cage, Sonatas and Interludes for Prepared Piano (1948).
- John Chowning, Phonée (1981).
- Jim Denley, title track of Dark Matter (Tall Poppies 1991).
- Gustav Mahler, Das Lied von der Erde (1908-9).
- Jean-Claude Risset, Inharmonic Soundscapes (1977).
- Pierre Henry, Orphée (1953).
- Arnold Schoenberg, Farben, Opus 16 No. 3 (1909).
- Richard Wagner, Das Rheingold, prelude (1854).

Timbre, Dynamics and Register

- Luciano Berio, Sequenza III (1966).
- György Ligeti, Chamber Concerto (1969-70).
- Edgard Varèse, Ionisation (1930-33).

IMPROVISATIONS

Start and finish the session with a free or structured improvisation.

1 Improvise a solo using a sound from your high, middle and low registers, juxtaposing one against another to create a sense of structure.

2 Create a solo for voice or an instrument, using a single note. Try to create 'meaning' by exploring dynamic contrast and shape.

3 Explore sound envelopes with your voice and a single note, concentrating on different attack, sustain and decay shapes.

4 Sing the envelope for a passing car in any register. Try it with other voices, each person beginning the sound shape independently. The result will be a rich sound shape continually expanding and contracting.

5 Create a palette of sounds which are different in:
   • duration
   • shape
   • timbre
   • dynamic
   • register

Construct a short solo or group piece for voice using these sounds only.

6 Build up a complex sound structure with several voices, each person repeating one unique sound event defined by timbre, register and envelope.

7 Explore different sound structures using register, timbre and envelope. One structure could explore all the registers while another deliberately reduces the register bringing all the sounds very close together.

8 With your voice or instrument, create a sound event concentrating on all three parts of the sound: attack, sustain and decay. The sound event should be about 15 seconds long. For example, start the sound with a shrill, high pitch followed by a rapidly descending hum leading into sparsely articulated soft pops which gradually die out.

9 Sing a single note exploring variations in duration and loudness only. Use silences whenever you wish. How were you able to create meaning with just these two parameters?

6 THE VIBRATING SOUND

Good, good, good, good vibrations.   The Beach Boys (1966)

In the last chapter the basic parameters of music were introduced. Sound, like a molecule, consists of smaller units, the arrangement of which controls the type of material it makes up: like the difference between gold and lead. In sound, the arrangement of smaller units controls its timbre. This chapter provides some background to the physical nature of sound and instruments.

1 VIBRATIONS AND FREQUENCY

Whenever a source gives out a sound, it vibrates. For a sound to be heard it must disturb air particles at a number of vibrations per second. The ear transfers these vibrations into neurological signals which the brain registers as a pitch or sound. When a tuning fork is struck and immersed in water, it creates tiny waves, demonstrating the motion of the tuning fork. The pitch of a sound is determined by its frequency, i.e. the number of vibrations or cycles per second (c.p.s.). For example, a tuning fork tuned to middle C vibrates at 262 cycles or vibrations per second. This means that the metal fork moves back and forth at a rate of 262 times per second! A low sound vibrates at a lower number of cycles per second than a high sound. This is why we use the expression 'tuning' a car engine. A well-tuned engine is one that runs at the most efficient number of rotations or cycles per second.

 Activity 1
We can experience frequency with our lips. Form the sound 'p' with your lips and blow gently. If the channel of air is constant your lips should start vibrating at a low frequency. Repeat the exercise blowing harder and tightening your lips. The sound produced will have a higher frequency because your lips are vibrating at a faster rate. This is how register is defined. The sound of breaking glass has a higher frequency than the low rumble of a lawn mower.

NATURAL FREQUENCY

When physical objects are activated they undergo a sudden deformation and correction which causes a disturbance of air particles. The struck physical object vibrates at a frequency characteristic of the object itself. The frequency at which the object sounds is called its natural frequency. A glass placed on a table top is not in a state of tension because no force is being applied to it. Striking the glass therefore activates the object's natural frequency. In contrast, a guitar string is tightly wound and under pressure; so when the string is plucked, the resulting sound is not the string's natural frequency.

 Activity 2
Explore the natural frequencies of some empty bottles of different sizes by blowing across the lip of each.

2 AMPLITUDE

Amplitude is the measure of the amount of vibration displaced. If you imagine a pendulum with a swing of six feet either side, it has a wider amplitude than a pendulum with only a two-foot swing. The wider the amplitude the louder the sound. The loudness envelope introduced in the last chapter is really an amplitude envelope. An amplitude envelope measures the growth and decay of volume. This damping or decay of a sound as it comes to rest is due to friction and the energy lost in the conversion of vibration into sound. Compare the decay or damping time of a piano chord to a drum beat.

The amplitude envelope differs according to the instrument and the way it is played as Figure 11 illustrates:

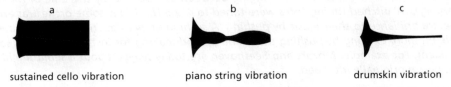

a	b	c
sustained cello vibration	piano string vibration	drumskin vibration

Figure 11: *Three amplitude envelopes.*

Activity 3

Draw the amplitude envelopes of a bell ringing and a dog bark.

Special Topic 1

Frequency, Pitch, Tuning and Scales

Frequency and Pitch

All sounds emit frequencies which can be low, middle or high in register. However the term register does not give us a precise understanding regarding the subtle differences between two or more frequencies within a register band. Pitch enables us to discriminate between two sounds so that we can say that one is lower or higher than the other. Low frequencies correspond to low pitches, high frequencies correspond to high pitches. While all sounds consist of a complex number of frequencies, we associate pitch with that part of the sound we hear as having the most dominant frequency. The shrill of a dentist's drill, or the low hum of a car engine are defined by pitch. If the sound of a broken window glass pane sounds higher in register to another broken window glass pane, it will be because the first has a higher pitch.

In musical instruments we use the word pitch when referring to a constant tone. This means that the pitch is unambiguously definite and happens at a constant rate over and over again. In opera, a bass singer wavering in pitch will mean that his tone is unreliable. Consequently, we say he has a bad sense of pitch. A good tone played by a saxophonist will mean the pitch is reliable and in tune with itself and the other instruments.

Pitch is a perception and there are ways to change it psychoacoustically. Try listening to a note but block your right ear; then block your left ear. For most people the pitch will be different in each ear. Another example is virtual pitch. If all the harmonics or partials of a note are heard except the fundamental, we still perceive the pitch of the note to be that missing fundamental. This is how we think we can hear a bass guitar in a small radio speaker when it is physically impossible to hear the actual bass note fundamental. (See page 56)

$\rightarrow$

➡ **Tuning: The determining of pitch structures for instruments**

Tuning can mean two things, depending on whether it is referring to

1 an absolute measurement; or

2 the pitch structure of a particular instrument.

1 In order for instruments to be compatible with each other they are tuned to the concert note 'A' (this is the first note you hear played by the oboe when the orchestra starts to tune up). The world standard for tuning was set in 1939 and set concert 'A' at 440Hz. The term A = 440Hz (Hz meaning cycles per second) means that the note 'A' is defined as the pitch heard when an object vibrates at 440Hz. Over the years the frequencies of notes have risen.

A brilliant acoustician Helmholtz, back in 1877 noted that there were pipe organs, built in previous centuries, having a concert 'A' ranging between 374–567 Hz. By the time of Handel (18th century), 'A' pitched tuning forks were tuned to 422.5 Hz. Today some orchestras are adding extra brilliance to their music by pushing 'A' as high at 444 Hz. This makes the music that little bit more exciting by pushing the sound up and making for instance the brass sound more brilliant. For example, Mozart and Beethoven are today played about a semitone higher than they were originally intended.

2 Tuning is a compromise, an approximation and requires a lot of mathematical calculations. The calculations alter the size of various intervals (distance betwen notes) so that the tuning system can be functional. To be able to play a piano in any key a tuning system called equal temperament is required, a mathematically derived tuning where an octave is in a ratio of 1:2 and all the semitones in between are $^{12}\sqrt{2}$ apart.

Scales: A set of pitched steps that melody and harmony play on

Once the instrument adopts a tuning system, it is possible to construct scales. The word comes from the Latin 'Scala' meaning ladder. In the Western musical system the building blocks for scales are defined by some pattern based on semitones. The semitone is the smallest unit available in the modern western tuning system. Scales will be formed from combinations of semitones (S) and tones (T – equalling two semitones).

The major scale always has the following steps TTSTTTS; the steps of the natural minor scale are TSTTTST. These patterns create a sense of leaning or pulling towards a home note called the tonic which is the first note of the scale. The C major scale's home note is C, it being the first step of the scale: CTDTEsFTGTATBsC.

Every culture has their scales, often surprisingly similar. There is the 5 note or pentatonic scale, the Arabic 17 note scale, the whole tone and chromatic scales and the many Hindu scales which serve as the basis for the Indian ragas (See Appendix 5).

The Chromatic Scale: The twelve equal steps of an octave

The chromatic scale divides the octave into twelve equal semitone steps. The scale is best represented by all the white and black keys on a conventional piano keyboard. Because no interval in the chromatic scale is different to any other, there is no pull to a home note as is the case in major and minor scales. It is a scale without a key. However it is a scale that allows composers to dip into to shift from one tonal (key) centre to another. It is associated with the music of Wagner and the late Romantics at the end of the 19th century, when it was often impossible to identify the home, and indeed tonality was often implied rather than defined.

A.A and R.V.

Special Topic 2
Amplification
Altering the Relationship of One Sound to Another

Amplification is magnification. The Australian choreographer Graeme Watson observed that amplification is a twentieth-century phenomenon. It is liable to happen whenever art and technology mix. A film amplifies an actor and a valve or transistor can amplify a musician.

In audio it was the invention of the triode valve by Lee de Forest in 1906 that transformed the world of music and sound. It led to the invention of the electronic microphone whereby sound could be amplified electrically rather than acoustically. At first microphones were not very sensitive, and quiet instruments such as violins still needed acoustic amplification. In time, more subtle sonic textures became available on recordings and this led to a reassessment of the relationship between musical sounds. A whisper could be amplified to the same volume as a shout. The style of singing known as crooning, popularised by Bing Crosby, was only possible because amplification allowed a quiet and intimate singing voice to be heard against a band. This re-ordering of sound relationships was taken to its extreme in electronic dance and art music. Often, real acoustic spaces were replaced by new virtual spaces.

The heart of any amplification system is the mixing desk. This controls the amplification of a signal (or its opposite, attenuation) as it flows through the system. Relative sound levels or even parts of the audio spectrum (tone controls) can be changed. If no amplification or attenuation is present, the system is said to be at 'unity gain'.

The rock concert is the most extreme manifestation of amplification. More subtle use is made by sound enhancement systems used in theatres and concert halls. The Royal Festival Hall in London has an amplification system which can change the perception of the acoustic space of the hall itself. Groups such as Nine Inch Nails have exploited the redefinition of sound relationships to the full. *A.A.*

3 RESONANCE

> ...in 14th-century Europe, church bells were rung and cannons fired in the belief that the attendant noise would somehow ward off hail.   Joseph Moran and Michael Morgan[13]

Resonance occurs when the frequency of a vibration is the same as the natural frequency of an object. The result is an increase in amplitude (i.e. loudness). Imagine two children, one pushing the other on a swing. When the force of the child pushing coincides with the periodic cycle of the child on the swing, the amplitude of the swing increases. If the child pushing applies a force out of time with the swing, the forces act in opposition, interrupting the cycle and probably breaking a few limbs as well.

Another example of resonance is the sympathetic vibration of a window as an aeroplane flies overhead. The vibration from the aeroplane activates the natural frequency of the window causing it to vibrate. Resonance can be very powerful and, if ignored, very destructive. We have all heard a story of an opera singer whose voice could shatter a crystal glass. If the frequency of the singer's voice coincides with the frequency of the glass, it vibrates sympathetically; if the singer's voice is loud enough, the glass will break.

If a tuning fork is struck and held against a wooden box it causes another form of resonance. The regularly repeating vibrations of the tuning fork set the air inside into motion. The box becomes a resonator amplifying the sound. The cylindrical pipes underneath a marimba, vibraphone or xylophone combine both forms of resonance, the natural frequency of the pipe and enclosed air, so that it only resonates when the wooden key above is struck.

Special Topic 3
The Rumble of Thunder

During a thunderstorm, we may be startled by a sudden, sharp clap of thunder that is followed by a low rumble that persists for tens of seconds. Why the rumble?... the speed of light is so great that we see an entire lightning bolt instantly. Sound waves are generated all along the lightning path, but sound waves are considerably slower than light waves. This means that the first thunder we hear is from the part of the bolt that is closest to us (that is, where it strikes the ground). Subsequent sound waves reach us from portions of the bolt that are progressively further away from our ears (that is, at higher altitudes). The net result is a lingering rumble.   *Joseph Moran and Michael Morgan*[14]

The resonating chambers of a violin or guitar have many resonant frequencies involving the body of the resonating chamber and the air enclosed. The soundboard of the piano acts as a resonator as it vibrates in response to the piano strings.

HARMONIC SERIES (OVERTONES)

A note played or sung is actually a complicated unit of acoustic components. The combination of components produces the particular timbre of a sound. A sound's timbre is similar to a recipe, consisting of particular ingredients used in different ways at different stages in the cooking process. An important ingredient of any sound's timbre is its harmonics or overtones.

The German acoustician and physicist Hermann von Helmholtz conducted pioneering research into the harmonic series. He demonstrated that a sound is really a compound of frequencies vibrating in relation to each other (similar to the colour green consisting of blue and yellow). He found that any compound sound consists of a dominant tone, which he called the fundamental tone (frequency), to which all the higher tones or overtones are related. The combination produces the individual character of the sound.

> [The ear,] when its attention has been properly directed to the effect of the vibrations which strike it, does not hear merely that one musical tone whose pitch is determined by the period of the vibration ... but in addition ... becomes aware of a whole series of higher musical tones, which we call the harmonic upper partial tones, and sometimes simply the upper partials of the whole musical tone or note.   Hermann von Helmholtz[15]

Listening Example 16: Demonstration of a fundamental tone plus overtones
In this example the pure tone of a fundamental becomes gradually richer as each of the first seven overtones are added.

A vibrating guitar string demonstrates the complexity of sound. When a guitar string is plucked, the string will vibrate at different rates simultaneously. There are many vibrating patterns present ranging from low to high. These vibrations will vibrate according to a simple rule in which each vibration is a multiple of the lowest vibration. Figure 12 schematically represents the first five vibrations of a guitar string when plucked. While the lowest vibration (the fundamental) is vibrating, vibration two vibrates at twice the speed of the fundamental, vibration three at three times the speed of the fundamental, vibration four at four times the speed of the fundamental, and so on.

Figure 12: *Schematic representation of a guitar string vibrating.*

Each of these vibrations is an overtone. It is the combination of overtones, the shape of the resonator and the material from which it is made that creates the complete timbre of the sound.

The first two vibrations would look like this:

Figure 13: *The first two vibrations of a guitar string.*

The single vibration is the fundamental and the double vibration (vibrating at twice the speed) is the first overtone. The point of minimal vibration (where the ellipse is narrowest) is called the node and the point of maximal vibration (where the ellipse is widest) is the antinode (its opposite).[16]

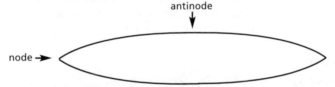

Figure 14: *The node and antinode of a vibrating string.*

The term harmonic is used when a player activates a sound from the node point of a string or column of air. Any instrument that uses a vibrating string or column of air (such as a violin or a flute) can produce harmonic sounds. This was discovered by Pythagoras (c.582-500BC). Touching a node half-way down the string will produce a harmonic an octave above the fundamental, two-thirds down the string will produce a harmonic an octave and a fifth above the fundamental, three-quarters down the string will produce a harmonic two octaves above the fundamental and so on.

While the harmonic series is crucial to an instrument or voice's timbre, it is only part of the story. Sounds also have non-harmonic tones which are important. These are vibrations that, unlike the harmonic series, do not fit into a predictable pattern. The timbre of a gong, for example, is a rich soup of harmonic and non-harmonic tones, noise and other elements.

Activity 4
Overtones can be heard in the sympathetic vibrations of a piano. Silently press down A2 (located in the second-lowest octave) with your left hand and play an accented staccato attack with your right using one of the overtone frequencies in the stave below. The accented tones played by the right hand will cause the overtone of the note held down by the left hand to vibrate sympathetically (i.e. resonate). Now try accenting the notes

➤ without holding down the fundamental note or notes not belonging to this particular harmonic series. If the hammers of the piano are functioning properly you should not be able to produce any sympathetic resonance.

Figure 15: *The first 8 frequencies of the harmonic series mapped onto a stave.*

4 SUMMARY

All sounds are vibrations perceived by the ears. The louder the sound, the greater its amplitude. When a sound source vibrates, it emits a natural set of frequency vibrations. Frequency determines pitch and resonance. Any sound consists of several components, some more dominant than others. While the harmonic series is an important aspect of timbre, sounds are affected by many other elements, such as non-harmonic tones and instrument design. In simple terms, the timbre of a sound consists of a fundamental tone combined with the various overtones or upper partials. The presence or absence of these overtones or partials gives the sound its particular timbre. A complex sound like a gong has all its particular overtones present whereas a simpler sound, such as a flute, is more likely to have a minimal number of overtones, which is why it sounds so pure. In general, the richer the sound, the more overtones are present.

5 QUESTIONS

1 What is frequency?

2 What is the relationship between frequency and pitch?

3 What is natural frequency?

4 What is amplitude?

5 What is resonance?

6 What is the harmonic series?

7 What are nodes and antinodes?

Special Topic 4
Upper Harmonics and Their Vibrations

The relationship between the fundamental frequency and its overtones is based on very simple arithmetic in which the upper partials are multiples of the fundamental. For example: if the fundamental tone of a sound is 100 vibrations per second, then the first overtone will have twice as many vibrations per second, i.e. 200. The second overtone will have three times as many (300) and so on. The harmonic series can be formulated as:

A complex tone = y (fundamental) + 2y (first overtone) + 3y (second overtone) + 4y + 5y etc

If the fundamental (1st harmonic) is a low C vibrating at 65.4 cycles per second then:
the 2nd harmonic (1st overtone) vibrates at 130.8 cycles per second (65.4 x 2)
the 3rd harmonic (2nd overtone) vibrates at 196.2 cycles per second (65.4 x 3)
the 4th harmonic (3rd overtone) vibrates at 261.6 cycles per second (65.4 x 4)

➤

→ the 5th harmonic (4th overtone) vibrates at 327.0 cycles per second (65.4 x 5)
the 6th harmonic (5th overtone) vibrates at 392.4 cycles per second (65.4 x 6)
the 7th harmonic (6th overtone) vibrates at 457.8 cycles per second (65.4 x 7)
the 8th harmonic (7th overtone) vibrates at 523.2 cycles per second (65.4 x8)
and so on.

Theoretically this could go on forever. The formula for calculating the frequency of any overtone is:

nth overtone = fundamental frequency y (n+1)

For example, the 19th overtone = 110 cycles/sec x 20 (19+1) = 2200 cycles per second.

Note: Overtones and harmonic series offer an exciting and complex world. Since the advent of digital synthesis there has been a huge amount of research in the area of timbral construction. The Yamaha DX7 keyboard, which was very popular in the early 1980s with rock bands, is one such example. A lot of the work in digital synthesis has been pioneered by the American composer John Chowning.   R.V.

FURTHER LISTENING

- A.J.M. Houtsma, T.D. Rossing and W.M. Wagenaars, *Auditory Demonstrations*, Institute for Perception Research, Eindhoven, The Netherlands (Philips 1987).

- Warren Burt, *Three Inverse Genera (1989)* on Austral Voices: For Telegraph Wires, Tuning Forks, Computer-Driven Piano, Psaltery, Whirly, Cello, Synthesizer and Ruined Piano (New Albion 1990).

- Jimi Hendrix, 'Driving South' (1967), The BBC Sessions (MCA 1998).

- David Hykes with the Harmonic Choir, *Hearing Solar Winds* (Ocora 1983).

- Harry Partch, *Delusion of the Fury* (1966).

- Karlheinz Stockhausen, *Stimmung* (1968).

- Javanese gamelan music.

IMPROVISATIONS

Start and finish the session with a free or structured improvisation.

1 Using your voice or an instrument, make sounds which are timbrally similar and dissimilar. Improvise a solo exploring similarities and dissimilarities of timbre.

2 Explore the natural resonances in your body with your voice. Sing the vowel 'a' (as in 'bath') and 'e' (as in 'feed') in a low register. Although the pitch is the same the timbre changes. The vowel 'e' resonates in the nasal register which has higher upper partials, whereas the vowel 'a' sounds in the chest which has lower partials. Explore notes from your chest register and different parts of your head and throat registers. You should be able to feel these parts of your body vibrate as you sing.

3 If you have access to a string instrument or air-column instrument explore the harmonic series, composing sounds that are only made from the natural harmonics.

COMPOSITION PROJECT 2

NOTATION EXERCISE PART 1

Choose a sound location and transcribe the sonic event. Use symbols of your own invention. Give a key at the beginning of your transcription to all the symbols in the work. The event may last a second, a minute or more.

If you need help, refer to Questions to Ask a Piece of Music and More Questions in Chapter 4. Listen to each sound's attack, sustain and decay, its register and loudness. A good way of identifying the different parts is by mimicking the sound vocally. Make your notation signs visually gestural. For example, something loud could be represented by a bigger sign than something soft. If speech is involved, write it down and try to represent the musicality of the way the performer is to speak. Be aware of all the sounds you are hearing, from the most distant to the most obvious. If you cannot represent a sound with something that describes it visually, invent a symbol that is explained by a key or composer's notes. Explain in your exercise how time, pitch difference, register and volume are to be interpreted.

PERFORMANCE EXERCISE

Present the transcription of your sound location so that it can be easily performed by a group. For example, everyone could have their own copy or part; or your transcription could be large enough for everyone to be able to read it easily.

NOTATION EXERCISE PART 2

The purpose of this sound composition is to explore the effect of different combinations of sounds and sound orders.

Compose a work between one and two minutes long, combining sounds you hear around you: for example, an aeroplane flying in the distance, a glass of water being stirred with a spoon followed by a dog bark and the hum of a vacuum cleaner.

Referring to Appendix 1, Representing Sounds, devise a notation system that effectively expresses your composition. The above example could be represented visually like this:

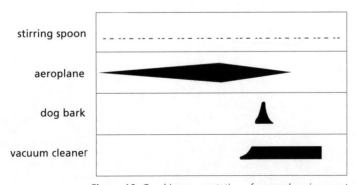

Figure 16: *Graphic representation of a sound environment.*

You may wish to record these sounds on two or more cassette tapes and play them back simultaneously on separate tape recorders. It is important to time the entry of each sound carefully. The composition could then be notated like this

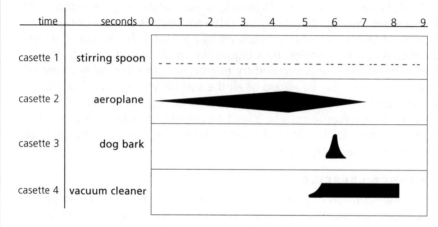

Figure 17: *Notation for tape recorders.*

THE VIBRATING INSTRUMENT

A sound is made when an instrument, voice or object is set in vibration by some force. A sound can be produced in a variety of ways and these can be used to classify them into families. Sounds are continually manipulated, changed and placed in new contexts in order to produce new ways of hearing.

CHAPTER 7 — The Vibrating Instrument

Key concepts or themes	Signals and controllers Aerophones, chordophones, idiophones, membrano-phones and electrophones
Special Topics	1 Transients and Controllers 2 The Electric Guitar 3 Bowed, Stroked, Strummed and Plucked 4 Banged, Hit, Rattled and Shaken 5 Blown and Tongued 6 Switched On and Amplified
Improvisations	

CHAPTER 8 — Old Sounds, New Contexts ... New Sounds, Old Contexts

Key concepts or themes	Syncretism, fixed and mobile traditions, new contexts, the changing role of instruments, new and extended instrumental techniques, changing traditional performance practices, prerecorded music and sampling
Special Topics	1 Music of the Indian Subcontinent 2 Cross-currents 3 Africa 4 Albert Ayler (1936-1971) 5 The Spiritual
Improvisations	

CHAPTER 9 — Resonating Instruments and Spaces

Key concepts or themes	Reverberation, resonating spaces, sound sculptures and installations
Special Topics	1 Reverberation 2 In Music Everything Has its Sonic and Spectral Space 3 Greg Schiemer's *Spectral Dance*
Improvisations	

Composition Project 3

7 THE VIBRATING INSTRUMENT

Any musical instrument requires... a method of playing (input or stimulus)
... the object being played, and a resulting sound (output or response).

Allen Strange[17]

One of the most exciting aspects of music-making is the infinite variety of ways a sound can be made: a jazz drummer changing from wooden sticks to brushes; a rock'n'roll guitarist creating feedback from the amplifier or using foot pedals to produce a 'wah wah' sound, flanging, phasing or overdriven distortion. The manipulation, transformation or subtle variation of sound is an essential part of any musician's search for expression. Understanding the components of a sound allows a musician to take control of what is otherwise a random process of trial and error.

1 SIGNALS AND CONTROLLERS

Any sound has three basic components:

1 a controller;

2 something that vibrates; and

3 a signal.

The CONTROLLER is a force that can be applied either to create the sound or to change it; the OBJECT that is set into vibration can be an instrument, voice or surface; and the SIGNAL is the sound created.

The controller can be applied as an input (e.g. crescendo or decrescendo) or via an implement or process that changes the sound after its initial attack (e.g. a trumpet mute, a guitar tremolo bar or an effects unit). Fingering, bowing and pressure are all controllers that go into producing a violin note. Changing the controller (the quality of the applied force) changes the output of the sound. Random movements of the tongue give a song a slurred effect. In this case, the random tongue movement is the controller, the sound of the song is its signal and the vocal chords are the objects set into vibration.

The lush piano repertoire of the nineteenth and early twentieth century – Chopin, Liszt, Brahms, Ravel and Debussy – can be largely attributed to the invention of the sustain pedal. This is a form of controller that enables sounds to be held over and combined. The invention of the tremolo bar had a similar revolutionary effect in the twentieth century on the sound-world of the electric guitar. The slide guitar is a common example of changing the normal controllers of the guitar sound. The player alternates between traditional playing and slide guitar which uses a metal tube over the index finger producing a succession of glissandi. The plectrum used to pluck the strings is also a controller. One of the most rewarding products of music-making in all cultures is the continual modification of instruments and sound-producing objects.

Cage's *Sonatas and Interludes for Prepared Piano* (1948) are a famous example of the use of controllers. Rubbers, screws, paper clips and other non-pianistic controllers are inserted among the strings. The signal produced when the piano is played is a combination of the vibrations from the strings and the controllers. Each controller filters out different transient frequencies. Although the preparation of the piano in *Sonatas and Interludes* is unconventional, the manner of playing is not. The pianist still sits at the keyboard and plays the keys. However, this application of force is also a controller and it can be changed too.

Special Topic 1
Transients and Controllers

The effect of different controllers on an instrument can be quite dramatic. Each means of attack can activate a different aspect of the instrument's sound. Compare tapping a table top with your fingernails and the palm of your hand. These different controllers are crucial to the defining characteristics of the sound. The aspect of the signal most affected by the controller is its 'transients'. Crudely stated, transients are the initial sound frequencies activated by the controller. A hard mallet striking a tuning fork produces higher ('brighter') transient frequencies than a soft mallet. R.V.

Listening Example 17: Demonstration of prepared piano sounds

In this example, screws, rubbers and wooden clothes pegs have been inserted between the strings of the piano to create an enigmatic percussive sound.

Activity 1
Investigate the relationship between controller and signal in the following exercises:

1 Place your foot on the sustain pedal and whistle inside the piano. As you whistle listen to the sympathetic resonances of the activated strings.

2 Explore the sounds created by hitting the strings with different types of implements (glass, wooden sticks etc).

3 Put a microphone inside the piano and play. Listen to the internal mechanism become a part of your playing.

4 Silently hold down a chord without using the sustain pedal. Sing the notes of the chord and listen to the strings vibrate sympathetically.

The microphone has made possible the production of an extraordinary array of sounds. Its ability to transform sounds so that they appear to come from a large amplified space is a simple example of how it acts as a controller. The composer, music producer and software developer Greg White discussed this potential in an interview with the author:

> The microphone is an active instrument because one is able to control tone and timbre. It is not a passive receiver of sounds. The microphone transforms a performance into a different sonic event due to its position in the recording studio and the choice of microphone quality. High quality does not necessarily mean the best, as sometimes a bad or cheap microphone produces the desired sound. Microphone placement can create different types of acoustic spaces, such as a very close intimate space in which one hears a lot of surface detail of the acoustic event; or it can be placed further away which will produce a distant microphone sound. A lot will also depend on the room's reverberation. By placing several microphones in different parts of a space around a performer one is able to produce layered perspectives of the same sound. One is able to hear a multiplicity of recorded perspectives which is impossible to do with one microphone alone.

The microphone also makes it possible to apply other controllers after it has transformed an acoustic signal into a electronic one.

Listening Example 18: *The Naked Kiss*, Andy Arthurs (1997)
In this song the voice takes on a new timbre through the use of flanging. Flanging is an electronic process by which a signal, in this case the voice, is moved in and out of phase with itself. It is often achieved electronically by mixing a continually varying delay with the original signal, creating a 'whooshing' or 'churning' sound as in this example. Electronic processing of signals is discussed in more detail in Chapter 8.

Special Topic 2
The Electric Guitar

The electric guitar is a remarkable instrument which relies completely on electricity and amplifiers to produce a sound. Apart from the fingerboard, the shape of the guitar has no effect on the sound it makes. Because it has no soundboard, without amplification the strings only produce very faint and feeble vibrations. However, the addition of electromagnets (pick-ups) transforms these feeble vibrations into electronic sound waves which can be fed through an amplifier to magnify the sound. Often guitarists channel sound through a special effects unit before sending it on to the amplifier. The unit looks like a small box with a foot pedal and several can be arranged in front of a guitarist or mounted on a rack which is controlled by a dial or button. These effects units apply distortion or transform the sound with delays such as flangers and chorus effects. Using a selection of units, a guitarist can build up an orchestra of effects.

R.V.

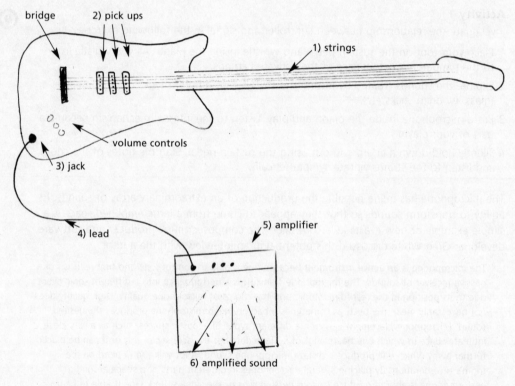

Figure 18: *The electric guitar*

2 INSTRUMENTAL CLASSIFICATIONS

There are many ways of classifying instruments and every culture uses different terms of reference. A study of the subject is a book in itself. The first Western attempt at a universal instrumental classification was created by the acoustician and organologist Victor-Charles Mahillon, who published a catalogue of musical instruments in 1893. This was later revised by Erich von Hornbostel and Curt Sachs in 1914. Instruments were categorised in a general way according to the manner in which they were sounded or structured. In some instruments the primary vibrating part is a reed; in others, a string. The sound is created by a material or column of air in vibration. It can be sounded inside an enclosed space, such as a pipe or above an enclosed chamber, such as a guitar. A book can be made to act like a reed by holding it closed and blowing; the force of the air causes the pages to vibrate against each other, causing a sound. The aspects of sound discussed in Chapter 6 (vibration, amplitude, resonance and overtones), play an important role in the quality and articulation of any sound.[18]

There are five instrumental classifications: chordophones, aerophones, membranophones, idiophones and electrophones, and each of these has subcategories according to the way the instrument is played:

CHORDOPHONES

Chordophones generate sound from a vibrating string, usually attached to a resonator. An elastic band over a shoe box is a chordophone. There is a huge number of these instruments, including the violin, guitar, harp, piano, zither and dulcimer.

subcategories	examples
a striking	dulcimer, clavichord, piano
b plucking	harp, guitar, mandolin, harpsichord
c bowing	violin, viola, double bass, cello
d rubbing	hurdy-gurdy

Special Topic 3
Bowed, Stroked, Strummed and Plucked –
Mainly Strings Attached

The Orchestra
The strings are the mainstay of the orchestra; some orchestras consisting solely of strings. The string section delivers most of the melody and a fair amount of the harmony too. String players with a well-developed rhythmic sense are harder to find, although the Electric Light Orchestra was notable for the precision of its cellos and the Kronos Quartet is typical of a movement to bring a new smartness to the rhythmic side of string playing. The classical orchestra usually contains several pairs ('desks') of each of the following stringed instruments:

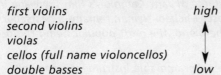

first violins	*high*
second violins	↑
violas	↕
cellos (full name violoncellos)	↓
double basses	*low*

We usually see strings being 'bowed' – causing the strings to vibrate in a continuous note by scraping. A violin can also be plucked (pizzicato) or even struck. It is also often referred to as a 'fiddle', which is a more general term usually used for folk instruments such as the Irish and Eastern fiddles, and other versions of the instrument from various parts of the world. The hurdy-gurdy is a mechanically-bowed folk instrument usually associated with Romanies and Eastern Europe. The 'bow' is driven by a wheel on a handle. The hurdy-gurdy usually has one melody string and several drone strings.

The stringed instruments used in orchestras before the eighteenth century were similar to their contemporary counterparts but they had six strings tuned a fourth apart rather than the current four strings tuned a fifth apart.

→

➜ *The other stringed instrument in the orchestra is the harp, an enormous instrument with octaves of strings whose pitch can be adjusted chromatically. The strings of the harp are all open with no means of damping, so that they create a rippling reverberation when the harpist's fingers pass across them.*

The World

Every country and every era has its share of stringed and plucked instruments. The list is almost endless, but some more common ones include the classical harp; the ancient lute; the sitar, sarod and tamboura from the Indian subcontinent; the koto from Japan; the quatro and charango from South America; the zither and Baroque clavichord from Europe; the berimbao from Africa and South America; and the jaw harp (or Jews harp) from Asia.

Musical Hybrids

There are two well-known hybrid string-percussion instruments: the guitar and the piano. They are interestingly the two most common instruments in the Western world.

The Piano and the Keyboard

One of the distinguishing features of the piano, apart from its sound, is the mechanism it uses: the keyboard. A keyboard is a mechanical transducer, translating finger velocity into gestural or electrical energies. Some other examples of stringed keyboard instruments are the harpsichord, celeste and clavichord. However, not all keyboard instruments are stringed, for example the organ, synthesiser and some tuned percussion.

On a harpsichord, striking a key causes a string to be plucked and no dynamic variation is possible. However, a piano key strikes the strings with a hammer and allows degrees of velocity. The full name for the piano is pianoforte *which in Italian means 'soft-loud', illustrating its capacity for dynamic and timbral variation.*

The contemporary piano keyboard, with its 12 semitonal chromatic steps to the octave is made up of seven white notes (natural) and five sharp ($\sharp$) or flat ($\flat$) black notes. (Incidentally on a harpsichord the black and white notes are often reversed.)

The piano has inspired composers ever since its invention in Florence by Bartolommeo Cristofori in 1709. Its versatility has lent itself to composers such as Bartók, Stravinsky and Cage who used it percussively. Cage 'prepared' the piano so that different materials struck the strings, some dampened considerably more than others. To the nineteenth-century composer it was a complete orchestra. Liszt fully explored its piano *and its* forte*, and Chopin created pieces of sheer beauty and melodic charm. By the early twentieth century almost every middle-class home in the West had a piano, creating an enormous market for sheet music. The early Broadwood 'square' piano was the subject of Jane Campion's film* The Piano *in 1992. The music for this film by the minimalist composer Michael Nyman remains a bestseller. Today there are many designs and shapes for the piano, the most popular being the domestic upright, and the most lavish, the grand piano.*

In 1897 Edwin S. Votley patented the Pianola, a programmable instrument using rolls of perforated cardboard, which allowed it to play on its own. This concept has had a new lease of life since 1984 with the invention of the Musical Instrument Digital Interface micro-processor. MIDI allows an electronic piano-type keyboard to control anything from notes on a synthesiser, to notes on an acoustic piano, so long as it is set up electronically and mechanically to receive MIDI. It can even be used to trigger lights in a theatre, open doors or pour coffee.

The Guitar

Perhaps the best-known stringed instrument is the six-stringed guitar with a fretted finger-board. The guitar is usually strummed or plucked. Classical or Spanish guitars have become immensely popular worldwide, as well as the more recent metal-stringed versions which of ➜

→ course include the electric guitar. The guitar has a long history and many relations. Three or four string guitars have been excavated in Egypt that date back as far as the fourth century. More often the guitar is associated with Spain and Flamenco music, and from there with Latin America, from whence it eventually spread in various versions to the rest of the world. Each country makes the guitar its own. The stylistic playing of West African guitar music, for instance, is far removed from the classical style of John Williams or the sensuous innovative work of rock musicians like Mark Knopfler.   *A.A.*

IDIOPHONES

Idiophones are made from naturally sounding materials which do not require the application of tension, unlike chordophones or membranophones (drums). In other words they naturally resonate. A hub cap is an idiophone.

subcategories	examples
a striking	marimba, xylophone, woodblock, cymbals, metal chimes, metal rods
b plucking	kalimba, jaw harp, a ruler held down on a table top
c rubbing and scraping	crystal glasses or wine glasses with water, guiro
d shaking	rattles, maracas
e stamping	a resonating wooden floor

Special Topic 4
Banged, Hit, Rattled and Shaken –
A Cocktail of Percussion

If rhythm is the heart-beat of music, percussion must be the heart itself, the pacemaker of the orchestra. Percussion essentially means drums, but what is less widely appreciated is that it also includes any instrument that is struck. So the xylophone, the marimba and even the piano are classified as 'tuned' percussion. Kettle drums (also known as timpani) can be tuned and adjusted during playing by a foot pedal. Even if a violin is plucked in a particularly snappy way, as frequently happens in Bartók's string quartets, it is called a 'percussive' sound. Any drum with a vibrating membrane (termed a 'membranophone' – while those composed of metal, wood or some other material are called 'idiophones') has a resonant frequency. This frequency is determined by the volume of air trapped between the hitting surface (the skin) and the outer casing (the shell). The larger the volume, the lower the resonating note. There is a pitch component to all acoustic percussion instruments.

The percussion section of most orchestras is very small. Overt or complex rhythm was not a feature of Western art music until the early twentieth century when composers such as Stravinsky encouraged its re-evaluation. But in rock music, the drum kit pounding out a 4/4 rhythm is ubiquitous. Usually it comprises a bass (or kick) drum, a snare (or side) drum, two small cymbals which crash together to 'tick-tock' the tempo (collectively named the high-hat), a few tuned tom-toms and a number of overhead cymbals to add splash and brightness. The cymbals are perhaps the least tuned percussion instruments but they cover a wide spectrum of noise which allows them to blend with instruments in any register or key.

Rock has its origins in African music where the simplicity of 4/4 or 6/8 rhythms are often enhanced by much more complex syncopations and polyrhythms. African percussion has spread across the globe; the South American rhythms and Latin American percussion instruments such as the congas, the bongos, the frame and talking drums mostly derive from Africa.

Drums usually lay down the tempo and metre while the smaller percussion instruments – tambourines, shakers, cabassas and castanets – excitedly dance around them.   *A.A.*

MEMBRANOPHONES

Membranophones generate sound from a membrane stretched over an opening. A bass drum is a membranophone.

subcategories	examples
a striking	bongo, conga, bass drum
b friction	rope drum (a drum using a cord pulled through a hole in the membrane causing it to vibrate.)
c blowing	kazoo

AEROPHONES

Aerophones generate sound from a vibrating column of air. A bottle is an aerophone when a breath of air across the lip causes it to vibrate. Aerophones are classified according to the way the air column is activated. Each of the reeds below works in a different way:

- A mechanical reed works by vibrating at the resonant frequency of the column of air in the body of the instrument.
- An air reed is an opening or aperture that produces sound when air pressure is applied to it.
- A lip reed is made by the player's lips vibrating at the resonant frequency of the column of air in the body of the instrument.

subcategories	examples
a mechanical reed	clarinet, oboe, bassoon, saxophone, bagpipe, gumleaf, blowing into a closed book
b air reed	flute, recorder, pan-pipes, ocarina, whistle, an empty bottle
c lip reed	trumpet, trombone, French horn, tuba, a garden hose
d free aerophone	bull-roarer, open pipes activated by wind or rapid movement through the air.

Special Topic 5
Blown and Tongued –
The Sound of the Wind

Wind instruments produce notes by exciting a column of air to vibrate. Holes in the side of the instrument can be opened or closed with the fingers or keys to effectively change the length of the pipe, thereby altering its resonant frequency, which determines the note. The only orchestral instrument that does not work this way is the trombone, which has a variable pipe (the slide) to alter the length of the air column.

In fact any pipe will do. The Australian composer and performer Linsey Pollak makes wind music using lengths of hose, hollowed-out carrots, tubular camping stools and other everyday items. The size of the bore of the tube and whether it opens at one or both ends affects the timbre and method of tuning. The wind instruments of any culture, such as the Australian Aboriginal didjeridu or the Chinese bamboo flute, generally derive from the materials to hand. Apart for some rare exceptions, the wind family play one note at a time.

The wind section of the orchestra is much less homogeneous than the strings, and adds the most noticeable changes of colour (or timbres) to the sound of the orchestra. They are divided into two groups, the woodwind and the brass. The woodwinds are further subdivided into those which:

→

➤ • *have a vibrating reed as a sound source (double reed – the oboes, bassoons and cor anglais; and single reed – various clarinets)*

• *are sparked into life by blowing across a hole, like blowing across the top of a bottle (flutes and piccolos – deriving from whistles and fifes).*

Anyone who has heard the plaintive cry of an oboe or the sweetness of the clarinet in its upper registers, or the haunting melodies and almost comic grunts of the bassoon will understand how much variety these instruments can bring to music. The sound of some wind instruments can be idiosyncratic in themselves. For instance, the velvety low notes of a clarinet have a very different tonal flavour to its upper register.

The brass is a completely different bunch. Generally these instruments come into their own when things are getting hot and exciting; their brilliant upper partials put a zizz into the orchestral colour. The orchestral brass family consists of:

trumpet	high
french horn	
trombone	
tuba	low

Their sound can be dramatically changed by 'mutes'. A trumpet with a mute can sound reedy, or if blocked and unblocked with the hand can make a 'wah wah' sound. Muted brass are used a lot in jazz, blending perfectly with the saxophone to form the 'horn section'.

The saxophone is a relatively recent invention of the mid-nineteenth century. It is a hybrid instrument, producing sound in a similar way to the clarinet but made of metal so that it has some of the qualities of a brass instrument. It is versatile and highly expressive. The four most common members of the family of saxes are the high soprano, the alto, the tenor and the throaty baritone sax.

Another instrument that has its own family is the mouth organ or harmonica, particularly popularised by Larry Adler. The 'harp', as it is called colloquially, has proved to be indispensable to blues, rhythm'n'blues and rock music. Most harmonicas play in one key only. It consists of a line of fixed-pitch double-reeds which make two notes – one when sucked and the other when blown. The player moves the instrument across the mouth to select the notes.

There is also a series of wind instruments which uses bellows rather than the breath to blow them. These include countless bagpipes from all over the world, the accordion and the pipe organ. The pipe organ has been pivotal to Christian worship. There are organs in almost every church and cathedral in the world. Some of them are immense and would have once required a team of people to supply the puff to keep them going. The steam organ on the other hand was central to the atmosphere of the fun fair. A.A.

ELECTROPHONES

Electrophones produce sound from a vibrating loudspeaker driven by an amplifier. Classification is made according to the way the input signal is amplified.

• All of these instruments are acoustic, but they become electrophones when their sound is amplified electrically.

• A vibrating member is an instrument that relies on mechanical vibration but cannot be sounded acoustically. The vibration must be amplified electrically.

• An electronic instrument has no vibrating parts. Sound is created by electronic oscillators and other circuits.

subcategories	examples
a acoustic	amplified guitar
b vibrating member	electric piano, electric guitar
c electronic	synthesisers, electronic organ

Special Topic 6
Switched On and Amplified –
Twiddling the Knobs and Pumping Up the Volume

Music was turned on when Lee de Forest invented the valve in the early twentieth century. For the first time electrical signals could be amplified. However, the significance of this invention is much greater than might at first be imagined. Here are just a few of its results:

- home entertainment (the phonograph)
- 'crooning': a style of singing which relied on the sound of a quiet, intimate voice over a big band sound
- the electric organ, vibraphone and guitar; the synthesiser and sampler
- rock'n'roll
- electronic and acousmatic music
- home recording, reducing the cost of making a record so much that it has become available to just about anyone.

Cynics would say that the one good thing about electronic instruments is that you can turn them off. To some they are the death of music and to others they are its saviour. Electric music (electrified acoustic music) and electronic music (music generated electronically) are areas still in their infancy and therefore, where most development is taking place.

We continue the story of the guitar with the great instrumental success story of the twentieth century – the electric guitar. Invented in the early 1930s principally by Adolph Rickenbacker, it was first popularised by Charlie Christian. There followed other legendary names – in particular Leo Fender and Les Paul. Les Paul was able to make good jazz/rock music out of the technology in the early 1950s. His recordings are well worth hearing. By the 1960s progressive rock bands, inspired by the likes of Jimi Hendrix (who many still consider the greatest of all rock guitarists), were using the Gibson electric guitar to sing out with controlled feedback.

What is its magic? There is no visible soundboard apart from the amplifier to which it is plugged in. The sound signal is sent to the 'amp', having first been sensed by pick-ups. The placing and quality of these pick-ups is of vital importance. Pick-ups near the bridge are much harsher than the more mellow sound of those near the centre of the string. But what has given the electric guitar the edge over any synthesiser to date, is its availability to be modulated by human touch. All guitarists superimpose their musical personality over the sounds they play. With the aid of effects pedals, the electric guitar can become a rhythmic instrument, a melodic instrument or savage and sexy. The electric bass guitar is just as important and versatile in a less flamboyant way.

The synthesiser is the name given to a vast array of instruments that generate sound electronically. The 'synth' is usually a keyboard instrument and the sounds it can make are almost infinite. Early synthesisers used oscillators to generate sounds which were then filtered, modulated and amplified. Today sounds are more likely to be stored as a 'wave-table' and altered digitally. But there is still a way to go before this will become a true organic performance tool like the electric guitar. The challenge is to create an instrument that offers musical control over its vast range of parameters.

There are many other electronic musical instruments, from the early and successful theremin and the ondes martenot, beloved by Messiaen, through to a plethora of microprocessor-controlled instruments today. A few will take their place beside more established instruments; many more will never be heard of again – which is as much up to marketing and luck as the intrinsic qualities of the instruments.

The synthesiser has been a double outcast, considered a wild rock-music instrument by classical music lovers and an artificial, cold instrument by 'heavy rock' devotees. This attitude is now changing in the popular music world which seems thirsty for new sounds and timbres. Many brilliant musicians have been turned on to the drug of the new electronic timbral palette forever.

A.A.

Activity 2

1 Change or replace the controller of a sound-producing instrument.

2 Build or design a new instrument which sets something into vibration over or within a resonator.

3 SUMMARY

The design of an instrument influences the sound it produces. In Chapter 6 the timbre of sound was discussed. In this chapter the factors that influence its production were introduced. Sound production has three components: a controller, something that vibrates and a signal. The signal is the sound that results after all the controllers have been applied to activate the sound. The controller can be applied via a clarinet reed buzzing away in a mouthpiece, the vibrating lips of a trumpeter's embouchure or finger pressure applied to the instrument. There are many types of sound-producing instruments which can be categorised according to their structure and how they are played. Each instrument creates vibrations which can be acted upon to produce signals called sound.

4 QUESTIONS

1 What are the three elements required to make a sound?

2 What characterises these three elements?

3 What is a transient?

4 What are the five classifications of instruments and sound-producing objects?

5 What are three controls that can be created with the mouth? For example, whistling requires the mouth to form a small aperture through which a constant stream of air passes.

FURTHER READING

- David Sawyer, *Vibrations: Making Unorthodox Musical Instruments*, London: Cambridge University Press (1977).

- Reinhold Banek and Jon Scoville, *Sound Designs: A Handbook of Musical Instrument Building*, Berkeley, California: Ten Speed Press (1995).

FURTHER LISTENING

- Michael Atherton, *Australian Made... Australian Played* (Sounds Australian 1990).*

- John Cage, Sonatas and Interludes (1948).

- Brian Eno, *Discreet Music* (Island 1975).

- Jimi Hendrix, *Are you Experienced?* (Track 1967).

- Led Zeppelin, *Led Zeppelin III* (Atlantic 1970).

- The Merry-Go-Round, 'Time Will Show the Wiser' on *The Best of The Merry-Go Round* (Rhino 1983).

- Prince, *Sign O' The Times*, Disc 1, tracks 1, 4, 5 and 8, Disc 2, tracks 2 and 3, (Paisley Park 1987).

IMPROVISATIONS

Start and finish the session with a free or structured improvisation.

1 Explore different uses of controllers on your voice. For example, sing with your fingers in your mouth or try different positions and movements of your tongue. Does the signal radically change with different controllers?

2 Explore the different types of sounds available to a microphone, tape recorder and loud-speaker. Place the microphone in front of the tape recorder speaker while it is recording, to create feedback sounds.

3 Improvise on a 'prepared' piano or guitar. How do the sounds change the way you think about the instrument?

8 OLD SOUNDS, NEW CONTEXTS ...
NEW SOUNDS, OLD CONTEXTS

An old Ponca ... was heard to hum a familiar Omaha song. He was asked, 'Where did you learn the song?' 'Among the Omaha,' he replied. 'When did you learn it?' 'When I was a lad.' 'Have you always sung it as you sing it now?' With a look of astonishment he replied: 'There is but one way to sing a song!' Alice C. Fletcher and Francis La Flesche[19]

The Algerian popular music known as rai started early in this century as transcriptions of the unaccompanied tribal songs of the interior for the saxophones and violins played by dance bands in the coastal cities. As this process continued, the influences of Algeria's Spanish, Moroccan and French communities were felt (with a particular emphasis on Flamenco). In recent years a new rai has emerged, called pop-rai, that incorporates Western rock and disco rhythms for synthesizers and drums. Peter Spencer[20]

The history of music is a history of social interaction. When two different cultural groups come into contact, inevitably the music from each group eventually shows the influence of the other. Musicologists call this syncretism.

> Syncretism ... refers to the process by which old meanings are ascribed to new elements or by which new values change the cultural significance of old forms. Alan P. Merriam[21]

Music which avoids syncretism, like the Omaha song, is music that preserves traditional values. It is part of the preservation of social, religious or cultural values in a community. A change in the music implies a change in the community.

The musician's search for new sounds is also a search for a new musical vocabulary. An unwanted sound within a particular musical vocabulary may be classed as a noise – it depends upon the listener's criteria for defining a meaningful sound structure. The pleasure derived from listening is very subjective.

1 OLD AND NEW CONTEXTS

Traditions can be classified into two categories: mobile and fixed. A mobile tradition is one undergoing syncretism, such as *rai*, mentioned above.

A mobile tradition is dynamic. It continually questions its practice and searches for new modes of musical expression through sounds, contexts or ways of playing. Jazz is one such example. Consider the development over the decades across ragtime, New Orleans jazz, swing, bop, cool, free jazz and jazz rock. Or compare a radio or television advertisement from the fifties with one from the nineties: this is another tradition that is continually in flux. It cannot afford to be fixed; it has to change with the ethos and ethics of the time.

The fixed tradition is one in which conventions never change and both composers and performers work within these fixed conventions. The sounds are old and respected, the context and meaning is always the same. This is exemplified by such grand musical traditions as Japanese court music and traditional blues.

Listening Example 19: 'Ecce Dominus', Gregorian Chant
The Gregorian chant is an example of a fixed music tradition. It was sung for the liturgy in cathedrals for hundreds of years and is still used today in traditional liturgical rites.

Listening Example 20: *Lascivious Serenade*, **Edward Primrose (1998)**

The Australian composer Edward Primrose has written a series of works for instrumental combinations from around the world, including tabla (India), ud (Middle East), saz (Turkey), medieval psaltery and hurdy-gurdy, saxophone, violin, synthesiser and voice. The mixture of instruments creates a wonderful new sound-world as unrelated traditions come into exotic combination.

Another example of the use of instruments from diverse traditions is 'Freedom Now' by the Australian Aboriginal rock band Yothu Yindi. In this song the didjeridu is played in a context that has nothing to do with its original environment. The combination of the traditional instrument and Western rock'n'roll lets the music speak to people who are familiar with either musical tradition.

Special Topic 1
Music of the Indian Subcontinent –
Where the Subtleties of Melody Encapsulate an Entire Musical Culture

The depth of Indian and Pakistani musical history is overwhelming – from the exquisite raga *to the spiritually powerful* qawwali, *the delightful* ghazal *and ubiquitous music of the Indian film industry. Eastern music is nowhere more seductive to an inquiring Western mind than here in this artistically rich subcontinent.*

The explosion of Western interest in Indian music was spearheaded in the 1960s by the Beatles and Ravi Shankar. The music which most caught their attention, and has been the most popular ever since with non-Eastern audiences, is the raga. *To define* raga *(pronounced 'raag') is almost to define Hindustani music itself. Each* raga *is based on one of a series of scales, some of which are easier for Western ears to assimilate than others. Their equivalent would be the ancient Greek modes, except that where there are eight modes there are around two hundred* ragas, *some of which may be different when ascending and descending (like the melodic minor scale). There are different* ragas *for the different times of day, the* yaman *probably being the most popular, which is a late evening* raga.

To listen to a raga *on CD it is preferable to hear it at the appropriate time of day and in a still and calm environment. The magic will infuse you. A live performance is even better. Out of the stillness comes the slow meditative* alaap, *the presentation of the* raga. *The four-stringed* tamboura *(or another drone instrument) accompanies the melody instrument (usually a sitar or sarod) with its own set of 'sympathetic' or resonating strings. In a 'true' live performance, a private party, this* alaap *and its free rhythmic exposition may last for several hours. On CD it can only take a few minutes. The essence of Indian music is improvisation around the* raga.

The two central sections (the johl *and* jhala *sections) introduce the rhythmic elements. When eventually the tabla or another percussive drum enters (the* gath *section) the rhythm heats up. These complex rhythms, or* taals, *are more numerous even than the* ragas *and are again improvisational. Without a score, the inventiveness and sensitivity of the performer is therefore pivotal. Eventually the intensity and interplay between the performers builds to a climax.*

A lighter branch of this North Indian classical music is the ghazal, *a song-based form incorporating poetry and music, which has become the cornerstone of the Indian film music industry. A similar form is the romantically inclined* thumri.

Most recent interest in music of this area has concentrated on Islamic Sufi devotional music called qawwali *from Pakistan. This is essentially a vocal music, accompanied by harmonium and some percussion. The melodic lines are liquid, led by a performer known as a* qawwal. *Its most famous exponent in the West was Nusrat Fateh Ali Khan. He led a group of singers and performers (all men) in a style which used repetition and improvisation to achieve a trance-like mood. It is truly inspirational music, moving and powerful for both the performers and its increasingly large audiences.*   *A.A.*

2 NEW SOUNDS, NEW CONTEXTS

The innovative use of an instrument or its placement in a new context makes a musical tradition mobile. A new context allows the listener to hear the instrument or sound afresh and creates possibilities that did not exist before.

Some of the approaches to performance practice or instrumental writing which can change a musical tradition are:

- providing a new context,
- changing the role and function of the instrument,
- introducing a new or extended instrumental technique or
- changing the instrument's traditional mode of performance.

NEW CONTEXTS

The placement of a recognised sound in a new or foreign environment has long been an important technique in music. Musicians have often freely mixed and combined the music

Special Topic 2
Cross-currents

'A great big melting pot, big enough to take the world and all it's got.'　　**Blue Mink**

African slavery in North America has been credited with the origin of the spiritual, gospel, jazz, blues, R&B (rhythm and blues), rock'n'roll, funk, rap and soul. Little did the slave owners of the Americas or the Caribbean realise how much more they were dragging across the ocean than unpaid work. In nineteenth-century North America, the African slaves sang working songs together (Negro spirituals). Later, around the turn of the century when conditions were marginally improved, the blues emerged. Usually one person would stoically sing of living conditions and general discrimination. Their hopes vested in God were encapsulated in the gospel song. But the desire to play and celebrate eventually surfaced in a more instrumental form, jazz. And this was embraced by the white community too. So the story of the influence of Africa continued in jazz, developing and mixing with blues to become R&B which in turn begat rock'n'roll, and in time, funk and rap. Gospel music found a contemporary spiritual home in soul music – some of the most moving songs you can hear today.

In South America, especially the Caribbean, the results were very different. As well as the African and Latin influences, South American music has a third influence from the indigenous Indians, most notably in their use of the pan-pipes. The music has given us salsa, samba, bossa nova, chicha, lambada and tango. South American music is famous for its passionate, syncopated dance rhythms and swing – a very physical music. The composer Heitor Villa-Lobos, who started his career playing the cello and guitar in the cafés of Rio, fused South American traditions with Western art music. More recently, the turbulent politics of the region have spawned 'new song', a highly allegorical and subversive style of music.

In the United Kingdom and Europe, each wave of immigrants has made its mark on the music of its adoptive country. Zap Mama, an all-female group from Belgium, are a prime example, as were Osibisa in London in the 1970s and the countless soukous bands in Paris. Reggae came from Africa via the Caribbean. And similarly rap, which hails from black urban USA, has taken over the city streets of Europe.

In Africa itself the flow has also been two-way. Zaire has embraced the electric guitar and adapted it to their own style of plucked-string playing. Jazz has been reimported into west Africa. The line-up of a black South African band may look remarkably similar to any in London, New York or Paris, but the sound is distinctive and in demand worldwide.　　*A.A.*

of their own traditions with music from other cultures or earlier styles. This is probably
the basis of musical evolution. Consider the influence of jazz on music around the world
or the influence of Arabic music on the West in the sixth century. Rock 'n' roll was
the product of interaction between gospel and country and western. The combination
of diverse sounds and patterns often produces interesting paradoxes. The reconciliation
of the two opposing styles, if successful, often leads to the formation of new musical
tradition.

The following pieces offer three different approaches to the harpsichord.

Listening Example 21: *La Nanete*, François Couperin (1716)

The harpsichord is primarily associated with the Baroque. It began to lose prominence
in the latter part of the eighteenth century when it was superseded by the fortepiano,
a later development of the harpsichord which offered a much wider range of volume and
a richer tone. The fortepiano could project further in public spaces as well as hold its
own in larger ensembles. Traditional harpsichord music explores counterpoint, to which
this instrument is ideally suited due to the quick decay of the harpsichord sound envelope.
Prominent characteristics of the music are rapid note movement as exemplified in the
ornamentation of the melody, and the vertical collision of notes to form particular
harmonic relationships.

In 'Fixing a Hole' by the Beatles (1967), the harpsichord plays an accompaniment usually
given to the piano. The sound of the Baroque instrument takes on new life in the context
of pop music. The album it featured on, *Sergeant Pepper's Lonely Hearts Club Band*, was
revolutionary in its time for precisely the reasons discussed in this chapter. Many of the
sounds on the album proposed new conventions, incorporating technological innovations
from the avant-garde electronic music of the period.

Listening Example 22: Demonstration of harpsichord combined with percussion

In this example a harpsichord is pitted against a barrage of percussion sounds. The harmonic and textural context is completely different from the previous two examples.
We hear the sound of the harpsichord in its unadulterated rawness and vitality. In the
Western concert tradition the percussion ensemble belongs purely to the twentieth century
and the clusters, registral juxtapositions and textural overlays – normally associated with
the musical vocabulary of the mid-twentieth century – are played here on an instrument
which flourished two centuries before.

It is through these 'assaults' on the assumed practices of harpsichord performance
methods that this instrument continually changes, freeing itself from a particular moment
in history.

The practice of mixing tribal or folk music from another culture with pop music is very
common. Deep Forest perfected this technique in the song 'Sweet Lullaby' (1992).
An earlier example can be found in 'A Secret Life' by Brian Eno and David Byrne. In this
song Samira Tewfik sings an Egyptian popular song over a background of ambient guitar
and percussion sounds. The Egyptian song has been lifted virtually completely intact from
its original context and placed in an environment for which it was never intended.

Special Topic 3
Africa –
Rhythm, Blues, Blacks, Whites

The diversity of the vast continent of Africa is obvious from a glance at the map. But what binds it together? What makes a piece of music essentially African?

So central is music to African culture that although African languages have myriad terms for song forms and dances, they seldom have a single word for music itself. As Jim Chapman, Lecturer in World Music at the Queensland University of Technology, said: 'Everyone in Africa sings, so to call someone a singer is similar to calling someone a breather'.

From the djembe *to the modern drum kit and the marimba to the unique talking drum, in every African country, rhythm drives the music. With such complex rhythmic and polyrhythmic structures there is little room for equivalently elaborate modulating harmonies. Of course there are exceptions; the harmonies of some of the choral music, which is distinctly African, were developed during European colonisation. However, the root of most African harmony is modal or pentatonic. The ubiquitous thumb piano often has as few as five notes. Interestingly the interweaving of these modal instruments often creates textures akin to contemporary minimalist music by composers such as Philip Glass.*

In many African languages, like many Asian ones, tones are an essential part of pronunciation. That is, sometimes the same collection of consonants and vowels can mean something radically different depending upon the pitch and inflection used. Vocal melody has to take this into account, and in fact is often determined by the linguistic content. Yoruba *drumming and singing from Nigeria is an example.*

Until recently African music was mainly transmitted orally. It was never written down but passed on through families or master musicians. This gave it life and currency, but also made it more susceptible to outside influences such as Islam and more recently the West.

Many Christian churches in Africa were hostile to African music-making, in particular to the drumming at its heart. Western music practice was in many cases foisted upon the indigenous population and became the benchmark for 'good' music. However, the colonial practice of ignoring the traditional music ironically allowed it to flourish outside the official music-making channels. The culture was too resilient to be eradicated. In time new influences were grafted on, creating fresh musical forms, such as the choral music in South Africa.

More recently, since the 1930s, new technology has been stirring the cross-cultural currents. Audio recording centres created the first archives of traditional music and new instruments have been introduced. A.A.

FURTHER LISTENING

- *Papa Wemba (Zaire)*
- *Angelique Kidjo (African tonal music)*
- *Geoffrey Oryema (Uganda)*
- *Youssou N'Dour (West Africa)*
- *Salif Keita & the Ambassadors (West Africa)*
- *Bhundu Boys (Zimbabwe)*
- *Miriam Makeba (South Africa)*
- *Ladysmith Black Mambazo (South Africa)*

CHANGING THE ROLE OF INSTRUMENTS

The roles instruments play in music is an essential part of the composition's construction. Sometimes the role of the instrument is so novel that it creates a revolution and a new way of thinking. Changing the role of an instrument can produce a new sound, new sonic relationships, or a new textural organisation. In the next two examples you will hear two completely different approaches to the role of the drum kit.

Listening Example 23: *The Naked Kiss*, Andy Arthurs (1997)
In this example the drum kit has a purely rhythmic function providing a back beat.

'Fever', sung by Peggy Lee, is an excellent example of the use of a drum kit in a variety of roles. In this song the beat is articulated mainly by finger clicks and to a lesser extent the double bass. The drum kit's role, on the other hand, has been changed from rhythmic to melodic. Its role is purely timbral, providing colour and texture as it comments on the text. It is also eruptive as it freely interjects in the song, producing a much more expressive piece of music.

Listening Example 24: Drumkit Improvisation
In this example the drum kit has been freed from its traditional rhythmic role of supporting the main melodic instruments with a steady rhythmic beat. Its role now is purely gestural and textural in which rhythms become layers of sounds allowing timbre to predominate.

EXTENDED INSTRUMENTAL TECHNIQUES
The history of instrumental practice is essentially the history of instruments extended beyond their normal practice. Chopin's piano works were written to develop the piano's range. Bach's *Well Tempered Clavier* was written to show the potential of the equal tempered tuning system.

The opening bassoon melody of Stravinsky's *Le sacre du printemps* was one of the early examples in the twentieth century of extended instrumental techniques. Playing the bassoon in its top register was unheard of in 1913 and considered too difficult to be practical. *Le sacre du printemps* caused its first audience to riot but today it is part of the standard repertoire. *Le sacre du printemps* is full of new instrumental sonorities and remains an orchestral masterpiece of the twentieth century in the field of new sounds for orchestra.

The unleashing of instrumental timbral qualities to explore and liberate pure sound is the predominant feature of virtually all forms of music in the second half of the twentieth century. Sound shapes and particular types of timbral articulations become motivic units; and development is achieved by the juxtaposition and variation of sonic shapes. Often the traditional concept of melody is gone completely. The instrument becomes the source of a sensuous outpouring of new sound. This is what made Jimi Hendrix a unique guitar player in the 1960s.

Listening Example 25: *Tango*, Richard Vella (1990)
In this example the clarinet plays glissandi, multiphonics (two or more notes at the same time) and extreme register leaps.

The liberation of sound has also led to the incorporation of all sounds into the sonic canvas. Sounds from the environment, domestic sounds, any sound can become a compositional input.

Listening Example 26: *Dark Matter*, Jim Denley (1991)

The flautist completely avoids any suggestion of melody in this piece. Instead he creates units of sound which are extended and then interrupted. Sound becomes a mobile, highly fluid unit of time, each with its own identifiable sensuous quality. The musician explores different types of blowing sounds and accents, two or more notes at once (called multi-phonics), and the instrument's harmonic series by whistling into it.

Listening Example 27: *Genesis*, Andy Arthurs (1997)

This example combines bird calls, didjeridu, electronic manipulations of trombone sounds and pre-recorded drum sounds in an evocative sonic tapestry.

CHANGING THE INSTRUMENT'S TRADITIONAL MODE OF PERFORMANCE

John Cage's prepared piano techniques, discussed in the previous chapter, are also examples of changing an instrument's traditional mode of performance. There are many other examples of this approach in which composers or musicians have changed or modified some aspect of an instrument in order to create a new sound. In 'Vocalise' by George Crumb, part of his exotic work *Vox balaenae* (1971) *(The Voice of the Whale)*, the music is produced by silently pressing down a chord on the piano keyboard and strumming

Special Topic 4
Albert Ayler (1936-1971) –
Free Jazz Techniques

Albert Ayler was a New York jazz musician who extended the boundaries of saxophone technique. His style was expressive, ecstatic, primal, often atonal and, at the same time, simple and poignant. He was one of the many musicians – along with Ornette Coleman, Cecil Taylor, Pharoah Sanders and Archie Shepp – who developed avant-garde free jazz in the 1960s. The free jazz movement was a reaction against mainstream jazz which had become confined by convention and popular among the white community. Many black musicians used free jazz both to extend the form and as a political expression of black America.

Many of Ayler's recordings transgress the traditions of not only his own instrument but also the others in his band. His version of George Gershwin's famous 'Summertime' (1935), on the album My Name is Albert Ayler, makes beautifully expressive use of the saxophone. The solo is no longer driven by motivic and thematic development. Instead, the melody is transformed by new sounds and articulations. Ayler incorporates pitch bends, pure timbral eruptions of colour, register leaps, squeaks and textural bursts. The instrument moans and wails like an animal. Each sound is crucial to the song's emotional and formal conception.

In Spirits *(1964) on the* Spirits Rejoice *album, the drums and double bass have been completely freed of their traditional homophonic rhythmic role of supporting the main melodic instrument. Their function is purely textural. The independence of the instrument parts creates more complexity. The concept of a beat has been completely abandoned. Movement is created by phrasing, rhythmic counterpoint and textural shape. Instead of a steady rhythmic pulse with supportive harmonic changes, the accompanying musicians anticipate the beginning of each player's phrase, and play textural shapes of varying intensity, polyrhythms.*   R.V.

SELECT DISCOGRAPHY

- Witches and Devils *(Freedom 1964).*
- Free Jazz *(Debut 1962).*
- Spirits Rejoice *(ESP 1965).*
- *Albert Ayler,* The Last Album *(Impulse 1969).*

the strings like a harp. The cello plays harmonics only, producing an eerie melody in its top register. In both instruments the composer has explored new timbres. It is as if he were revealing another 'personality' of the instruments by investigating qualities not usually associated with them. The high-pitched harmonics of the cello are also reminiscent of the sounds of whales.

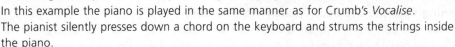

Listening Example 28: Example of a piano played from the inside
In this example the piano is played in the same manner as for Crumb's *Vocalise*. The pianist silently presses down a chord on the keyboard and strums the strings inside the piano.

3 THE INFLUENCE OF ELECTRONIC AND DIGITAL TECHNOLOGY

In the early 1950s composers started exploiting the potential of the tape recorder. They would record a sound and then manipulate it by playing it backwards, slowing it down, cutting it into smaller pieces, re-combining and joining disparate sounds, overdubbing other sounds or creating interesting repetitive cycles called tape loops. The style of composing was called *musique concrète* and was largely pioneered by the French composer Pierre Schaeffer. See Special Topic 2, The Autonomous Aural Object, in Chapter 20.

Electronic processing was another significant development of the 1950s which allowed composers to manipulate sounds by electronic controllers. This transformed familiar sounds and produced an array of completely new ones. An important factor was the sudden discovery by musicians of the potential of the microphone in performance and recording.

One of the most famous electronic works of the 1960s was *Microphonie* by the German composer Karlheinz Stockhausen. In this piece, the microphone becomes an instrument, acting as an interface between the tam-tam (a gong) and the controlling filters. In this work, all sounds are based on the tam-tam. The manipulations are all electronic, using microphones, filters which select parts of the sound and potentiometers. As this piece demonstrates, the microphone need not always play a silent part in performance. In *Microphonie* different uses radically change sounds through distortion or close-up recording.

Cheaper technology has made sound mixing widely available and has revitalised both musical practice and listening, especially in popular music. Units such as flangers and phasers were commonly used in the 1970s by rock'n'roll guitarists. Flanges and phases are delay techniques in which a sound is played back upon itself creating a much richer result.

Sampling, which encodes recorded sounds digitally in a keyboard, computer or sampler unit, has enabled composers to transfer sounds from virtually any context into any other. It has become common practice to make new recordings composed entirely from samples. The popular music industry has dominated this approach, often constructing complete recordings from other recorded sounds except, possibly, for the vocalist. Traditional instruments can be combined with helicopters, gun shots, a crying baby, voices and electronic and synthesised sounds. In fact, anything is possible – the pleasure of music is essentially the realisation that music is the unfolding of sound within the endless possibilities of new, old and revitalised musical environments.

One of the most famous examples of sampling can be heard in Laurie Anderson's 'O Superman' (1982). This was one of the first instances of a music recording defined by the technology of sampling. For example, the recorded note 'Ha' is a perfect repetition of the spoken articulation every time it is used; the singer's voice has also been manipulated by a harmoniser which transforms it into a chord.

Listening Example 29: *Fantasy Island*, Andy Arthurs and Philip Chambon

Apart from the main soloist and guitar, all the sounds on this recording are samples played back via a keyboard sequencer. The sampled vocal sounds are put on a loop to create rhythms with a precision impossible for a human performer to produce.

Listening Example 30: *Orchid*, Greg White (1994)

In 'Orchid' the clarinettist is required to control two pedals at certain moments in performance. One pedal selects samples of recordings and manipulations of earlier music by the same composer; the other controls the tempo of the playback samples. The samples function to accompany or oppose the clarinet, resulting in a more complex surface of textures.

Listening Example 31: *Splinter*, Jon Drummond (1998)

This example, like listening to a cymbal from the inside and outside at the same time, has been created by manipulating aspects of the sampled sound. The sound has been created by using 'phase vocoding' and 'granular synthesis'. Phase vocoding changes the pitch of the sound without affecting the tempo while granular synthesis dissects the sound into tiny pieces like grains of sound. The composer can then manipulate the register, envelope and attack of each 'grain', play them backwards, combine them with others and so on. Detail is highlighted, new sound envelopes created and the cymbal becomes a microcosm of sound events.

4 SUMMARY

The search for new sounds is an exciting and ever-changing musical practice which allows some very expressive ways of playing. Playing within a fixed musical tradition can be just as rewarding, requiring discipline and technique. A mobile musical tradition essentially explores new means of emotional expression when older ways become perhaps clichéd, out of fashion or less challenging. This does not necessarily mean that they are never used again. What one era considers unimportant or obsolete, another rediscovers. The availability of technology enables music to be mixed and revitalised. Sound becomes liberated. A recorded sound can be re-combined in an infinite number of ways. It is in the continual revitalising, recontextualising and extension of sonic gestures and techniques that music becomes a dynamic and exciting form.

5 QUESTIONS

1 What is syncretism?

2 What is a fixed tradition?

3 What is a mobile tradition?

4 What are the four approaches which can affect a musical tradition?

5 List some of the aspects of electronic and digital technology.

Special Topic 5

The Spiritual –
Music Born From Slavery

The spiritual, often referred to as the Negro spiritual, was the first cross-cultural music produced by Africa and the West. The harmonies do not modulate and indeed are often pentatonic (as for example in 'Swing Low Sweet Chariot'). However the harmonic progressions, usually in the Protestant hymn tradition, were built on small motifs just as in west African music, which was the area from which most American slaves were taken. The call-and-response technique which originated in Africa was adapted in the spiritual and used in extended improvisations.

Although slaves were prohibited from dancing or playing instruments, religious worship was not banned. The slaves would sing a spiritual and often bend their knees to bring them closer to their God, not of heaven, but the earth. They used syncopated and polyrhythmic sections, something quite rare in the European art music tradition before 1900, and although the singing was without instruments (a cappella), it was often accompanied by quite complex clapping rhythms.

Native African slaves were forced to stop practising their own religions and so adapted the music and words of Christian worship, both to fulfil a spiritual need and also to carry subversive messages in code. Singing about Moses who led the Jews out of slavery in Egypt, for example, was a powerful analogy. This was also an important part of the language of the conductors of the underground railroad, the 'freedom train'. The spiritual was the basis of later black Christian gospel music, which in turn spawned soul music. A.A.

FURTHER LISTENING

- Peter Jenkin, *A Day in the Life of a Clarinet* (Tall Poppies 1990).
- Jim Denley, *Dark Matter* (Tall Poppies 1991).
- George Crumb, *Vox Balaenae (The Voice of the Whale)* 'Vocalise' (1971).
- The Beatles 'Fixing a Hole', *Sergeant Pepper's Lonely Hearts Club Band* (Parlophone 1967).

Cultural Interaction

- King Sunny Adé, *Juju Music* (Mango 1982).
- Mango (Island).
- Youssou N'Dour, *Set* (Virgin 1990).
- *Irakere-Irakere* (CBS/Columbia). A Cuban jazz band.
- *Out of Africa* (Rykodisc 1988). This is an excellent compilation of 1980s African pop styles.

Old Sounds, New Contexts

- Brigid Burke and Rainer Linz, *Intersect,* (NMA 1997).*
- Miles Davis, *Star People* (Columbia 1983).

New Contexts

- The Beach Boys, 'Good Vibrations', *Smiley Smile* (Capitol 1967).
- Beastie Boys, *Ill Communication* (Grand Royale/Capitol 1994).
- Björk, tracks 3, 8 and 11, *Debut* (Elektra 1993).

- Deep Forest, 'Sweet Lullaby', *Deep Forest* (Epic 1992).
- Joni Mitchell, track 2, *The Hissing of Summer Lawns* (Assylum 1975).
- The Residents, *Third Reich'n'Roll* (Ralph 1976). ‡
- Swordfish, track 3, *Genii* (Volition 1994). ‡
- Frank Zappa, Disc 1, tracks 8 and 10, Disc 2, tracks 1, 2 and 14,
  The Best Band You Never Heard In Your Life (Barking Pumpkin 1991). ‡

Changing Role of Instruments
- Laurie Anderson, tracks 3, 4, 10, 11 and 12, *Bright Red* (Warners 1994).
- The Dirty Three, self-titled album (Torn & Frayed 1994). ‡
- Einstürzende Neubauten, *Strategien Gegen Architecturen* (Mute 1983). ‡
- Kraftwerk, *Autobahn* (Vertigo 1974) and *Radio-Activity* (Capitol 1975). ‡
- The Velvet Underground, tracks 4, 6, 7, 10 and 11,
  The Velvet Underground and Nico (Verve 1967).

Extended Instrumental Techniques
- Luciano Berio, *Sequenza V* (1968).
- Björk, tracks 2, 3, 4 and 9, *Post* (Elektra 1995).
- James Brown, tracks 2, 3, 11, 14 and 16, *The CD of JB* (Polydor 1985).
- Nick Cave, tracks 1,2,4 and 10, *From Her To Eternity* (Mute 1984). ‡
- Frith & Kaiser, *With Enemies Like These, Who Needs Friends* (SST 1987).
- Jimi Hendrix, 'Star Spangled Banner' (1969).
- Yoko Ono, John Lennon, *Plastic Ono Band* (Apple 1970).
- Salvatore Sciarrino, Capriccio No. 1 (1976).
- Sonic Youth, tracks 3, 4, 7, 8 and 9, *EVOL* (SST 1986). ‡
- Witold Szalonek, *Pierikiana* (1979).
- Frank Zappa, Disc 1, *Uncle Meat* (Bizarre 1968). ‡

IMPROVISATIONS

Start and finish the session with a free or structured improvisation.

1 Improvise or compose a work using a performance technique foreign to its environment, e.g. create a rhythm section made from sounds unrelated to drums, such as hitting the ends of pipes with the soles of a pair of shoes.

2 Explore approaches to sounds with your voice or an instrument that go beyond their normal performance practices. Create a work in which these approaches are an important part of the composition.

3 If you have a microphone and amplification equipment, explore the radical and subtle effects microphone placement has upon a sound made by your voice, an instrument, a surface or an object.

9 RESONATING INSTRUMENTS AND SPACES

Then the celestial harmony sounded and all the earth marvelled.
Hildegard von Bingen (1098-1179)[22]

Soundwaves are activated within an enclosed space producing vibrations. The timbre of these vibrations is dependent on the quality and construction of the enclosed space. The sound of a bell varies depending on whether the clapper is made of soft or hard metal and the shape of the bell. Each violin has a unique sound depending on the nature of its wood, varnish, bow, etc. The sound of an instrument is enhanced by its resonator which radiates the sound waves. The resonator can be an enclosed pipe, as in a flute; or a wooden box, as in a violin. The soundboard inside the enclosed space of a piano is the resonator which enables the piano's tone to be radiated and amplified. The resonator of a guitar is the enclosing wooden case which amplifies the plucked, vibrating strings. The enclosed space causes amplification by reflecting the sound waves inside the case and adding to the overall sound.

1 RESONATING SPACES

Large architectural spaces are like gigantic resonating chambers. This is due to reverberation. Reverberation occurs when sounds are reflected off the walls of an enclosed space. As well as the direct sound waves reaching your ears, there are others behaving like billiard balls as they bounce off all the surfaces. A dead reverberant space is one with minimal reflection while a live reverberant space has a lot of reflection.

The reverberation of a space greatly affects the way we perceive a sound or music.
A marble foyer has a different sound from one that is carpeted. An indoor basketball court is a huge resonating and vibrating chamber in which the sound of the ball bouncing, the yells of the players and their stamping and running are triggers. Buildings can be designed to be acoustically efficient or functional. The choice of materials is a major factor. A foyer made of concrete reflects sound more, resulting in long decaying and blurred sounds; the same foyer furnished with carpet and curtains sounds clearer as the carpet and curtains absorb the sound in the space.

The relationship between an articulated sound and its environment is crucial to how it is perceived. In the Australian bush, the cooee call is used to locate people. The reverberation and placement of the call gives the listener information about how far away the caller is.

Listening Example 32: Gregorian Chant, 'Hodie Christus Natus Est' (anon.)
Because medieval cathedrals are predominantly made of stone and marble the reverberation time is relatively slow. The slow organic quality of the Gregorian chant allows each sound to be heard clearly. If the music were sung more quickly the reflection of all the sounds would cause the music to blur as the decay of one sound event mixes with the attack of the next.

Listening Example 33: Church bell from Margherita Piazza, Venice, recorded by Trevor Pearce (1988)
The church bell in any town or city is a wonderful example of a signal resounding in a reverberant space. The bell can be heard over a great distance as its sound waves bounce along walls, buildings and travel over open fields.

Special Topic 1
Reverberation

When we hear the sound of an instrument emitting from a room, our ears receive sound waves from a variety of sources. First we hear the direct sound coming from the instrument. These are the sound waves that have not been reflected by any surface. Then, those sound waves which have been reflected off the room's surfaces begin to reach our ears. Obviously these arrive later because their journey is longer. The following simple diagram demonstrates reverberation.

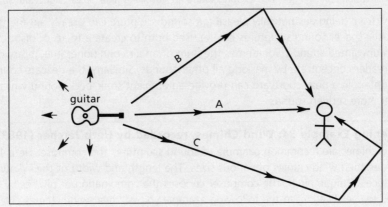

Figure 19: *Reverberation.*

Soundwave A reaches our ears first, taking the shortest route and not experiencing reflection. Soundwave B has a longer journey, reaching our ears via the right hand side of the room. Soundwave C is reflected off two walls and therefore takes the longest time to reach us. It follows that because soundwave A has the shortest route to travel and the shortest travel time, it is more concentrated and is therefore perceived as the loudest while soundwave C is perceived as the softest.

Recording engineers exploit this phenomenon: with the help of a reverberation unit, they can increase the loudness or brightness of background reverberation and mix it with foreground reverberation to create a rich sound which would be virtually impossible to produce naturally. R.V.

Activity 1
Environment excursion: Go to a public area such as a hotel foyer, tunnel, courtyard or mall. Listen to the overall soundspace as if it were an instrument and all the sounds made in it were its components. Does the environment you are listening to have a lot of reverberation? If so, what would stop unnecessary reverberation? Are there other sounds contributing to the overall environment which add to or detract from the soundspace?

2 SOUND SCULPTURES AND INSTALLATIONS

Many sound artists and composers design sounds for specific contexts or spaces. Sound can be used to create a relaxing environment in a public place or to create new and unexpected experiences of familiar surroundings. A sound installation can be as simple as a set of loudspeakers transmitting bird sounds in a underground railway station or it could be a structure specially designed for interaction. The placement of sounds in specific spaces is generically termed sound sculpture. The term 'Site Specific' is used for works created for a specific location such as an old building or railway station.

Sound sculptures and installations are specifically designed sound-producing instruments, resonators or transmitters that explore a sound in a particular context. The sound sculpture is a visual and auditory experience. The composer is equally concerned with the visual design of the sculpture as its sound. In her book *Sounds in Space* the composer Ros Bandt writes:

> Sound sculpture is the organisation of sound in space. It is a way of thinking and working with the sounds around us. Sound sculpture is the bringing together of visual art and musical art. The fusion makes a new and exciting sound art, involving time, space, sight, and sound.[23]

Apart from being aesthetically pleasing a sound sculpture can greatly aid the design of acoustic space. Sound sculptures can be used both to create a focus or distract attention from unwanted sounds. Sometimes the hum of an air conditioner in a library helps the reader concentrate by masking all other sounds. Similarly, the delicate sounds of a fountain in a busy courtyard can provide an ambient sonic background which neutralises other more sudden sounds.

Listening Example 34: Wind Chimes, recorded by Herb Jercher (1983)
Wind chimes are a common example of sound sculpture. The composer Herb Jercher has designed wind chimes of various sizes. The length and width of the cylindrical pipes produce a unique pitch. The composer chooses the combination of pitches by cutting the pipes to specification. In the following example you will hear wind chimes cut to lengths varying between four feet and twelve inches.

Listening Example 35: 'Ocean Bells', *Glass and Clay*, Ros Bandt (1982)
Ros Bandt is a pioneer of sound sculpture. She has built elaborate wind chimes made from diverse materials, invented instruments and explored the many relationships of sound in acoustic space. (An example of her improvisations in a wheat silo was given in Chapter 3.) Her work 'Ocean Bells' is performed on a chime called a 'flagong'. The flagong is an original playable sound sculpture. It is a percussion instrument made from flagons and bottles from which the bottoms have been removed to make bell structures which are suspended from a wooden frame. It consists of thirty-one microtonal glass bells which are rearranged for each piece so that the instrument constantly changes. The vertical rack is played with mallets of different types and the sculpture has been influenced by Harry Partch's chamber bowls.

Both Ros Bandt and Herb Jercher have designed sound playgrounds in which all the instruments have been made from found objects from industrial sites and factories. The collection of instruments has been designed like a children's playground; participants are encouraged to go from one instrument to the next like children going from the monkey bars to the swings; the difference is that each piece of equipment is a musical sound source. The result is an interactive free sculpture which can be played by several people at once.

Activity 2
Choose a location to construct a sound environment installation which will add to the overall soundscape. Does the space have reverberation? What sculptural materials would be appropriate to the space? Does the installation explore natural phenomena such as wind, birds or rainfall?

3 SUMMARY

The sound artist and composer of sound sculptures and installations have turned the traditional concept of music-making on its head. They acknowledge the important role of context as well as sound structure. Sound sculptures can be specially designed structures which are visually and sonically pleasing, or completely designed environments such as museums or office foyers.

Special Topic 2
In Music Everything Has Its Sonic and Spectral Space

The advent of computers has meant that not just sound but parameters such as attack, sustain and decay can now be augmented. Computers can amplifiy all the body's senses and actions.

Perspective is the perception of physical positioning using visual or aural clues. In art the vanishing point is the furthest point the eye can see. Similarly, when a sound becomes too quiet to hear it seems to have slipped beyond the aural vanishing point. Acoustic reflections (reverberation) are also sonic clues about the position of a sound in space. Hearing a more distant sound involves not only hearing the direct sound but also indirect sound emissions, as it bounces off the landscape and objects. Sometimes the source of a sound is obscured by something closer. This changes the tone of the sound, the obstruction absorbing the higher, brighter frequencies.

By working with new technologies composers have been able to extend the manipulation of sound texture, i.e. orchestration, beyond anything their predecessors might have dreamed possible. For example, because all sounds can now be amplified, a rustle of paper can be matched to the roar of an aeroplane. Although it requires new skills, at the heart is still the art of listening and making aesthetic and musical judgements. For example, as a trombone gets louder it also becomes harsher. This harshness relates to the increase in loudness – or the level – of the upper partials or harmonics. A synthesiser can develop this raspiness further by adding more and more overtones until the trombone sound dissolves into noise. Just as the development of digital special effects has allowed the cinema to venture into the super-real, the synthesist can now not only orchestrate a piece, but create the orchestra itself. Compared to earlier centuries therefore, the repertory of sounds available to late twentieth-century composers is virtually unlimited.

'Electrical instruments will make available any and all sounds that can be heard.' John Cage (1937)

Stereo was invented to give recordings greater depth. Today with multi-speaker PA setups, antiphony (i.e. call and response technique) is back with a vengeance. Pink Floyd and Jean-Michel Jarre achieve wonderful ambiences, way beyond the physical spaces in which they perform.

Digital reverberation allows musicians to create long or unusual sound decays. A cathedral might have a decay time of ten seconds due to its many hard, reflective surfaces, like a mirror maze, diffusing the sound. But a digital reverberation unit can create an decay time as long as 100 seconds. The reverberation time can be changed throughout the piece and even programmed to grow, rather than decay, creating feedback.

Straight tone controls (equalisation) can bring a sound forward or send it backwards too. For example, if the middle frequencies are boosted, the sound appears to come nearer. On a sound-mixing console these frequencies are often referred to as 'presence'.

With all these perspective-altering parameters, the new century will continue to hold exciting challenges for composers and performers. A.A.

The designing of sounds for specific spaces is an exciting area. As we have become aware of noise pollution and the effects of sound in our daily lives, the designing of sounds in public spaces has become more important. Sounds in space can be public and private. The playing of a stereo at home is an example of saturating a space with a new sound environment. Flight paths are massive examples of a large public space saturated by particular sounds. As we move into a more technologically dependent society, the construction and role of sounds will become an important consideration. Not only sound, but also its relationship to its environment – its context – create meaning and sensibility. In the next chapters we will be looking at specially-constructed musical environments or spaces.

4 QUESTIONS

1 What is reverberation?

2 What is a sound sculpture?

3 What is a sound installation?

4 Compare the projection of sounds heard in two contrasting enclosed public spaces.

FURTHER READING

Rebecca Coyle (ed.), *Sounds Australian*, No. 45: 'Sound Music Noise – Music and Sound Art in Australia', Sydney: Australian Music Centre, Autumn, 1995.

Ros Bandt, *Sounds in Space: Wind Chimes and Sound Sculptures*, Melbourne: Victorian Arts Council of Adult Education, 1985.

R. Murray Schafer, *The Tuning of the World*, New York: Knopf, 1977.

FURTHER LISTENING

• *Austral Voices: For Telegraph Wires, Tuning Forks, Computer-Driven Piano, Psaltery, Whirly, Cello, Synthesizer and Ruined Piano* (New Albion 1990).

• Ros Bandt, *Improvisations in Acoustic Chambers* (Move 1979).

• Ros Bandt, *Glass and Clay* (Move 1995).

Special Topic 3
Greg Schiemer's Spectral Dance –
Designing Interactive Computer Instruments

The Australian composer Greg Schiemer (b. 1949) belongs to an emerging group of international composers who are pioneers in the design of interactive computer instruments.
Spectral Dance, like many of his previous compositions, is a unique instrumental design
involving gesture, interactivity, space and timbral synthesis. Spectral Dance is a 'free music'
machine that spontaneously generates timbres beyond the control of the composer's
imagination. Its performances create an illusion of control, but the illusion is never without
a surprise, both for the composer or performer, as well as for the audience.

An important aspect of Spectral Dance is the use of computer-generated algorithms.
Algorithmic composition consists of a set of steps (procedures) which the composer
programs the computer to do. Each step must be very clear, methodical and unambiguous.
The computer processes these steps to determine the musical details of a composition
required by the composer. Processes, like algorithms, take responsibility for some of the
minute detail, thereby allowing composers to focus on more global aspects of musical design.
Analogue systems built by some composers in the 1960s were used to create interactive
processes that worked in real time, blurring lines of demarcation between composer and
performer and between performer and audience. As computers evolved over several decades,
so too did algorithmic composition. Once a means for composers like Hiller or Xenakis
to specify the minute musical detail of complex scores, algorithmic composition has come
to include systems that make spontaneous musical decisions.

Spectral Dance is a hybrid design in which two different technologies are brought together:
the UFO, a mobile tunable oscillator mounted in a plastic kitchenware container and attached
to a short rope which a performer swings to produce pitch shift Doppler effects; and the
MIDI Tool Box, a microcontroller (mini computer) system Schiemer built with a set of tools
allowing composers to create their own interactive composition algorithms. A Doppler effect
is a perceived shift in pitch when a sound passes by. A good example of a Doppler effect can
be heard by a passenger when a train passes by a railway crossing signal: once the train moves
away from the signal, the passenger perceives a shift in railway signal's pitch.

As an improvising machine Spectral Dance involves a performer swinging a UFO which acts as
a trigger for new sound events. A microphone placed in the centre of the performance space
picks up the UFO signal and converts it into a digital signal recognised by the MIDI Tool Box.
The MIDI Tool Box algorithm transforms these into MIDI signals which in turn produce complex
timbres on the Yamaha FB01 synthesiser. Interaction with the system affects timbral changes
in ways that the performer cannot always anticipate.   R.V.

Listening Example 36: Spectral Dance, Greg Schiemer (1991)

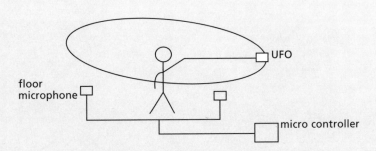

Figure 20: System configuration used for Spectral Dance by Greg Schiemer.

IMPROVISATIONS

Start and finish the session with a free or structured improvisation.

1 With your voice or instrument, play or improvise a work in different acoustic environments such as a church hall, basketball court, hotel foyer or a carpeted room. How does the space you are performing in affect the music? Does it have a lot of reverberation or only a little? What types of materials is the space made from?

2 Explore the space with your voice or instrument to discover how reflected waves reach the ear. You could also do this by listening to someone else make sounds while you walk to different locations. Improvise a solo that explores the acoustic qualities of the space.

3 Choose a musical gesture or song which interacts with a location in such a way that the two become intricately related in combination. Sing a sad song in a corner or recite a poem in different locations. This is called activating a space. The space becomes 'alive' because of the choice of song or music.

COMPOSITION PROJECT 3

The purpose of this composition is to think in terms of timbre, time and register and loudness.

TIMBRE

Compose a two- to four-minute work for voices, instruments, found sounds or any combination of these. You may wish to use a tape recorder or computer sequencer and sampler.

The work should utilise the basic parameters of sound-making: register and/or pitch, sound shape, loudness, timbre and duration. Notate the work using any type of notation that is appropriate to the people and instruments available.

You may wish to explore and combine different timbral groups (such as wind sounds with guitar sounds), or separate each timbral group as if they were characters in a story. Try to create a composite sound in which different instruments or voice sounds are part of a larger structure.

For example, the sound could begin with a low male voice becoming louder and wider in register followed by a high register guitar chord. It might look something like this:

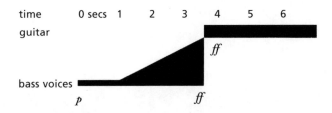

Figure 21: *Representation of timbres in relation to time.*

TEACHING STRATEGIES FOR IMPROVISATION

IMPROVISATION ...

- is a valuable tool for understanding creative and musical thinking.
- can involve working with existing or known structures from which one explores new possibilities, combinations or outcomes.
- is real-time interaction and involves spontaneous decision-making either consciously or unconsciously.

Improvisation is a valuable tool for understanding creative and musical thinking.

For most people it is a mystery of mythological size. But improvisation is not necessarily about virtuosity. People who don't understand a great impro solo may attribute it to a divine soul. The soloist is a shamanic figure exposing universal truth. But in our day-to-day lives, normal conversation is improvisation: you never really know exactly what you're going to say next. The speaker has a concept which is expressed in a familiar, personal vocabulary. With more than just words, the concept can be articulated in the speaker's patterns of speech, meaningless utterances ('er' and 'hmm'), favourite words and expressions. We trust our personal vocabularies to communicate a larger idea. A good dinner party conversation is like an ensemble improvisation: it meanders, transforms, interrupts, overlays two conversations at once, jump-cuts to new topics.

Improvisation can involve working with existing or known structures from which new possibilities, combinations or outcomes are explored.

Improvisation is a process for the investigation of sound, starting from a known set of criteria and progressing towards an unknown result. The known criteria can be a chord progression, the traits of the musician's instrument or voice, a set of sound parameters, the limited technique of the student player or the attributes of a group of people who choose to play together. Anything can be used as the basis for an improvisation because the creation of the process is as important as the outcome.

Improvisation is real-time interaction and involves spontaneous decision-making either consciously or unconsciously.

In many situations our problem-solving techniques depend on a process of reflection: we allow time to inform our decision-making process. Using learnt methods of problem-solving, improvisation enables us to understand, in real time, how we might approach a longer-term problem or issue in the absence of reflection. Reflection allows us to research, learn or consider new possibilities, which are crucial to cognitive development. It is through reflection that we propose new solutions. In contrast, improvisation tests reflective thinking and allows for unpremeditated outcomes.

By exploring and reflecting, the user can develop a sense of musical thinking based on doing. The 'doing' informs the 'thinking' and the 'thinking' informs the 'doing'. This is called critical practice. The improvisation exercises combined with the modules in Parts 1 and 2 enable the student to develop two modes of learning:

1 Experiential Learning

Experimental learning is deep level learning relying on real time decision making. These learning experiences can be quite profound. Through trial and error the student develops a 'hands on' relationship and understanding of the material in question. This kind of learning develops a vocabulary of performance and critical practice which expands with each improvisation. Musical thinking is learned by doing, and should happen independently from the learning approach required in the modules. Unlike more traditional teaching methods, which require the performer to acquire a solid theoretical grounding first, improvisation develops an experiential relationship to structure, patterns and transformations. The experience enables students to comprehend concepts and complex structures introduced in the modules since they will already have applied these ideas in practice.

2 Conceptual Learning

This type of learning involves the application of introduced concepts to given situations. The student is taught patterns and structures generically and learns to identify these patterns in different contexts. In experiential learning the student applies conceptual terms to already learnt experiences. Conceptual learning enables the student to explore generic concepts through experiment.

The improvisation sessions enable both these learning strategies to be negotiated. Improvisation intensifies the learning experience via pattern recognition application and experience. The student applies concepts introduced in the modules to the experiences learnt in the improvisation sessions. Conversely, the improvisation sessions provide a rich set of experiences for the student to learn abstract concepts. As a result, conceptual learning problems tend to be avoided once the performer has some experience of these problems in practice.

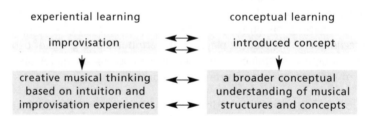

Figure 22: *Two independent learning strategies.*

GETTING STARTED

It is recommended that the teacher conduct regular sessions on improvisation, referring to the guide below, to overcome inhibition among students and develop their confidence and familiarity with its concepts. Some may wish to spend comparatively more time at the beginning of the course on these activities.

Ideally, the improvisation sessions should run concurrently with the chapters in this book. Time is always limited in the classroom, especially when classes are large. This problem can be overcome to some extent by breaking the class into smaller groups of five or six (accommodation permitting). Each group will be able to work independently if the students are responsible for the group's direction and are clear about the program's purpose.

Alternatively the program can be taught by forming a demonstration group followed by class discussion of the improvisation activity. Afterwards each student should try the improvisation or composition exercise at home.

To dispel the myths of improvisation in the classroom, use an ordinary object in the first exercise. For example, try exploring what can be done simply by playing with the tuner and volume control of a radio; or by tapping a table top or tearing paper. Make the students realise that the improvisation process is real-time exploratory interaction between their cognitive processes, sensory experience and the limitations of the object or instrument of inquiry. Always let the sound lead the student and never impose a direction. After each improvisation discuss its qualities.

Once the students have overcome their initial inhibitions, each session ought to start with a group improvisation. A physical warm-up may be appropriate. After a period of improvising and exploratory work, move on to the composition exercises or the tasks related to the chapter.

In every class there will probably be egotists, shy people and others who are resistant or fearful of looking foolish. Each group will have its own identity. By forming smaller groups of duets, trios and even solos, it is possible to combine and separate different personalities and make sure that all the students are involved. Separate the egotists from the shy ones if the improvisation is not working. This can happen with the enthusiastic and the inexperienced. But keep in mind it is important not to discourage the keen ones. Encourage the group to start up on its own without your input and to be self-motivated.

Students generally start with stylistic improvisations such as blues. Always allow the group to choose the warm-up, whether it is a rhythmic pattern or a rock'n'roll riff. Modal improvisations are good as they allow relative freedom. It is best to keep to one mode and usually something simple like the Dorian mode in D. If the improvisation begins well, use it as the basis for developing their musical thinking by applying the chapter's lessons. For example, discuss the role of register or the instrumental relationships.

Inexperienced improvisers are generally poor ensemble listeners because they tend to be focussed on their own performance. After each improvisation ask all the students what they thought. If they comment that it was too loud, for example, obviously the next impro should focus on this quality: performing as softly as possible. This process develops critical awareness in the students of the music-making process.

How the class develops from there depends on the teacher and how the group is working. If the group gets stuck, refer to the exercises at the end of each chapter. Whenever appropriate, introduce relevant musical vocabulary. If the group says they liked something about an improvisation, ask them why. It is important that they learn to put their experience of music into words. Try to get them to be descriptive in their musical language and to use musical terms rather than accepting a statement like 'it sounded good'. Avoid promoting personal interests over other forms of music; otherwise students may interpret these as the approved method or sound. The teacher's role is to monitor, not to lead, and he or she should only step in when there is a problem that cannot be resolved by the students themselves. Be open to all their endeavours: naive as they may sound, they are all valuable starting points. If a student offers a simple folk song, using tonic and dominant, then this is the musical material to work with. In most cases the student will make up something intuitively.

It is wise to perform a duet with everybody in the class so that teacher and student build up a sense of trust. In these improvisations make sure that the student is always supported. Lead and interact sometimes, but most often, provide a sense of security and create a musical basis that will allow the student to perform. Always make them sound good. This does wonders for self-confidence and motivation.

It is the teacher's role in this course to develop the student's intuitive thinking through the exercises of inquiry provided. However, any student open to intuitive learning is also vulnerable to criticism and it is easy to discourage creativity unintentionally. Always be open and always encourage; a useful technique that can help prevent such misunderstandings is to encourage self-observation in students rather than self-critical stances.

STRATEGIES

As a teaching strategy, improvisation encourages:

1 different aspects of musical intelligence, such as pitch discrimination, pattern recognition, register and time;

2 real-time interaction and inquiry, encouraging the development of a critical practice in music;

3 group learning and collaboration;

4 directorial and communication skills through composition;

5 the questioning of assumptions and beliefs about sound and music; and

6 risk-taking.

The following exercises develop creative thinking whenever the group gets stuck or runs into problems.

1 Focussing Exercise: Listening, *Not Thinking*, About What You Are Doing

i Listen, Don't Think

This exercise is played on a drum or surface. Tell the student to start playing without thinking about the sound. Whatever sound is made first, that is the beginning and the student has to respond to it. If the side of the drum is scraped by accident, the scrape is the beginning of the piece. If students are really listening, they will know what to do next.

Students often break off when they becomes aware of attention. If they focus on the sound, then it won't matter to them who is watching. It will be clear to both listener and performer when they are focussed.

ii Playing in the Dark

If your students feel inhibited during a vocal improvisation, ask them to close their eyes (even turn out the light). Listen to each other and then sing or say or make a sound.

2 Repetition and Variation

Making a student continually repeat a solo often reveals the patterns, formulas or habits they are relying on. The processes discussed here empower the student to make observations about a particular action and then decide whether this action is an inhibiting factor or has further potential.

i Repetition

Ask a student to play or sing a solo about one minute long. When it is finished, ask for another and another until you have heard at least ten more. Point out the repeating patterns.

ii What Have I Done and What Haven't I Done?

Get the student to analyse the music by asking 'What have I done?' and then 'What haven't I done?' For example, if a guitarist repeatedly plays pentatonics up and down the fretboard, then put it into words: the guitarist should say 'I am always playing pentatonics up and down the fretboard'. Follow this with a question: 'What haven't I done?' This will offer any number of suggestions, such as 'play another finger form-ation that is not based on pentatonics' or 'Play in one register concentrating on the permutation of those available notes'. Other students can be quite inventive until they reach a point when it suddenly becomes obvious they no longer know what to do. This is an indication that they have gone through their bag of tricks and have at last exhausted themselves. This is where you apply the 'What haven't I done?' technique.

3 One-Parameter Exercise

i Improvisation Using One Note Only

This will force the student or group to explore other parameters, such dynamics, timbre and rhythm.

ii Exploring One Parameter

Ask a group to explore just one parameter, such as register, dynamics, or playing an instrument in a certain way. This develops a sense of critical thinking about the students' relationship to music and their instruments.

4 Freeing-Up Processes

i Play As Fast As Possible

Don't think about what you are doing, keep saying to the student, 'faster'. In getting the student to play as fast as possible, you are stopping them from thinking about what they doing.

ii Change an Aspect of the Performance

For example, put a slide on a guitar, play the inside of a piano instead of the keys, or sing with paper in the mouth. This makes students think differently about their instruments.

iii Solos, Duets and Smaller Groups

Using smaller groups and continually changing combinations creates freshness and allows new relationships to develop. A duet may be easier than a solo because it takes the pressure off the individual having to perform alone.

iv Extending Horizons

If you think the group is getting stuck in a style, take the style and interrogate it in different ways. For example, explore different phrase lengths, accent different parts of the beat, explore register shifts or go against the natural way they play or sing.

v Clapping Games

Ask two people talk to each other via clapping. This develops a sense of listening. Generally students start by copying each other. If that is the case, take them to the next step so that they clap independently of each other creating polyphonic sound.

5 Developing a Sense of Ensemble Listening

i Accompanying

One person starts playing, others pick up on one aspect of the solo and elaborate in a supporting role.

ii Avoiding Copying and Repetition

When students feel insecure they try to copy each other. Try to get them to think in contrasts or opposites to break this pattern. If someone does something high and fast, then someone else should do something low and slow. Try to get them to avoid repeating themselves. Suggest that they do a solo based on no repetition of phrases.

6 Aleatoric Improvisations

These are processes based on indeterminate procedures such as a random sequence of events, musical decisions based on actions such as throwing a dice or other types of processes in which the outcome is not certain.

i Set up procedures such as playing as quickly as possible or in contrasting registers until the conductor cues otherwise.

ii Improvise with found objects like chains or dragging chairs on the floor.

7 Structural Improvisations

i Take an idea and vary some aspect of it by expanding, contracting, transforming or distorting it. Pass it around the group and listen to how the sound is changed and shaped.

This process is largely based on composing through improvisation. Improvisation has been and always will be a reliable process from which to produce original music.

SUMMING UP

These are just a few strategies for making a group less inhibited and more musically aware. Improvisation classes often take a path independent of the listening program. If this happens the teacher should not try to force it back. If an improvisation group develops a sense of autonomy the teacher's role is to discuss the musical implications of the work the group is doing, referring wherever possible to *Sounds in Space, Sounds in Time*.

Finally, one cannot underestimate our capacity for hearing and listening. The improvisation exercises will allow students to develop their listening skills very quickly and give them time to enter the creative-thinking process. Through repetition, an improvisation solo becomes a valuable means of unfolding or unlocking those hidden creative thoughts embedded in us all. We allow time and process to inform our decision-making by setting into play unconscious processes with the conscious ones.

> Man has the 'fastest ears' in history. They can record many things at once with great rapidity, compressing time and space in a panorama of sound. They can discriminate acute nuances in talking, laughing, crying, groaning, shrieking – street sounds, factory sounds, nature sounds, as well as the gamut of human emotions and feeling.
> Joseph Eger[24]

PART 2

SOUNDS IN TIME

THE MUSICAL MIX

4 module

Music, like language, requires punctuation and detail to create meaning and expression. The detail of music-making is often called articulation. Sounds are generally either differentiated into identifiable layers or blended to form new sounds. When combined with articulation, these layers and blends form the basic building blocks of musical clarity.

CHAPTER 10   **The Musical Surface: Articulation**

Key concepts or themes   Articulation
                                Staccato, legato, glissando and portamento

         Special Topics   1 Glissando or Portamento?
                                2 Articulation and Symbols
                                3 Miles Davis (1926-1991)

         Improvisations

CHAPTER 11   **The Musical Mix: Layering**

Key concepts or themes   Layering

         Special Topics   1 The Computer Sequencer and Songwriting

         Improvisations

CHAPTER 12   **The Musical Mix: Blending**

Key concepts or themes   Blending

         Special Topics   1 'Criss-Cross', Thelonious Monk (1957)
                                2 Sound Synthesis – Think of a Sound You Have
                                  Never Heard and Create It

         Improvisations

Composition Project 4

10 THE MUSICAL SURFACE: ARTICULATION

Articulation: 1a the act or process of articulating speech. b the adjustments and movements of speech organs involved in pronouncing
a particular sound, taken as a whole. c any of these adjustments and
movements. d any speech sound... 8 (music) the manner of performing
a passage...

Expression: ...3 the manner or form in which a thing is expressed in words;
wording; phrasing. 4 the power of expressing in words... 5 indication
of feeling, spirit, character, etc, as on the face, in the voice, or in artistic
execution. 6 a look or intonation as expressing feeling... 8 the act of expressing
or representing, as by symbols. 9 (maths) a symbol or a combination of symbols
serving to express something. *The Macquarie Dictionary (Australia)*

The musical surface is a constantly and subtly changing environment. It is this continual
change which holds our interest: something loud followed by something quiet; some
sounds separated or detached and others joined together; sometimes there are slides and
bends, at other times, sudden leaps and abrupt endings. All these minute details come
together under the general term ARTICULATION.

Articulation refers to the way a sound is played with respect to its loudness, duration,
tone colour or timbre, shape or pitch. They are the basic building blocks of music which
are combined and mixed to produce complex sound structures. Music articulation allows
for a sense of nuance and expression. There are many types of articulation and they
function in the same manner as punctuation in writing. A person who articulates well
is someone who speaks clearly; every syllable and word is pronounced and stressed. Any
piece of music relies on combinations of basic musical punctuation and syntax to produce
meaning. A piece without articulation would be bland, lacking colour, differentiation and
nuance. If a score makes no specifications for articulation, the performers provide their
own to give the music expression.

1 SOME BASIC BUILDING BLOCKS FOR THE ARTICULATION OF SOUND SHAPES

In this section basic articulations will be introduced with their symbols. Traditionally, types
of articulation are expressed in Italian.

GETTING TO THE POINT: STACCATO

Staccato means short. In terms of sound shape, a staccato has an instantaneous attack,
no sustain, and an instantaneous decay. In performance terms, a staccato directs the
performer to play a sound as briefly as possible. This creates a gap between the notes.
The faster the staccato notes, the less noticeable the gap and vice versa. If you listen
closely to a clock ticking, you can hear each tick as a staccato articulation. Can you hear
the small pause between the end of each tick and the start of the next tock? In musical
notation staccato is represented by a dot (Figure 23) above or under the note; the dot
provides an accurate visual representation regarding the performance of the sound. The
opposite of staccato is tenuto, meaning 'play for the full value of the note'.

Listening Example 37: Vocal demonstration of staccato

In this example a short phrase is sung normally and then repeated with staccato
articulation. The envelope of the singer's voice suddenly changes shape.

A WELL-POLISHED SURFACE: LEGATO

Legato means 'smooth' and indicates a sound with no perceptible interruption between two sounds or notes so that each note is joined to the next. Can you imagine what a clock would sound like if it were ticking legato? While the word 'legato' is often used as a general indication for smoothness, there are different ways to indicate legato depending on the instrument. For keyboard and percussion instruments with sustain sounds such as a piano or vibraphone, a curved line (Figure 23) is used over the notes required to be performed smoothly. For vocal music, a curved line is used also. This line is called a slur and it is often the case that legato and slur are used synonymously. For woodwind, violin and brass instruments, the word 'legato' is used at the appropriate place to indicate smoothness. A slur is used to indicate playing in one breath or bow. Sometimes a broken slurred line is used to indicate a legato phrase in wind, brass and string instruments.

Figure 23: *Staccato and legato.*

Listening Example 38: Vocal demonstration of legato
In this example the same short exercise as for Listening Example 37 is sung normally and then repeated with legato articulation.

A very fast jazz saxophone, as exemplified by Charlie Parker (1920-55), is an excellent example of legato or slurring. By its very nature the saxophone is an ideal instrument for slurring as its note articulation time (attack time) is slower than, for example, a piano's, which is instantaneous. Where a pianist's finger acts like a hammer, instantly sounding the string, the saxophonist's breath takes time to pass through the mouthpiece and down into the tube of the instrument. Consequently the attack time of each note is almost hidden. At very fast speeds, legatos – such as the one played by Parker in 'Ko-Ko' (1945) – give an effect of liquid shape.

The combination of legato and staccato makes a musical line very expressive. The opening guitar solo in Led Zeppelin's song 'Since I've Been Loving You' (1970), for example, elegantly combines the two. The first four notes are clearly articulated and detached while the remaining notes are slurred together.

Listening Example 39: Sonata in C, K545, Third Movement, Wolfgang Amadeus Mozart (1788)
In this example the combination of staccato and legato gives the piece its musical sensibility. This is an example of why Mozart's music is often so tricky to play, each note demanding a particular nuance of expression.

Sliding or Bending: Glissando and Portamento
Glissando and portamento are essentially pitch slides (or bends), meaning a shift up or down in pitch. They are represented by an oblique line (Figure 24) or sometimes a wavy line which indicates pitch direction.

Figure 24: *Glissando and portamento signs.*

Activity 1

Sing the first line of the Christmas carol 'Silent Night', sliding from syllable to syllable:

Si ╱ ╲lent ╲night ╱ho ╱ ╲ly ╲night

Si - lent night Ho -.........ly night

Figure 25: 'Silent Night' notated with pitch bends.

The expressive power of the glissando and even more so, the portamento, cannot be underestimated. In many types of music the whole style is defined by pitch slides. Most popular and folk singing styles capitalise on pitch bends in various ways for their expressiveness (e.g. guitar solos and blues singing). A very famous example of a pitch slide can be found in the opening of George Gershwin's *Rhapsody in Blue* (1924).

 Listening Example 40: Vocal demonstration of pitch bends

The melody is sung first with pitch bends and then without. The expressiveness of this solo is created by the slight pitch bends between the notes.

Listening Example 41: Trombone melody using pitch slides

The trombone's use of a slide to articulate notes makes it an ideal instrument for portamento.

Listening Example 42: *Asp 3*, Brigid Burke and Rainer Linz (1996)

This duet for clarinet and electronics is completely based on glissando. Movement is created by various types of slides using different speeds and register sweeps. It is hauntingly beautiful, full of harmonic colour and invention.

 Activity 2

Listen to someone speaking, especially if it is in a language you don't understand. Listen to the subtle pitch inflections, the changing rhythms of the voice, the vocal utterances and sounds and the creation of accent by exclamation.

Special Topic 1
Glissando or Portamento?
Which term is used depends upon the type of instrument in question

Portamento is used for slides on instruments which do not have frets or fixed gradations of pitch, such as violins, trombones and the voice. Glissando is used for instruments such as the piano, harp and guitar. No matter how quickly a glissando is played, one can still hear a progression through the discrete pitches. The portamento, on the other hand, is one continuous slide in which no discrete progression can be heard. Quickly running your hand over a piano keyboard is an example of a glissando whereas a wailing police siren is an example of a portamento. A pitch bend such as stretching a string with the finger while playing on a guitar is a portamento, but sliding the finger up or down the guitar string over the frets is a glissando.

There is a lot of ambiguity in the use of these two terms. In many situations, a glissando is used to refer to a large sweep while small slides between two adjacent pitches is referred to as a portamento. Although technically incorrect, you should be aware of such vernacular uses of these terms.

R.V.

2 SUMMARY

Articulation is inextricably linked to the physical sound of a piece of music. It provides clarity, colour and expression. There are many types of articulation. In this chapter we have only dealt with some of the basics concerning loudness, duration, shape and quality. Each instrument has a broad range of articulations created by its own idiosyncrasies. The violin, viola, cello and double bass, for example, have a huge range of articulations provided by the almost infinite number of bow-pressure combinations possible on the strings. Articulation is fundamental to style. The pitch bend gives the blues its expressive quality, whereas the portamento and glissando were never used by Baroque composers, for whom the production of exact and discrete sounds was the aesthetic ideal.

3 QUESTIONS

1 What is articulation?

2 What is staccato?

3 What is tenuto?

4 What is legato?

5 What is glissando?

6 What is portamento?

7 Why is articulation important?

Special Topic 2
Articulation and Symbols

Articulation gives the musical surface a sense of physicality and shape. It is for this reason that many systems of musical notation or representation include symbols for articulation. For example, in traditional notation, a slide in pitch is represented by an ascending or descending line (/or\ ); a very short sound is represented by a dot while a sound to be articulated for its full duration (tenuto) is represented by a horizontal line (–). The symbols we have already seen for increasing and decreasing loudness (crescendo <, decrescendo >) illustrate this physical expressiveness. So informative are these symbols that it is possible to communicate musical meaning or expression with nothing more than articulation signs. R.V.

Activity 3

Sing the following graphic score. In this exercise each vertical line represents a sung note. Staccato and legato articulations are provided.

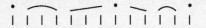

Figure 26: *Staccato, legato and slide symbols combined.*

Special Topic 3
Miles Davis (1926-1991)

The jazz trumpeter Miles Davis was a master of articulation. The range of nuances he could produce from the trumpet was extraordinary, from the most subtle inflection to notes that lay somewhere between pitch and timbre. When listening to Davis perform, one hears a musician thinking in real time. The variation within each type of articulation is immense: bending and sliding, the use of staccato, combinations of pitch slides and staccato, portamento, legato and →

➤ half-legato and pitch wavers. Sometimes a note is 'chewed' and 'savoured', other times there is a pure and golden precision to the pitching. The use of the mute adds to this expressivity. The mute takes the top edge off the sound by modifying the trumpet's transients. The attack has fewer high frequencies, giving more presence to the middle and low frequencies of the trumpet sound.

Unlike Dizzy Gillespie and Louis Armstrong, Davis' virtuosity does not focus on speed but nuance and expressivity with minimal use of notes. The space between the notes is just as important as the sound. The use of articulation in this music is comparable to the demands of playing Mozart. The jazz arranger, Gil Evans, once said of him, 'Miles couldn't play like Louis [Armstrong] because the sound would interfere with his thoughts. Miles had to start with almost no sound and then develop one as he went along, a sound suitable for the ideas he wanted to express. He couldn't afford to trust those thoughts to an old means of expression'.[25]

Each of Davis' solos on Kind of Blue (1959) is clearly articulated.[26] This album is a typical display of the diversity of his style. John Coltrane (tenor sax) and Cannonball Adderley (alto sax) also exploit a wide range of articulations on this album.

R.V.

FURTHER LISTENING

- Miles Davis, 'Round Midnight (Columbia 1956).
- Miles Davis, 'My Funny Valentine', Cookin' (Original Jazz Classics 1956). This piece displays slurs, smears, pitch bending and half-valve squeezes. A transcription of this exquisite solo can be found in Ian Carr, Miles Davis: a Critical Biography, London: Quartet Books 1982, pp. 260-1.
- Johnny Hodges, title track, Passion Flower (Bluebird 1940-1946).
- Laughing Clowns, Golden Days (When Giants Walked the Earth) (Hot 1995). ‡
- Led Zeppelin, 'Since I've Been Loving You', Led Zepplin III (Atlantic 1970).
- W.A. Mozart. Any of the piano sonatas.
- 'Flagellation Song', Music of the Fulani Niger/Northern Dahomey (UNESCO 1988). African vocal technique is an important forerunner of Afro-American vocal traditions.
- Charlie Parker, 'Ko-Ko' (1945).
- Prince, Sign O' The Times (Paisley Park 1987).
- Queen, Greatest Hits (EMI 1983).

GLISSANDO AND PORTAMENTO

- George Gershwin, Rhapsody in Blue (1924). (The opening clarinet phrase is a famous example of a pitch bend.)
- P.J. Harvey, tracks 2, 5, 8, 11 and 14, 4-Track Demos (Island 1993).
- Polvo, Today's Active Lifestyles (Merge 1993).
- The Beach Boys, 'Good Vibrations', Smiley Smile (Capitol 1967).
- Iannis Xenakis, Polytope (1967).
- Arnold Schoenberg, 'Mondstrucke' Pierrot lunaire, (1912).
- The vocal line from any country and western song.

IMPROVISATIONS

Start and finish the session with a free or structured improvisation.

1 Improvise a solo exploring as many different types of articulation as possible. Try to make the articulations relate to a musical statement rather than making them randomly.

2 Use various articulations randomly on a repeating pulse to create a more complex structure.

3 Play or sing one note exploring as many different ways of articulating this note as possible. How do the articulations create variety and meaning?

11 THE MUSICAL MIX: LAYERING

Spread half the ricotta mixture over the base of the loaf, layer over this
the filling, then sprinkle with nuts.   Margaret Fulton[27]

Chapter 10 demonstrated the crucial role articulation plays in the construction of musical surface. The way sounds are combined is also important. There are essentially two approaches to the construction of musical surface: layering and blending. Layering involves separating the parts while blending (discussed in Chapter 12) involves fusing or merging.

Layering is like using colours to distinguish one thing from another (for example, using different coloured labels for identification) whereas blending is like mixing colours to make something new.

1 STACKING IT UP

Layering is probably the most elementary organisational technique: stacking up one sound on top of another. Any sound perceived together with a different sound automatically becomes layered.

Listening Example 43: *Isis*, Chris Blackwell

Most pop songs and dance music rely on layering to create structure. Each layer is heard distinctly and differentiated by a specific timbre or combination of timbres. In *Isis* each new layer is denoted by a specific combination of instruments, such as the beginning layer played by the synthesiser and shaker, and culminating finally with the piano. Often, but not always, this produces a hierarchy of layers; sometimes, however, the layers are equally balanced. As each new sound layer is introduced all the other layers recede into the middle or background.

In *Cortège du sage* (bars 69-71) from Igor Stravinsky's *Le sacre du printemps* (1913), the layers of sound stack up gradually, eventually combining no less than 15 in a wall of sound. The layering in this piece is not as hierarchical as Chesworth's *Layer on Layer* and its approach, called STRATIFICATION, will be discussed in Chapter 20. However, in both these works certain techniques are employed to avoid aural confusion. Register allocation, rhythmic difference and timbre are three important devices. The importance of allocating registers was most obvious in Listening Example 11 (drum registers) which achieved its musical sensibility by associating certain rhythmic gestures with the high, middle and low registers. In any piece of music built around layering, each layer has to be distinctive from the others.

Activity 1

A simple example of layering is singing a round such as 'Row, Row, Row Your Boat' with a group of people.

2 SUMMARY

Layering is one of the most fundamental means of organising music. For layering to be perceived, each layer must be distinguishable. This is achieved mainly through timbre differentiation, register allocation and distinctive rhythmic patterns. Other approaches use loudness or the overlaying of identifiable sound shapes.

3 QUESTIONS

1 What is layering?

2 Can you name a work that demonstrates layering?

3 What are the important factors that determine layering?

Special Topic 1

The Computer Sequencer and Songwriting

A computer sequencer's window gives a very clear graphic representation of the concept of layering in a piece of music. Each layer is called a track. On the left side of the sequencer window each track is identified by an instrument or a description. On the right, each layer has a graphic, describing its activity. The composer or songwriter simply stacks up the layers. A piece might begin with a drum beat or bass line. This can be made into a repeating loop. Melodies, harmonies, other sounds, effects, voices, etc can then be laid over this basic pattern. Layer by layer, the music is created. Before the invention of the computer sequencer, multi-track tape recorders were used for this process. For this reason sequencers are designed to look like tape recorders with virtual buttons, faders, monitoring levels, etc. R.V.

R	M	S	track	length	instrument	path	1	5	9	13	17	21
			1	8	drums	4						
			3	16	guitar	5						
			2	8	bass	6						

Figure 27: *A sequencer window showing layered tracks.*

FURTHER LISTENING

- King Sunny Adé, *Juju Music* (Mango 1982). Adé has presented up to 30 or more musicians on stage playing rhythmically interlocking layers.
- Miles Davis, *On The Corner* (Columbia 1972).
- Miles Davis, *Bitches' Brew* (Columbia 1969).
- Gustav Mahler, Symphony No. 1, Second Movement (1888).
- Igor Stravinsky, *L'Histoire du Soldat* (1918).
- Igor Stravinsky, *Le sacre du printemps* (1913).
- Zap Mamma, *Sabsylma* (Crammed Discs 1994).
- Stan Kenton, *New Concepts in Artistry and Rhythm* (Capitol 1952). The opening 30 seconds demonstrate layering.
- Thirteenth-century isorythmic motets from the period of Petrus de Cruce (c.1300).
- Kate Bush, 'Running Up That Hill', *Hounds of Love* (EMI 1985).

IMPROVISATIONS

Start and finish the session with a free or structured improvisation.

1 Improvise a sung or spoken vocal pattern in a group. Each person contributes a different layer with his or her voice, exploring a certain register and sound quality. Try improvisations which include sounds both contrasting and compatible to the initial layer.

2 Repeat the first exercise with instruments, found sounds or a computer sequencer.

12 THE MUSICAL MIX: BLENDING

Combine the basil, nuts, garlic and salt, and grind in a food processor
or with a pestle, crushing the ingredients to form a paste. Add the grated
cheese and grind again until the mixture is blended.   Margaret Fulton[28]

1 BLENDING

The opposite approach to layering is blending. Here, sounds are blended or fused together
so that the individual parts or components lose their identity in a unified sound. According
to Robert Erickson in *Sound Structure in Music*:

> Blending or fusion is a precarious balance of forces where individual instrumental sounds lose
> their 'identifiability' and when an unexpected, or striking, or otherwise memorable fused sound
> is in the perceptual foreground.[29]

The effectiveness of a blended sound depends upon context, spatial location and duration.
In the Western choral tradition, a good choir sound is determined by how well the
individual voices fuse or blend together in a unified sound. Some excellent examples
of vocal blending can be found in recordings of Renaissance and Baroque vocal music.

Listening Example 44: 'Kyrie', *Missa L'homme arme*, Josquin des Prés
Listen to the homogeneous blend of voices in this example and the richness of the overall
tone. Imagine how it would sound if one of the voices had a thin or rasp-like sound. The
sensual and emotional effect of the piece would be transformed by the listener's
awareness of the individuality of the voices rather than their similarity.

Blending music can be just as colourful as blending paint. Blending is the basis of more
complex sound structures and will be discussed in Chapter 21. Combining different
instrumental attacks to form a composite, new sound is one approach.

Special Topic 1
'Criss-Cross', Thelonious Monk (1957)

*In 'Criss-Cross' by Thelonius Monk, the saxophone, vibraphone and piano create a new colour
by playing in unison. The piano does not always play together with the other two instruments
but when it does, the blended sound becomes much richer. This is largely due to the different
sound envelopes produced by the three instruments. The vibraphone has an instantaneous
attack with a medium decay while the saxophone's attack takes longer. The sustain time
of the saxophone is completely dependent upon the player's breath control. The piano has an
attack and sound envelope similar to the vibraphone's. As the vibraphone and piano sounds
decay, the saxophone reaches its peak and a sustain sound with no decay. We could draw the
three instruments' attacks and sound envelopes like this:*   R.V.

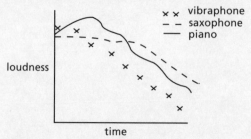

Figure 28: *Attack, sustain and decay of the piano, saxophone and vibraphone.*

Activity 1

In the following exercise a new sound is created by blending three different sound envelopes created by saying the sounds 'buh', 'slow' and 'till'.

'Buh' (as in 'but') has an instantaneous attack and a long decay on the 'h'. Its sound shape could be represented like this:

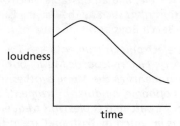

Figure 29: 'Buh'.

'Slow' has a relatively quick attack, a rise on the 's' reaching a peak on 'lo' with a long decay on 'ow':

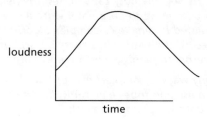

Figure 30: 'Slow'.

'Till' has an instantaneous attack as in 'buh' but a gradual decay on 'i' followed by a sustain on 'll' followed by another decay:

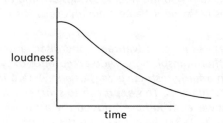

Figure 31: 'Till'.

Putting all three together produces this blended sound:

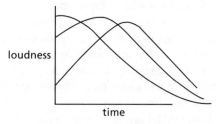

Figure 32: 'Buh' + 'slow' + 'till'.

Special Topic 2
Sound Synthesis – Think of a Sound You Have Never Heard and Create It

When the Russian Leon Thérémin invented his eponymous instrument in the 1920s, he had little idea what he was starting. The theremin is played without touching the instrument: one hand creates the sound by moving between two electrodes and the other controls the dynamics. The sound it makes is a warble, like an unstable electronic siren. The theremin was used extensively in science fiction films such as The Day the Earth Stood Still and the 1960s television series, Lost in Space. The Beach Boys also made use of it in 'Good Vibrations' (1966).

There had been other attempts at electronic instruments (see The Early Years (1877-1945) in Appendix 2, Postcards from History: Electroacoustic Music) but it was the theremin that inspired such ground-breaking instruments as the Moog synthesiser. Robert Moog's early synthesisers of the 1960s were monophonic, modular instruments that took up a whole wall. They needed an enormous number of patching cables and frequent tuning. The first desktop synthesiser was the VCS3 which was invented by Tristram Cary in the early 1970s. Both the Moog and the VCS3 could be played with or without a piano-style keyboard.

By the 1980s, the introduction of digital wavetables and other microprocessor-controlled sound-generating devices transformed the synthesiser from an electronic enthusiast's toy into a musician's instrument. With its new memory capabilities, the performer could recall instantly any programmed sound from pure noise to pure note. Once a sound was in a digital format the numbers could be manipulated by simple or complex algorithms. The microprocessor-based sequencer could be used to record the synthesist's every musical gesture in performance in much the same way the piano roll recorded pianist's performances around the turn of the century.

Synthesisers are similar in many ways to samplers except that, instead of playing back bites of real sound, they generate noise and tones electronically. There are, in fact, many hybrid synthesisers that incorporate both sampling and synthesis in their architecture. One of the most comprehensive instruments was the Kurtsweil K2000.

Synthesisers have made available a vast sound palette to electronic musicians through a variety of synthesis methods. The most sophisticated to date is often referred to as 'acoustic modelling'. The component parts of a sound are noted with reference to its size, shape and density and how it is stimulated into making a sound (e.g. blowing, bowing or striking). Thus new virtual instruments with properties indistinguishable from an acoustic sound can be fabricated and played.

Just as written notation has its musical advantages and disadvantages, synthesis can also be a two-edged sword. Rather uninspiringly, wide acceptance of synthesisers has come about mainly through their use in a fairly restrictive way, as a keyboard instrument imitating, for the most part, other musical instruments. This approach to synthesised sounds forms the basis of General MIDI. Others, however, who have bridged the art/music divide, such as Brian Eno (b. 1948) and Wendy Carlos (b. 1939), have taken up the challenge to create a new musical aesthetic which emerges out of the medium itself. A.A.

Listening Example 45: Cadences, Deviations and Scarlatti, Elena Kats-Chernin (1995) performed by the Sydney Alpha Ensemble

In this example, the opening sound structure is a combination of all the low instruments in the ensemble. Not all the sounds happen at once. Each new part of the sound structure results from the contribution of another instrument to the overall event at that specific point in time. Using the same technique demonstrated in Activity 1, the composer has orchestrated the beginning, middle and end of this piece using different low instrumental timbres.

The fusing of instrumental attacks heard simultaneously is an example of vertical blending, whereas the progression from one timbre to another within a sound envelope or gesture is an example of horizontal blending. Both can occur at the same time.

2 SUMMARY

Blending is an important technique used in the creation of new sounds. It relies on fusing and similarity. The fusing of timbres to create a new sound component is an example of vertical blending, whereas the shift from one timbre to another within an attack-sustain-decay structure is an example of horizontal blending.

3 QUESTIONS

1 What is blending?

2 What is vertical blending?

3 What is horizontal blending?

4 Can you name a work that explores vertical blending?

5 Can you name a work that explores horizontal blending?

FURTHER LISTENING

- Luciano Berio, *O King* (1968). This piece blends voices with instruments.
- Thelonious Monk, title track, *Criss-Cross* (Columbia 1962-63).
- Sixteenth-century choral music.

IMPROVISATIONS

Start and finish the session with a free or structured improvisation.

1 Construct a new sound from a fusion of disparate elements. The sounds can be vocal, percussive, instrumental, found or a combination. When designing your sound, think about the sound envelope and which elements contribute to the attack, sustain and decay.

2 Improvise a vocal solo with at least one other person, which blends together all sounds in a unified sound surface.

COMPOSITION PROJECT 4

1 Collect sounds you find interesting on a tape recorder or sampler and computer sequencer, and layer them into a more complex sound structure. Each layer should be identifiable and contribute to your overall sound event.

2 Blend a collection of similar sounds on a multitrack recording system or, if you don't have this facility, use three or four cassette recorders to play the sounds simultaneously.

3 Compose a work for voices, instruments or both using all the concepts introduced in Module 4. The duration of the work should be two to four minutes.

When preparing your composition, take advantage of new sounds that can be created by blending sounds you have already collected. The blending may also require you to pay some attention to register, dynamics and sound shape. For example the combination of a high sound with a low sound implies a wide register space.

Think about the role articulation is playing in your piece: is it contributing to clarity, exploring the idiosyncrasies of an instrument or sound; or towards the construction of a larger sound shape?

Use any form of notation that communicates the sound you desire. Your composition should also take into account the concepts discussed in previous modules.

LISTENING SPACES

Our ears and brain work together to enable us to receive complex auditory information. When we listen to music or sounds we actively decide which sounds to listen to and which to exclude. In order to make sounds meaningful we contextualise them into zones called listening spaces.

CHAPTER 13	Listening Spaces: Musical Spaces
Key concepts or themes	Listening Spaces Musical Spaces
Special Topics	1 Dynamics and Structure
Improvisations	

CHAPTER 14	Aural Depths of Field
Key concepts or themes	Foreground Middleground Background
Improvisations	

CHAPTER 15	Listening Strategies
Key concepts or themes	Mobile Structures and Stable Structures
Special Topics	1 Two Examples of Music Perception 2 *Durations*, Morton Feldman (1961) 3 *Imaginary Landscape No. 4*, John Cage (1949)
Improvisations	

Composition Project 5

13 LISTENING SPACES: MUSICAL SPACES

The conception of 'space' is for us a sensation ... and if different senses have different spaces, we then have to consider whether ... correlations exist ... between visual and auditory sensation.   Fritz Winckel[30]

The word space can be used to refer to volume, area or distance. Volume is used to describe three-dimensional space, such as outer space or the size of a room. Area describes two-dimensional space such as a floor plan, or the length and width of a piece of paper. Linear space describes the distance between two points, either on a measure such as a ruler or in time ('I completed this task within the space of an hour'). Space has also come to be commonly applied to emotional states – 'he is in a bad space at the moment' is a poetic way to describe a bleak period in someone's life.

This chapter introduces the terms 'listening space' and 'musical space'. These terms are virtually interchangeable. Both are defined by the parameters of loudness, duration, register and sound quality. A listening space is like a photograph. The edges of the photograph indicate the limits of what the viewer can see. A musical space applies the same principles using the equivalent musical parameters: dynamics, rhythm, pitch and timbre.

1 SOUNDS AND THE LISTENING SPACE

Many pieces of music are designed to make the listener focus on specific events. Some are designed so that all the sounds are heard equally, while others are designed hierarchically so that some sounds are more prominent than others. A compact disk producer is primarily concerned with these issues when mixing a recording. The producer constantly has to decide which sounds are to be heard above which other sounds. When listening to a piece of music or sound we also apply limits to what we include, by blocking out sounds we do not want to hear. But there are no hard and fast rules about where the limits fall. Fundamentally, it all depends on how the listener wants to hear the sounds. Listening spaces are defined by perception: we decide what we want to include. A prominent sound for one person might be completely unnoticeable to someone else. This falls within the study of music cognition which examines the perception of the physical and psychological aspects of sound.

2 LISTENING SPACE DEFINED BY LOCATION

The sounds you hear in the room you are sitting in now define one space while the sounds you hear from outside define a larger or separate space. The dimensions of the room define the limits of what you hear inside and outside. As a listener, you may want to hear only the sounds in the room; or you may prefer to group these as a subset of all the sounds you can hear from both inside and outside. You might even decide to place all the sounds that can be heard within one metre of your ears within a small, intimate listening space. Imagine this scene:

I am in my kitchen. I am washing the dishes before I go to a concert to hear Mozart's Piano Concerto in B♭ major. I decide to listen to a record of the concerto while I wash up. The sounds of the piano, orchestra, my spontaneous singing, cutlery, crockery and water playfully merge into a rich and complex texture. The Mozart concerto sounds terrific. Then I go to the concert at the local town hall. The concerto is scheduled after the interval and, being a community event, the interval is marked by tea and biscuits. After the interval I sit in my seat and eagerly await the concerto. It starts, but to my dismay, the sound of stacking cups and saucers can be heard from the town hall canteen. I am annoyed.

In this example, the sounds of the dishes (i.e. their tone colour or quality) at home are part of the listening space, whereas the same type of sounds at the concert are not. In my kitchen, the sounds and music converge into one large space whereas the concert hall is clearly demarcated by wanted and unwanted sounds.

3 MOVEMENT WITHIN LISTENING SPACES

Dynamics and Movement

Imagine a recording of the same Mozart concerto. It starts with the Mozart concerto but in the middle of it, you hear the sounds of crockery being washed up and loudly put in a dish rack. While this is a single listening event consisting of a piano concerto and crockery sounds, it is also apparent that two events are occurring simultaneously. Imagine now that the volume of the crockery sounds gradually increases, reaches a peak and then slowly fades out. The slow fade in and out indicates that the crockery sounds are an intentional part of the recording. It also indicates that the person who mixed it wanted to hear the two groups of sounds contributing to a single event. The possibilities for the movement of sounds within the listening space are limitless.

'Bydlo' (The Ox Cart) from Mussorgsky's *Pictures at an Exhibition* (1874) is an evocative example of the use of dynamics to create a sense of movement. The image of the ox cart is created through repetitive rhythms. As the loudness increases the cart seems to approach; when it reaches its loudest point it passes directly in front of the observer; and as it dies away, the cart recedes into the distance.

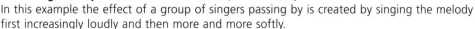

Listening Example 46: 'This Old Man' (traditional)
In this example the effect of a group of singers passing by is created by singing the melody first increasingly loudly and then more and more softly.

Special Topic 1
Dynamics and Structure

The manipulation of dynamics can greatly affect the way we hear a work. A world without dynamic change would be intolerable. Imagine a soundworld in which everything sounded at the same dynamic level as a car engine: your footsteps and breathing, the slam of a door, the rustle of paper. Beethoven was one of the first composers to utilise dynamics structurally. His association of phrase shape and dynamic indications creates a sense of movement in his music. In the opening of the Fifth Symphony, for example, he follows a distant phrase with a closer one.   *R.V.*

Listening Example 47: Ludwig van Beethoven, Symphony No. 5 (opening) (1808)
In this example the opening theme is played very loudly, fortissimo. A repeat is followed by a variation played by the string section at a much softer level, piano. Towards the end of the excerpt the music introduces a crescendo as all the other instruments, including the drums (timpani) join in. The excerpt concludes with a forte played by all instruments. The dynamics of the excerpt could be represented schematically as:

➤ *ff* *f*	*f*	*p*	*crescendo*	*f*
opening theme	repeat	variation on theme, violins	other instruments join in	conclusion, all instruments

If the dynamic indications were reversed the expressiveness and effect would be completely different. The music would begin with a repeated pianissimo, followed by a forte variation, which would then become a decrescendo leading to a piano conclusion.

Register Movement

It has been noted earlier that register is defined by frequency. Register (and therefore pitch) can also create a sense of movement. We interpret high register sounds as though they lie 'above' other sounds and low register sounds as though they lie 'below'. Sliding from high to low is a standard effect in cartoons and circus music for something falling. There is no physical relationship between the high sounds and altitude, yet psychoacoustically we interpret them that way.

Listening Example 48: *Charisma*, Iannis Xenakis (1971)
In this example the cello plays percussive sounds in its middle register. The clarinet enters with a very high squeal which slowly descends into the middle register and then works its way back up to the top; meanwhile the cello plays harmonics in a register higher than the clarinet. This example completely relies on movement around the registers.

TIME AND MOVEMENT

If a pulse tapping at regular intervals and at a moderate speed slowly increases, we usually say that it is speeding up. Just as a changing register can be used to symbolise a fall, speeding up a tempo is often interpreted as though spatial movement is getting faster. It is common for radio plays and films to use a faster tempo for a chase. While the music has not gone anywhere physically, the sense of movement can be quite compelling.

Movement is also implicit in musical terminology such as 'busy', 'lethargic', 'slow' and 'fast'. These are terms musicians call tempo indications or expressive indications and they usually relate to the number of actions applied to a particular period of time. For example, tapping a table ten times a second sounds more busy than two taps a second.

Listening Example 49: *Fantasie*, Alistair Riddell (1984)
In this example the piano is controlled by a computer. The gradual layering up of all the lines produces a complex texture. While the tempo does not change, one experiences a lot of activity and at the same time the illusion of slowing down as the melodies combine.

4 THE MUSICAL SPACE

A musical space is a more specific application of the term listening space. It consists of time, register and dynamics. The sound of crockery mixed with a Mozart concerto is an example of two independent listening spaces combining in one total musical space.

A musical space can be two-dimensional: register describes the space in terms of 'high' and 'low'; rhythm creates a 'distance' between two events and dynamics show events to be 'far away' or 'up close'. All of these are measured against a timeline.

In three-dimensional space two or more of these parameters come into play simultaneously. When register moves between high and low, tempo changes between fast and slow, and dynamics move back and forth between far away and up close, we experience the three dimensions of the musical space through the 'movements' of the sounds. *Charisma* by Iannis Xenakis, Listening Example 48, is an example of a three-dimensional musical space in which register, dynamics and time are in continual movement. Appendix 4, Movement and Musical Spaces, discusses musical spaces in more detail.

5 SUMMARY

A listening space is a perceived sonic event or events defined by limits. But these limits are completely arbitrary. There is no definitive listening space; where the space begins and ends depends completely on the listener and how he or she hears the sounds. Within any listening space the listener detects sounds approaching, receding, staying constant, going higher or lower and these movements create a virtual space. Musical spaces are listening spaces defined in musical terms: dynamics, register and rhythm. Each term measures a different parameter against time. When combined, the two-dimensional spaces of dynamics, register and duration create a three-dimensional model.

6 QUESTIONS

1 What defines a space?

2 What defines a listening space?

3 Why are dynamics, register and duration two-dimensional?

4 What effect can dynamics have on a listening space?

5 What effect can register have on a listening space?

6 What is a musical space?

FURTHER LISTENING

- Ludwig van Beethoven, Symphony No. 9, first movement (exposition) (1822-23).
- Warren Burt, *Three Inverse Genera* (1989), Austral Voices: For Telegraph Wires, Tuning Forks, Computer-Driven Piano, Psaltery, Whirly, Cello, Synthesizer and Ruined Piano (New Albion 1990).
- P.J. Harvey, tracks 1, 2, 5 and 8, *To Bring You My Love* (Island 1995).
- György Ligeti, *Lontano* (1967).
- Gustav Mahler, Symphony No. 1, first movement (1888).
- Mr Bungle, *Disco Volante* (Slash 1995). ‡
- Modest Mussorgsky, *Pictures at an Exhibition*, 'Bydlo' (1874).
- Edgard Varèse, *Intégrales* (1925).
- Iannis Xenakis, *Charisma* (1971).

IMPROVISATIONS

Start and finish the session with a free or structured improvisation.

1 Using only dynamics create a sense of distance and movement on a single note or sound. For example:

ff p   *mf*   *sfz*   *ff*   *ppp*   *pp*   *p*   *mf*   *f*

2 Interpret this diagram with your voice or instrument. Interpret the blocks as expanding and contracting register spaces.

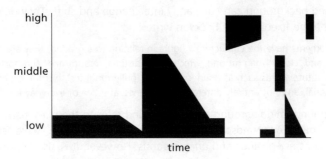

Figure 33: *Expanding and contracting register spaces.*

3 Create similar register studies of your own.

4 Improvise or compose a work showing a manipulation of space via dynamics and register.

14 AURAL DEPTHS OF FIELD

I wanted to open the window to hear the sea no longer
glass-paned. The tenor of the sea and the pitched gulls.
The beauty of the sea in its movement and mass.   Jeanette Winterson[31]

1 FOREGROUND, MIDDLEGROUND AND BACKGROUND

In any sound or combination of sounds, some aspects or elements seem to be more
prominent than others which seem to recede. To help differentiate between the elements,
we use the spatial terms foreground, middleground and background. The foreground,
middleground and background can constantly interchange and shift. They do not
necessarily have to be fixed. Robert Erickson writes:

> Foreground elements have the character of figure in relation to a ground; they are more distinct,
> more formed, and 'closer' than ground, which is less distinct, less formed, and 'farther away'.
> One could substitute words such as 'louder/softer' or 'duller/brighter', but the experience is
> undeniably spatial, and not entirely different from the visual space of everyday life.[32]

The terms foreground, middleground and background refer to the placement of sounds
within a piece of music or soundscape and how they influence the way we listen. In most
cases these positions are obvious and unambiguous. However, it is also important to
acknowledge the listener's own experience, whose particular relationship to a sound may
change the way he or she listens to the event.

Listening Example 50: *Ave Generosa*, Hildegard von Bingen
In this example a long sustained note is sung softly by the female voices giving the effect
of being 'behind' the solo female singer in the foreground. Can you imagine what this would
sound like if the main voice was in the background and the other voices in the foreground?

The continual shifting of material from foreground through middleground to background
is common to many styles of music. In some cases it is fundamental to the style and how
the composer or sound artist intends the piece to be heard. On the other hand, in a lot
of music the relationship between foreground, middleground and background is relatively
fixed. However, no matter how stable the structure is in a piece of music, there will always
be moments when the focus changes.

**Listening Example 51: *More Than Molecules*, Andy Arthurs and Philip Chambon
(c.1980)**
This piece opens with the bass guitar perceived in the foreground which is then replaced
by the female voice accompanied by a band. Notice the sudden shift of focus to the band
whenever the singer pauses; and the double foreground focus created whenever the guitar
plays a counter-melody accompaniment to the singer's melody. Can you imagine what the
piece would sound like if it were mixed so that the voice was softer than the
accompaniment?

Listening Example 52: Ludwig van Beethoven, Symphony No. 5, Ist movement (1808)
In this excerpt, the focus shifts from one instrument to another, beginning with the French
horns which are answered by the violins. As the horns recede into the background the
cello and double bass, playing a counter-melody, create a quick focus change between

→

themselves and the violins. Next the clarinets take up the foreground followed by the violins again and then the flutes. The excerpt is an excellent example of instruments constantly changing places to occupy the foreground.

Listening Example 53: Example of white noise

There are not many examples of music with neither foreground nor background. One example is called 'white noise' which is made by a television when it is turned to a non-broadcasting channel.

In 'Running Up That Hill' (1985) by Kate Bush each sound is introduced in the foreground, sequentially replacing the preceding sounds which recede into the middle or background. In order for this to succeed it is important that each new sound is formed and shaped distinctively. The first verse is structure as follows:

1st foreground:	crescendo on two long sustained notes
2nd foreground:	drum machine (first foreground recedes)
3rd foreground:	portamento violin sounds (drum machine recedes)
4th foreground:	voice solo with voice and chordal accompaniments in background.

A new background layer is added on the lines 'If I only could' consisting of a high pitched glass rattle. At the end of the first verse on the words 'If I only could', the portamento violin (layer three) becomes the foremost layer.

Activity 1

Choose a location for an excursion. Listen to all the sounds around you. You may wish to use a blindfold or close your eyes. Listen to what is in the foreground, middleground and background. Can you hear some sounds move from the background to the foreground and vice versa?

2 CHANGING ROLES: CONTINUAL VARIETY

The reader may ask why so much emphasis has been placed upon different types of focus. Imagine a house in which all the rooms, furniture and fittings were a single colour, or conversely, in which not one colour was repeated anywhere. In the first example all the items would blur into a general, single entity. In the second, the eye is over-stimulated, resulting in a constant and unstable focus. Each house has been designed to elicit a certain response from the viewer and music has similar design issues. A piece of music could begin with a single focus (a single 'colour'), which radically changes to a multiple focus (a 'multi-coloured scheme') and then shift to a completely new structure. The changes and roles assigned to the various parts are carefully planned. Each sound has a specific function so that the composer or performer (the 'designer') can communicate what he or she wants you to hear. What it all 'means' may be a difficult question to answer, as discussed in Chapter 1, but the way we hear the sounds relating to each other is crucial. Their design greatly influences our interpretation of the information.

3 SUMMARY

In order to distinguish between the sounds in a musical structure, the ear places them in a virtual space consisting of foreground, middleground and background layers. The characteristics defining each layer are not fixed. The perception of sound differs from one person to the next. Foreground sounds are those which stand out most to the listener, while background sounds are the least prominent. The middleground is that part of the musical space which lies between foreground and background. A foreground sound may be the loudest sound; but it could also be the most distinctive in timbre or shape. Foreground is what draws attention automatically. In many works of music and sound-scapes our perception continually shifts between the foreground, middleground and background.

4 QUESTIONS

1 What defines foreground?

2 What defines middleground?

3 What defines background?

4 Can you give an example of music with a stable foreground, middleground and background?

5. Can you give an example of music with a constantly changing foreground, middleground and background?

6 Can you give an example of music which begins with a stable foreground, middleground and background, which is then followed by an unstable foreground, middleground and background?

FURTHER LISTENING

- Kate Bush, 'Running Up That Hill', *Hounds of Love* (EMI 1985).
- W.A. Mozart, Concerto for Clarinet in A, K.622 (1791).

IMPROVISATIONS

Start and finish the session with a free or structured improvisation.

1 Improvise a solo with your voice or instrument which demonstrates easily identifiable sounds moving from background to foreground. Begin randomly and then try a solo which uses a strategy for shifting the sounds. For example, speaking a phrase first loudly and then softly.

2 Create a duet with another person exploring shifts between foreground, middleground and background. Use your voice, instrument, percussion or simply clap rhythms.

15 LISTENING STRATEGIES

Newton was prepared to admit ...that all motion is relative, but he maintained that ... in terms of the forces determining them, motions must be referred to absolute space as the frame of reference.   Ernest Nagel[33]

This chapter introduces some concepts referring to how we perceive sounds. The world is made up of a continual series of aural experiences and our ears have to be constantly on the alert to make sense of them. The more busy the world becomes, the more alert our listening has to be in order to make sense of the information. New environments force us to work harder at sifting through the information; familiar environments make the job easier by allowing us to make certain assumptions about what to expect.

Similarly, when listening to new music or sounds, our ears have to be attentive to make sense of the material. Some musical and sound structures call for more attention than others and it is the relationship between the sound's structure and the listener's attention that creates an engaging listening and communicative experience.

The study of how we perceive, categorise and respond to sounds is called music cognition and falls outside the parameters of this book. However, an introduction to certain concepts will allow further discussion of musical structures. When we perceive a sound we focus on it, giving it aural attention. The word 'focus' is used to indicate a site of activity involving the music's structure and the listener's aural attention.

1 MOBILE AND STABLE

The listening process constantly shifts focus between sounds, strands or layers of sound. A mobile listening musical structure relies on a perception of an active soundscape in which a lot of shifting takes place between the parts of the sound structure. A stable listening musical structure relies on the perception of a fixed order or hierarchy of sounds, allowing a certain amount of predicability. A stable structure assigns certain roles or functions to its sounds so that you, the listener, can predict what you will hear next. Listening Example 50, 'Ave Generosa', was an example of a stable structure in which the sounds conformed to a fixed hierarchy. The next piece is an example of a mobile structure.

Listening Example 54: Ludwig van Beethoven, Symphony No. 3 (*Eroica*) Op. 55, 2nd movement (excerpt) (1805)

In this example, the main melody is introduced by the second violins and then transferred to the first violins, followed by the violoncello section. Listen to what happens to the accompanying instruments when the main theme is played. They have a quality of their own. The focus is constantly transferred from one section to another with little predictability.

Listening Example 55: *Isis*, Chris Blackwell

Here the layers are quickly established, allowing the listener to focus on a hierarchy of sounds. Towards the end of the example the piano is obviously in the foreground while the bass, drums, percussion and synthesiser accompany in the background.

Listening Example 56: *Ricercare a 6*, J.S. Bach
This piece opens with a stable sound structure established by the violins in the foreground. The entrance of the other stringed instruments changes the sound structure into a highly mobile one. Does your focus constantly shift between the parts or settle on one instrumental sound?

2 SUMMARY

Listening spaces are like photographs: just as a frame confines a photograph, so our listening focus is limited. The frame of a photograph provides the limits for our listening focus. Much of what we define as listening space is dependent upon music cognition. This is due to each person's relationship to different sounds. Music cognition is the study of sounds as physiological and psychological phenomena. In the design of a musical environment, certain roles are attributed to certain sounds or instruments. These roles can be fixed or mobile. A sound structure in which the role of each sound is perceived to be fixed with little change in the foreground, middleground and background is called a stable structure. A structure in which sounds are perceived to continually change places – with a mobile foreground, middleground and background – is called a mobile structure.

3 QUESTIONS

1 What is a listening focus?

2 What defines a stable listening activity?

3 What defines a mobile listening activity?

FURTHER LISTENING

- J.S. Bach, *The Well Tempered Clavier* (c.1722).
- John Cage, *Imaginary Landscape No. 4* (1949).
- Miles Davis, *On The Corner* (Columbia 1972). All Davis' records from the late 1960s to 1975 are examples of textural music involving mobile structures.
- Morton Feldman, *Durations* (1961).
- Bill Haley and His Comets, title track, *Rock Around the Clock*, (DECCA 1955).
- The Orb, *Orbus Terrarum* (Island 1995).
- Gunther Schuller, *Transformation* (1957). This is an example of third-stream music which also uses klangfarben.
- Stan Kenton, *New Concepts in Artistry and Rhythm* (Capitol 1952).

Special Topic 1
Two Examples of Music Perception

The way we perceive sounds, and the procedures we put into place for listening to them are just as important as the sounds themselves. In some cases when we listen to sounds, certain aspects seem to be present even when they really are not. Our ears compensate by making us believe that what is missing is actually present. A sense of continuous falling, for example, can be achieved by overlapping two downward scales of exactly the same length and pitch. As one scale is about to end the other begins, creating the feeling of an endless downward spiral.

Two common examples of music perceptual strategies are the 'cocktail party effect' and 'streaming'. The cocktail party effect is produced by the technique of successfully separating wanted from unwanted sounds, as we do when concentrating the ear on a single conversation at a crowed party. Following a bass line or a guitar part separately in a song is another example of the cocktail party effect.

In streaming, the listener separates complex information into simpler components. The sound of a lawnmower or engine can be perceived to consist of a complex number of sounds. By focussing on the disparate components one appreciates the complexity of the whole sound. R.V.

Special Topic 2
Durations, Morton Feldman (1961)

In Durations, an important work of the 1960s, the composer has deliberately avoided any hierarchical organisation of the music. No sound is more important than any other. As a result, the structure is constantly mobile, the listening focus shifting from one sound strand to another. There is no predictability here, which makes it a more demanding piece of music to listen to.

One way Feldman has done this is by stipulating that all the instruments are to be played as softly as possible and declining to give any instructions for changes of loudness. He has notated the music as single notes without any indications of duration nor any attempt to organise the material vertically. As a result, sound changes radically from performance to performance. Listening to this work is like listening to the surrounding environment. Each listener hears the sounds receding and intruding into the foreground differently. R.V.

Special Topic 3
Imaginary Landscape No. 4, John Cage (1949)

Imaginary Landscape No. 4 is the fourth in a series of five works by John Cage scored for AM radios which use various types of electronically produced sounds. No. 4 has twelve parts and requires a conductor. Each radio is considered an instrument to be played by two people: one to work the tuner and the other to control the volume. The score consists of both instructions and notations: the player operating the tuner follows notes and rests with a change of station indicated by a radio frequency; the player operating the volume follows numbers representing the level of intensity. The duration of both dynamics is indicated by notes representing rhythmic values. The composer has no control over the detail of the performance: the type of material being broadcast depends on the station. Even the station itself may change depending on the city in which the piece is being performed. However, while the detail cannot be dictated, the composer does have formal control over the notated score which is the vehicle by which a certain series of actions produce sounds. In performance, this piece is an evocative landscape of radio programs sounding simultaneously; a collage of sounds which recede, disrupt, increase in magnitude, disappear and combine to form clouds of complex entities. See Special Topic 6, Indeterminacy, in Chapter 21 and Appendix 9, Generative Processes, for further reading. R.V.

IMPROVISATIONS

Start and finish the session with a free or structured improvisation.

1 Play a clapping game with another person so that you accompany each other, swapping parts around or playing together at the same time. The game will require you to decide when your playing is in the foreground, middleground and background. Try the game again with three or more people.

2 Do the same as in the previous clapping game with voices, instruments, sound-producing objects or a combination of all three.

3 Using at least two performers, perform the following graphic using any sustained note at any register. The length of the note is determined by the length of the dynamic indications. Discuss the sound structure that results.

First instrument or voice

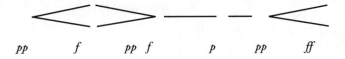

pp   *f*   *pp* *f*   *p*   *pp*   *ff*

Second instrument or voice

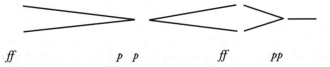

ff   *p* *p*   *ff*   *pp*

Figure 34: *A two-part work based on dynamics.*

COMPOSITION PROJECT 5

PART 1: RADIO COMPOSITION

This exercise explores foreground, middleground and background relationships using volume.

Compose a one-minute piece for four AM/FM radios, using only the volume control, the on/off button and the tuning dial. You may wish to assign different stations to each radio. If you decide to have the stations changing, be specific about the stations you want to hear: eg, FM 104.1, AM 873, short wave, etc. Use the following symbols for each activity:

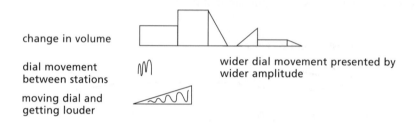

change in volume

dial movement
between stations

wider dial movement presented by
wider amplitude

moving dial and
getting louder

Figure 35: *Symbols for a radio composition.*

The following score is an example. Each vertical line marks a period of five seconds (this allows cueing). Each performer articulates the sound indicated by the symbol in terms of its placement within a five-second space. The following score indicates that Radio 1 begins with a short burst of sound at 3 seconds followed by a 5 second rest. On Radio 2 there is a short burst at about 2 seconds and a crescendo at 10 seconds. Radio 3 begins with a brief burst of sound followed by a rapid oscillation of the tuning dial at 5 seconds. Radio 4 explores crescendo with tuning oscillation and decrescendo.

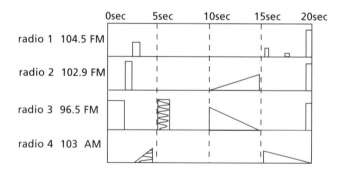

Figure 36: *Example of a score for four radios.*

PART 2: TIMBRAL COMPOSITION

Using any type of appropriate notation, compose a work of two to four minutes exploring:

- dynamic manipulation through the movement of sound between foreground, middleground and background,

- dynamic contrast,

- register expansion, contraction and contrast,

- timbre differentiation and combination,

- specially constructed sound shapes involving attack, sustain and decay.

The work may be for voices, instruments, sound-producing objects or a combination. You may wish to use a computer sequencer and sampler or a multi-track tape recording of pre-recorded sounds.

When composing this work think about the role of timbre and the function of all the sounds and gestures. Remember the work is an exercise. Its purpose is to demonstrate your awareness of the manipulation of sound structures and events.

HOMOGENOUS TEXTURES

The combination of sounds produced by layering or blending creates a musical environment called a texture. There are many types of textures and their chracteristics are defined by how sounds relate to each other and the role of time. Textures can be constructed from sounds which conform to a common concept of time or multiple concepts of time. The textures discussed in this module are based on sounds referring to a common concept of time producing a homogenous structure.

CHAPTER 16 — Texture

Key concepts or themes	Listening focus, hierarchical organisation, non-hierarchical organisation, density and parts and strands
Special Topics	1 Streaming 2 One Listener's Foreground is Another Listener's Background
Improvisations	

CHAPTER 17 — Homogenous Textures

Key concepts or themes	Time and Space Architectonic structures, single strands, alternating strands, parallel strands, hierarchical textures and multiple strands
Special Topics	1 Architectonic Structures and Metric Rhythm 2 Musical Gesture 3 Nineteenth-Century Terminology for Texture Archetypes 4 Phrases 5 '(You Make Me Feel Like a) Natural Woman', Carole King, sung by Aretha Franklin (1968)
Improvisations	

CHAPTER 18 — Spatialised Textures

Key concepts or themes	Perception, texture and time, counterpoint and contrapuntal thinking
Special Topics	1 Music Exists in a Space and Antiphony Exploits It 2 Stereo Panning 3 Klangfarben Melody 4 Heterophony and Rhythm 5 Op. 10 No. 1, Anton Webern (1913)
Improvisations	

Composition Project 6

16 TEXTURE

clouds of sound
a torrent of notes
a thunderous ending
a vacuum of silence

1 THE MUSICAL ENVIRONMENT

An environment is defined by an aggregate of objects, conditions and influences. We use the word in a variety of ways, be it weather patterns, workplace conditions or biological relationships. An environment is a system in which forces and factors are set against each other. If you look at a series of weather charts, you will find a complex array of signs, symbols and lines which indicate a constantly changing environment. All of these inform the meteorologist about the nature of the climate and changes in the atmosphere and are positioned to describe turbulence, stability, air pressure, temperature, etc.

In the musical environment, the forces at work are sounds and their parameters. Sometimes changing the role of one sound – making something much louder, for example – can have radical repercussions on the whole musical environment, while at other times such a change might have no effect at all. In music, different types of environments are referred to as 'texture'. Any combination of forces constitutes a texture and just as the weather can change in a moment, so too can musical textures.

2 TEXTURE

Texture refers to the way strands of sound intertwine and interweave with one another. All the elements of music contribute towards the quality of a musical texture, although not always at the same time. A piece of music can be based on a single texture or explore a combination of several. The textures involve register, timbre, duration, pitch and dynamics.

One way of thinking about texture is as a piece of fabric. A patchwork quilt uses a wide variety of fibres whereas silk consist of only one. It can also be thought of as a rock structure: granite consists of three or four minerals combined in a dense, tough texture while slate is made up of fine layers or sheaths of mudstone compacted together. In music, the word texture refers to the way sounds relate to one another when sounded 'vertically' (at the same time) and 'horizontally' (one after the other). Texture evokes a sense of physicality and invites the use of qualitative words such as 'dense', 'thick', 'sparse' and 'volatile'.

Textures can quickly change from one type or structure to another. This was demonstrated in Listening Example 56, *Ricercare*, by J.S. Bach. In that example, the music began with a stable melodic line which quickly changed to a highly mobile multi-layered structure. We often use qualitative expressions such as 'heavy' or 'light' to describe the density of a texture. Density refers to the number of parts sounding. A 'thin' texture has fewer parts or elements sounding than a thick texture.

Other qualitative words used to describe the density of a texture are 'opaque', 'transparent', 'sinewy' and 'dark'. When applying these words, try to understand the musical reason for their use. A 'transparent' texture, for example, probably involves sparseness, middle to high register, a soft dynamic and evolving attack envelopes.

Activity 1

Explore in a group different densities of a single note, such as a solo followed by various types of unison.

Activity 2

Sing these textures. Each one explores the basic elements of sound construction with the use of register, pitch, duration, dynamics and timbre.

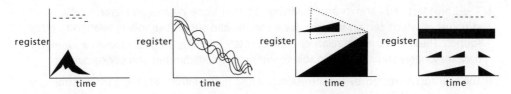

Figure 37: *Four visual examples of texture.*

Activity 3

Listen to the textures in Listening Examples 57 to 65. How would you

1 draw them?

2 describe them?

Listening Example 57: 'Eye of the Hurricane', Andy Arthurs & Phillip Chambon (1989)

Listening Example 58: 'Physic', *Intersect*, Brigid Burke and Rainer Linz (1997)

Listening Example 59: *Allegro*, Concerto Grosso in A minor, George Frederic Handel

Listening Example 60: *Icy*, Antoine Olivier

Listening Example 61: *Savanna Flyer*, Dennis Farnon

Listening Example 62: *Iyeya*, Vivien Ellis

Listening Example 63: 'Persephone sleeps amidst the blossoms', *Laquiem*, Andrée Greenwell (1991)

Listening Example 64: 'Sonata in C', K 545, 3rd movement, Wolfgang Amadeus Mozart (1788)

Listening Example 65: 'Oompah', St.Crustacean

3 TEXTURE AND LISTENING FOCUS

The terms introduced in the preceding chapters made it possible to discuss the sound activity of various textures. A texture could consist of foreground, middleground and background strands, which can either shift or remain stable; or it could consist wholly of high-register sustained sounds, slowly decaying in volume or soft, sparsely-placed middle-register sounds in the foreground with a low register hum in the background (like the sound of typing on a softly humming computer).

In any sound environment, sounds either relate to each other in a structured way or randomly. The way they relate influences the overall structure of the texture. The sound of someone singing a Christmas carol to a piano accompaniment is likely to have a hierarchical structure with the piano supporting the singer. However, if at the same time the sound of music from a radio is audible from another room, we become aware of two separate musical activities or listening foci. We may wish to shut out the radio music from our listening focus and concentrate solely on the hierarchical structure of the carol. However, should we take pleasure in the collision of the two separate musical spaces, then a simultaneous structure could be perceived. These two examples remind us of how subjective listening can be and the importance of the parameters of the musical space.

In these two scenarios the texture can be categorised according to the type of activity taking place.

i The Christmas carol and its accompaniment heard alone creates an hierarchical structure in which certain sounds play a specific and supportive role in relation to other sounds. These textures are relatively stable, often using layering techniques and relying on a reasonably static or predictable foreground, middleground and background.

ii The split focus created by the intrusion of radio music either sets the parts or strands in conflict, gives them independence from each other, or causes the focus to shift back and forth. These are non-hierarchical mobile textures in which the foreground, middleground and background are constantly in flux.

4 STREAMING INTO PARTS OR STRANDS

The traditional musical structures of the eighteenth and nineteenth centuries are primarily melodic or contrapuntal and they stream music into parts and strands by identifying the melodic and accompanying lines. In other periods different aspects of music were considered defining or crucial to the musical structure and it was streamed according to completely different criteria.

Most textures consist of a mass of information and to make sense of it, the ear streams it into parts or strands. A part or strand is something which can be heard as a unit. For example, it might be:

Special Topic 1
Streaming
Experiments in music cognition have shown that the ear streams (separates) complex material into simpler components. For example, while the following melodic line consists of a melody leaping between low and high notes, our ears stream the melody into two simultaneous strands, giving the impression of a two-part melody created by a single line:

Figure 38: *Melody implying two-part streaming.*

Figure 38 suggests the following strands:

Figure 39: *Separation of the melody in Figure 38 into two melodic streams.*

R.V.

1 the background guitar accompaniment or rhythm track to a song;

2 the melody of a song;

3 a freely moving strand or sound shape which recedes into the background or emerges in the foreground;

4 a distinct layer of sound such as the hum of an air-conditioning unit.

A texture can consist of a single strand, intertwining strands or multiples of strands. The relationship between the various strands defines the type of texture created. The excursion activities in previous chapters have demonstrated that a part or strand could be a bird call, car engine or someone speaking or coughing.

Activity 4
Draw a representation of a musical texture using musical signs where necessary, and imagine how it would sound.

5 SUMMARY

The texture of a particular sound shape is a musical environment in which the combination of all the parts or strands are woven together in a variety of ways. These elements can be set against each other or complement each other. Textures are often described in tactile terms: they can be 'thin', 'busy', 'dense', 'transparent' or 'delicate'. These metaphors inform us about the type of musical organisation: 'a cloud of sounds' has a different quality to 'a ripple of notes'. However, the metaphors do not tell us much about the musical activity. Consequently it is necessary to be more specific in the discussion of texture.
In Chapter 14 we heard how the degree of interplay between foreground, middleground and background layers directs the listening focus from one part or strand to another. Sometimes the interplay of these layers is stable, while at others the layers are highly mobile. Most musical works consist of several textures in sequence. These changing texture shapes create a sense of meaning and musical expression. In the next chapter, the different types of textures will be introduced.

6 QUESTIONS

1 What is texture in music?

2 What is streaming?

3 What is a part or strand?

4 What is the difference between an hierarchical and a non-hierarchical texture?

5 Give three examples of music that use different textures.

6 Give two examples of music that use similar textures.

FURTHER LISTENING

- Laurie Anderson, 'O Superman', *Big Science* (Warners 1982).
- J.S. Bach, Two-Part Inventions (c.1720).
- Brigid Burke and Rainer Linz, 'Physic', *Intersect* (NMA 1997).*
- Ornette Coleman, *At the Golden Circle, Stockholm I & II* (Blue Note 1965).
- Ornette Coleman and the London Philharmonic Orchestra, *Skies of America* (CBS 1972).

- Ornette Coleman, *Body Meta* (Harmolodic/Verve 1996).
- John Coltrane, arr. Eric Dolphy, 'Africa', *Africa: Brass I & II* (MCA 1961). This piece uses unconventional orchestration of the brass instruments to provide a 'whooping' vocal texture.
- Trilok Gurtu and Jan Garbarek, 'Once I Wished a Tree Upside Down', *Living Magic* (CPM 1991). This piece includes multiple percussion layers and synthesiser blended with saxophone and reverb effects.
- Steve Reich, *Vermont Counterpoint* (1982).
- Amanda Stewart, *I/T Selected Poems* (SPLIT Records 1998).*
- Frank Zappa, *Frank Zappa and the London Symphony Orchestra, Vols I & II*, conducted by Kent Nagano (Rykodisc 1986).
- Gregorian chant.
- Aboriginal song.

Special Topic 2
One Listener's Foreground is Another Listener's Background

There are no absolute rules for listening. Often sounds have particular associations for different listeners. Someone who lives next to a railway might feel quite differently about the sound of trains from someone who lives miles from public transport. Someone whose little brother is learning to play the violin (badly) might have a different relationship to the sound of the instrument from someone who collects violin recordings of all types. The associations sounds carry are important and the composer or arranger of a piece of music has only marginal control over how the listener hears the work. This is why texture is important. Textures provide a framework within which musical expression and information can be organised.

To understand the archetypes of texture it is essential that the listener be aware how he or she listens. There are basically two types of listening processes: wholistic and analytical. The wholistic listener perceives all sounds as a fused mass, paying little attention to any single aspect. This type of listening arouses sensory or emotional responses caused by the listener associating the musical event with other activities or experiences. The analytical listener focuses on individual parts or sounds, consciously piecing together the information to form a meaningful whole. This listener may be interested in the construction of a particular drum sound or the way two sounds combine and interact.

Between the two extremes of wholistic and analytical listening lies an associative listening process in which the listener associates a particular meaning with a certain sound event. These associations might be personal, cultural or communal. Sounds can trigger memories or bring to mind a story. Radio and television advertising consciously exploits this approach, associating cultural sound stereotypes with particular narratives, as for example, when an advertisement uses a new style of popular music to associate its product with fashionability; or when reverberation is used to suggest a large, grand room or space. R.V.

IMPROVISATIONS

Start and finish the session with a free or structured improvisation.

1 On an instrument, or vocally with another person, improvise a short work which continually moves from an hierarchical texture to a non-hierarchical texture.

2 Improvise a solo in which two or more parts seem to occur at once. How do you maintain clarity among the parts?

17 HOMOGENOUS TEXTURES

We're passing through time and space,
our ears are in excellent condition.   John Cage[34]

The musical environments introduced in this chapter are all 'homogenous' which means that they all rely upon a centralised or agreed conception of time or gesture. In an homogenous environment, all gestures belong to the same musical space. This is what playing 'in time' means: all the musical gestures conform to the same conception of time.

Metrically organised music (i.e. music 'with a beat'), such as pop music, is a very good example of an homogenous texture. In popular music, or any music with a functional beat, the musical hierarchy is architectonic. This means that every rhythmic layer reinforces every other layer, creating an homogenous time structure. The downbeat is a pivot or reference point from which everything else expands. However, there are other types of music, not based on a metric hierarchy, which are also homogenous archetypes. The essential characteristic of an homogenous environment is not conformity to a rhythm but simply a central concept of musical time. It is here that the term musical gesture becomes important.

Gesture expresses in space what rhythm expresses in time. A gesture is the physiological equivalent of rhythm. It gives texture its identity and quality. A work of music could be composed of similar gestures – such as staccato attacks – that all conform to the same concept of time. While the gestures might be rhythmically different to each other, their similar quality identifies them as a group within the same musical space. In this musical space, all the gestures are in sympathy with each other or defined by each other, and this creates homogeneity of time and gesture.

Listening Example 66: Demonstration of a common musical space created by metric organisation
In this simple vocal example, all the parts conform to the same musical space. The beat holds everything together. All the parts articulate or refer to the beat.

Listening Example 67: Demonstration of common musical space created by gesture
In this example, a common musical space is created by similarity of musical gesture. Each singer refers to the same motif, making slight variations to it which are not sufficient to disrupt its overall continuity.

Activity 1
Sing rising scale runs of different lengths. If you have a group of singers, sing the runs randomly, each member finishing on a different note. This activity creates a homogenous texture which is gesturally based on a single concept: a rising scalar passage of indeterminate length.

1 HOMOGENOUS TEXTURE ARCHETYPES

The following environments are considered texture archetypes.[35] The archetype is a common structure or form which can be found in different contexts. It is a recognisable structure which has many manifestations. Weather patterns also have archetypes. For example, while no cold, wet windy day is exactly like any other, the factors, cold, wetness

Special Topic 1
Architectonic Structures and Metric Rhythm

The music with which we are mostly familiar (such as pop and nineteenth-century music) explores a temporal system based on metric hierarchy which is architectonic. This means that every level in the temporal hierarchy reinforces every other. The traditional hierarchical approach divides units of time into two and three which can in turn be divided into further units of two or three.

Listening Example 68: Demonstration of an architectonic structure

Tap out the time strata you hear or feel in this piece – there will be more than one. For example, the four beats to the bar, the downbeat of every fourth count or the brass chord accent on every sixteenth count. This example is a rigid demonstration of an architectonic structure using multiples of two. As a result, its concept of time is uniform, each level reinforcing the next. In most music, these levels are only implied.

The rules of perspective are to traditional landscape painting what architectonic structures are to metrical music. Landscape paintings all conform to the same rules of perspective: a sense of infinity is created as all of the lines converge at the vanishing point.

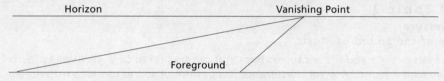

Figure 40: *The vanishing point*

Similarly, a sense of infinity is created when rhythmic values are divided sequentially according to a rule in which the rhythmic relationship is constant. In Figure 41, each rhythmic value can be subdivided into multiples of two or three to form a new layer. Conversely, each group of two or three notes forms another layer. This creates unity and theoretically can go on indefinitely.

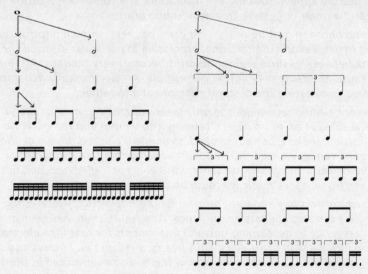

Figure 41: *Table of rhythmic values.*

and wind are the determinants. It doesn't matter if the temperature is five degrees or two degrees, it is still cold! Another example of an archetype is the concept of a soloist as someone performing in the foreground, accompanied by other musicians. This can apply to a soloist for a concerto or a lead guitarist in a rock'n'roll band. Both have a period of time in which to show off technique and musicianship.The purpose of these texture archetypes is to help identify the parts or strands of a piece of music or soundscape and their relationship to each other.

SINGLE STRAND: SINGLE AURAL FOCUS

Single aural focus is created by a single source of sound such as a melodic or rhythmic line, someone speaking alone, or even the sound of a buzzer on a film soundtrack.

Listening Example 69: *Ricercare a 6*, J.S. Bach

This is a traditional example of a single-strand texture. It is stable in that the listening focus is primarily on the totality of the opening melody. Each note is played so that it is even and well balanced against the next. The result is the homogenous, smooth surface.

Special Topic 2
Musical Gesture
The Cause of the Sound of Music

Every sound has a cause and if the cause is human it can be said to be a gesture: a physical action for making a sound. Any vocal utterance is a gesture. A sound cannot exist without a cause, which is silent, although the cause can exist alone. In most cases a cause or gesture without a sound would be musically meaningless. John Cage contributed to this debate with 4'33", a silent piece comprised of gesture alone.

Gesture does not define a sound. Hitting a cymbal results in a different sound from hitting a piano string. But equally hitting a cymbal results in a different sound to stroking a cymbal. The main parameters that define the 'personality' of a sound are its physical shape, and the material and gesture applied to stimulate it sonically. The combination of the sonic properties of an object and a cause or gesture creates a 'sound print'.

The relationship between gesture and sound print has been thrown into focus by electronic music-making in general and digital signal processing in particular. Outside the real acoustic space, the link between gesture and sound print becomes very tenuous. Although every sound has a cause, the cause may not be perceptible. An electronically generated sound can be programmed, eliminating the gestural component altogether.

Until the advent of audio recording, the only means of creating musical sound was through the mechanical stimulation of an object, causing it to vibrate and resonate. An object can be banged, hit, rattled, shaken, bowed, stroked, strummed, plucked, blown or tongued; but now a recorded sound can be emitted from a loudspeaker without any apparent cause or gesture. A whole genre of music has grown up around this concept, called 'acousmatic' music. It could be said that electronic dance music is acousmatic.

Whilst music which lacks any apparent gesture can be intellectually interesting, disconnecting cause from effect can also alienate an audience. As a result, there has been a lot of energy invested more recently in developing gestural instruments for real-time electronic music-making. These include MIDI controllers, light beams, virtual-reality gloves and so on. One of the earliest gestural electronic instruments was the theremin, invented in the 1920s. In the 1980s the performance artist Laurie Anderson replaced the horsehair on a violin bow with magnetic tape, and the violin strings with a recording head. The sound sampler is a hybrid gestural instrument which plays the 'voice' of another musical instrument with the gestural characteristics of the keyboard. A.A.

A single-strand texture need not have only one sound or instrumental source. The melody can be played in unison with all instruments performing the same material in the same rhythm and pitch; or by octave doubling, in which some of the parts perform the same material an octave above or below. The use of unison or doubling does not change the focus, but rather creates a more dense strand in which all the parts blend together, as the next example demonstrates.

Listening Example 70: Demonstration of unison and octave doubling
This is an example of gradual increase of density via unison and octave doubling. In it the melody is played five times. Each repetition introduces a new timbre. The first entry is played by the piano. The second, a string timbre, doubles the piano melody at an octave lower. The vibraphone enters playing an octave higher than the piano. The fourth entry, the marimba, plays in unison with the piano. The fifth entry, the bass guitar, plays an octave lower than the string timbre. Notice how the overall density of the texture gradually increases as the timbres merge, forming a new colour.

There are many examples of unison writing or performance. In the opening five bars of 'Gnomus', from Moussorgsky's *Pictures at an Exhibition* (1874) arranged by Maurice Ravel, the melody is played in octaves by the following instruments: clarinets, bassoons, contra-bassoon, viola, cello double bass and French horn. The dark sound created is a result of all the instruments blending together into a single focus.

ALTERNATING STRANDS: SPLIT AURAL FOCUS
When alternating sections of sound are sung or played it is often interpreted as a call-and-response. It divides the musical space into two areas of focus. Political chanting is a common example:

Leader: What do we want?
          Crowd: Funding!
Leader: When do we want it?
          Crowd: Now!

Listening Example 71: Demonstration of an alternating focus texture (call and response)
In this song the soloist sings short phrases which are answered by another singer. The structure of this call-and-response is relatively unstable, swapping back and forth between the soloist and the responding singer or group. However, within the parts themselves, as each part sounds, the focus is stable. The listening focus constantly changes from the soloist to the group.

PARALLEL STRANDS
Parallel Strands involve rhythmic unison but not pitch unison and are relatively stable. That is, all the parts play the same material but not in the same pitch as they would in a single-strand texture. The parallel movement of the parts creates a sense of depth.

Listening Example 72: An example of a scale as a single line and then in parallel motion
In this example a single melodic strand is intensified by the addition of another melody in the same time but at a different pitch. A third layer is then added over the other two to create a denser melodic structure consisting of three parallel rhythmic strands. Listen to the textural difference when the single strand is stated on its own again.

Listening Example 73: 'When I Was a Young Boy', Richard Vella (1999)

This listening example utilises all three of the texture types discussed so far:

1 a single-strand male voice solo,

2 alternating strands between the male solo and choir,

3 parallel moving strands in the male choir consisting of two pitches sung at the same time in the low bass voices.

STRANDS STRUCTURED HIERARCHICALLY

This type of texture uses a relatively stable foreground, middleground and background structure, with the middleground and background clearly supporting the foreground. Three archetypes belong in this category:

1 melody and drone

2 melody and accompaniment or fixed foreground with supportive middleground and background.

3 chordal style or vertical sonorities blending together to form a single unit in which one note stands out from the rest.

A Melody and Drone (Stable)

Melody and drone is essentially a combination of a single-strand texture with a sustained tone or group of repeated notes. One hears the drone as an accompaniment providing harmonic support and resonance to the single-strand texture. The drone functions like a pivotal point creating tension and relaxation between itself and the melody.

Listening Example 74: 'High Up', Richard Vella (1998)

This example uses a long sustained note sung by a male voice choir as a drone behind a lead singer's voice. Drones can be used beneath any kind of texture.

B Melody and Accompaniment (Stable)

This is a very common texture found in many song styles.

Listening Example 75: *If you want me*, Niqi Brown

After the introductory crescendo played by the synthesiser, the primary focus of the music is with the female vocal melody which clearly is in the foreground. The accompanying drums and guitar chords support the vocal line. Notice how the listening focus momentarily shifts whenever there is an accent in the drums or accompaniment. When the accompanying vocals sing in unison with the melody, they intensify rather than detract from the focus on the vocal melody. This piece is an excellent example of hierarchical organisation. Can you imagine how it would sound if the voices were absent or the accompanying lines were louder than the main vocal parts? Changing the hierarchical structure would change the way the texture is meant to be heard.

C Chordal Style (Relatively Stable)

In chordal style a melody is harmonised with other parts. Although the role of the parts is always to support the main melody, at times they can be heard independently. Whereas the parts in parallel strands play the same material at different pitches, in chordal style they are free to play different material from the main melody.

Listening Example 76: British National Anthem (excerpt)
Listen to the movement of the lower voices in this example as they sound with the top voice. If you had to sing this back, you would probably sing the top voice melody rather than one of the lower voices. The function of these voices is supportive. Listen as they move up or down in pitch. The movement of pitch creates a more unstable texture.

MULTIPLE STRANDS (MULTIPLE FOCUS CONTRIBUTING TO THE SAME TIME SPACE OR GESTURE)

This is a mobile listening structure in which several independent melodies or parts are played together. The listening focus constantly shifts from part to part. There are many types of multiple-strand textures, however this chapter introduces those of which the components either metrically or gesturally share a unified structure.

Listening Example 77: *Ricercare a 6*, J.S. Bach
The single-strand focus introduced in Listening Example 69 is transformed here into a multiple-strand focus as the other string parts enter. The focus constantly shifts from one part to another. No instrument takes priority. Parts share the focus, momentarily support each other, recede and emerge within this complex web. This style of writing, in which parts continually move and change in relation to each other, is called counterpoint.

Listening Example 78: African Frame Drums
In this example, the layers combine to form a highly active texture. The focus moves from one part to another.

2 SUMMARY

The relationship between the different parts of a texture constantly changes. Sometimes the elements approach and recede; at other times the foreground, middleground and background textures are fixed in a hierarchy into which other foci momentarily intrude. Understanding the texture archetypes allows one to begin to understand the roles sounds play in relation to each other.

The textures introduced in this chapter are common to many cultures. It is for this reason the term 'archetype' was introduced: archetypes are forms, models or patterns which can be represented in many ways. The elements which define them may be different, and their cultural associations and meanings may be diverse, but the basic structures remain the same. In order to classify these archetypes, the terms 'strand' and 'stream' are used to refer to their identifiable elements such as melody, chord, accompaniment and rhythm. However, a part or strand need not be a melody. It could be a gesture or a sound. The terms 'stable', 'unstable', 'strand', 'focus', 'foreground', 'middleground' and 'background' are crucial words in the listening vocabulary that enable us to perceive and understand the shifting relationships between sounds.

In this chapter all the sounds discussed have conformed to homogenous texture types. An homogenous texture is one in which all the parts or gestures conform to the same musical space. While it is important to be able to identify the archetypical textural environments, it is often the case that they have been further combined to form larger structures. The combinations of these textures give a sense of structural and musical meaning. Single-texture pieces are also possible. Shifting from one archetype to another gives music depth and density as the listening focus shifts from unstable to stable, foreground, middleground and background structures.

3 QUESTIONS

1 What defines a homogenous texture?

2 What is a musical gesture?

3 How does metric organisation define an homogenous time space?

4 What is a single-strand texture?

5 What is an alternating-strand texture?

6 What is a parallel-strand texture?

7 What are the three types of hierarchical textures?

8 What is a multiple-strand texture?

9 Can you give an example of each type of texture discussed in this chapter?

Special Topic 3
Nineteenth-Century Terminology for Texture Archetypes

The terms developed in the nineteenth century to describe musical textural activity were determined by criteria based on melodic organisation. The Western musical tradition is a contrapuntal one in which melodies are played against each other. Associated with this is the aesthetic of the balanced tone. Each note is performed so that it is evenly balanced against the next to create a pure, smooth surface. Changes to texture styles generally come about through instrumental and harmonic innovation. Baroque and earlier versions of counterpoint were mainly vocal musics. The instruments available were generally treated as if they were vocal parts. They provided simple textures and were treated as melodic instruments with little attention to variation in dynamics and articulation. The developments in instrumental building had a radical effect on orchestration. Suddenly composers were able to explore more exciting instrumental combinations and timbres. Orchestration is almost synonymous with instrumentation and therefore instrument development. At the same time, the musical language became more complex and dramatic with the introduction of adventurous key changes (made possible by the equal-temperament tuning system) dramatic effects such as tremolos, sustained and passing chords, extended harmonies and formal innovations such as the sonata, symphony, opera buffa and late eighteenth-century concerto. The net effect of these changes was a transition from a vocally-based music, in which instruments were considered as supporting or equivalent to the voice, to a music in which instrumental writing was independent of vocal writing styles.

If we look at the history of music in terms of these developments, the logic behind the traditional terms used in the nineteenth century becomes clear:

Monophony A single sound. This is a solo line largely representative of the plainchant period in which solo or unison voices sang single melodic lines. It was designed to be performed in a church, allowing lots of time for reverberation which created a slow organic quality of vocal delivery.

Antiphony The call-and-response structure so common in liturgical chant in which the cantor (priest or soloist) is answered by the congregation or choir.

Parallel motion Rhythmic-unison singing, harmonising in thirds or fourths. It came into existence after these intervals – considered dissonant in the medieval period – were accepted as a consonant harmony.

Homophony 'Same sound'. This was the beginning of melody and accompaniment in which all the parts support the melody.

Polyphony 'Many sounds'. This style is characteristic of the Baroque and Renaissance. As key changes were limited, movement was created through highly active individual parts →

→ continually set into play with each other. Development of material was primarily melodic, using such techniques as inversion, imitation, variation, retrograde, augmentation and diminution.(See Appendix 6.)

While this terminology was appropriate for music based on melodic organisation, tonality and smooth, even tone it is inadequate when applied to music based on other principals such as timbre, gesture, sound, different uses of rhythm or technological innovation. It is for this reason the terms single, alternating, hierarchical, multiple and parallel streaming (strands) are used as they are more representative of the listening strategy applied to textures.   R.V.

Special Topic 4
Phrases

It is often the case that the various parts in a musical texture can be heard as a series of phrases; each one seeming to have sense in relation to the previous one. Simply defined, a phrase is the smallest sequence of notes within a composition in which the listener hears a sense of unity. They are the building blocks from which a piece is constructed and when combined with each other they create formal structures such as melodies, verses, songs, improvisation solos and larger forms such as sonatas. Some people use the term sub-phrase to refer to incomplete identifiable units of music, such as a motif, which combine to form a phrase. This is probably because the term 'phrasing' is used to describe the way a performer shapes the motifs and units to give expression to a musical part. Phrases, when placed in sequence, can create

1 closure, and/or
2 a sense of process.

A melody consists of units (phrases and sub-phrases) which combine to form expansion, development and finally closure. One experiences a sense of opening out, a middle section and an end which is often called the cadence.

A sense of process is created when the phrases and sub-phrases combine to explore aspects of the musical material through variation, repetition, reduction and expansion. With phrases, one experiences a sense of argument presented in a similar way to language, with paragraphs and sentences made of clauses, phrases and connecting statements.

Phrases can be short or long. They can be combined organically to form a continuous melodic structure, such as Maurice Ravel's Bolero (1928), or form clearly defined sections such as those found in most national anthems. The 'period', a common phrase form, which uses antecedent and consequent structures is an example of musical gesture in homogenous time. An antecedent structure is an opening statement which creates a sense of expansion while a consequent structure is a closing statement which creates a sense of finality. Together they form a musical phrase by behaving like question and answer. The first two statements of 'Twinkle, Twinkle Little Star', for example, are antecedent and consequent structures. In this case the consequent signals closure by finishing on a home note of the scale:

Antecedent: Twinkle, twinkle little star,   (opening)
Consequent: How I wonder what you are.   (closure)

In answering the antecedent, the consequent complies with the same time and space relationship as the antecedent. A sequence of gestures need not use antecedent and consequent structures to create a homogenous time space. Songs consists of a series of phrases (each one called a verse) which may form a question and answer structure or develop or extend the previous phrases.

Compare the organisation of the phrase structure in '(You Make Me Feel Like a) Natural Woman' by Carole King, which forms an antecedent and consequent structure, and in 'Stairway to Heaven' by Led Zeppelin which repeats and extends before concluding.   R.V. →

→ **'(You Make Me Feel Like a) Natural Woman', Carole King (1968)**

Looking out on the morning rain,	(antecedent)
I use to feel so uninspired.	(consequent)
And when I knew I had to face another day,	(antecedent)
Lord it made me feel so tired.	(consequent and closure)

'Stairway to Heaven', Led Zeppelin (1971)

There's a lady who's sure,	(opening statement)
All that glitters is gold.	(varied repetition)
And she's buying a stairway	(extension)
to heaven.	(closure)

Special Topic 5

'(You Make Me Feel Like a) Natural Woman', Carole King, sung by Aretha Franklin (1968)

'Natural Woman' illustrates the use of both parallel, hierarchical strands (melody and accompaniment) and split-focus strands (call-and-response). This extraordinary arrangement is full of detail and fluid texture change. There are many shifts in focus between the band, female voices and the soloist – for example when the chorus sings 'ahoo' to reinforce the downbeat.

Lyric	Focus
First Verse	
looking out on the morning rain...	Melody and accompaniment.
Chorus	
'Cause you make me feel	Soloist and chorus sing in unison.
You make me feel	
You make me feel	
Like a natural woman.	Parallel strands descending, soloist (doubled with background reverb vocal) and bass guitar.
Woman.	Split focus with chorus.
Second Verse	Same as verse one.
When my soul...	
Chorus Followed by Extension	
Oh baby what you done to me	Split focus between soloist and chorus.
What you done to me	chorus
You make me feel so good inside	soloist
Good inside	chorus
And I just wanna be	soloist
Wanna be	chorus
Close to you, you make me feel so alive.	
Chorus and Fade Out	

FURTHER LISTENING

- Led Zeppelin 'Stairway to Heaven', *Led Zeppelin III* (Atlantic 1971).
- Aretha Franklin, '(You Make Me Feel Like a) Natural Woman', *Aretha: Lady Soul* (Atlantic 1967).

Single Strand: Single Aural Focus

• Sonny Rollins, 'It Could Happen to You', *The Sound of Sonny* (Original Jazz Classics 1957).

Alternating Strands: Split Aural Focus

• 'Lalle', 'Ere Ere' and 'Asibu' on *Music of the Fulani Niger/Northern Dahomey* (UNESCO 1988).

• Ebenezer Obey, 'To Ba Nwa I Re' *Out of Africa* (Rykodisc 1988).

Parallel Strands (Rhythmic Unison but not Pitch Unison, Relatively Stable)

• Most antiphonal responses in African folk music use improvised pitch but they are also structured in parallel strands.

• Nuages, Debussy (opening chords played by clarinets and bassoons).

Strands Structured Hierarchically

1 Melody and Drone (stable)
  • Stevie Wishart, untitled instrumental piece, *Gabriel's Greeting: Medieval English Christmas Music* (Hyperion 1993). The opening minute includes a hurdy-gurdy.
  • Byzantine Chant.
2 Melody and Accompaniment (stable)
  • Almost any popular song uses melody and accompaniment.
3 Chordal Style (relatively stable)
  • Supersax, *Supersax Plays Bird* (Capitol 1973). This record consists of Charlie Parker solos arranged for two alto, two tenor and one baritone saxophone section.
  • Stan Kenton, 'Opus in Pastels', *New Concepts in Artistry and Rhythm* (Capitol 1952). The saxophone section is a good example of chordal style.

Multiple Strands (Multiple Focus Contributing to the Same Time Space or Gesture)

• Charlie Parker, 'Chasin' the Bird' and 'Ah-Leu-Cha' (1947/8), *The Savoy Recordings Master Takes*, Vols I & II (Savoy 1976).

IMPROVISATIONS

Start and finish the session with a free or structured improvisation.

1 Improvise a solo over a repeating pattern which can be played by a performer, a drum machine or sequencer. Explore all the possible divisions of the beat via syncopations, accents and groupings. Try to introduce rhythms outside the time space so that the solo is not in the same time space as the repeating pattern.

2 Improvise a solo in which no divisive time is established. At no point in the solo should there be a beat or repetition. How does this change the way you play?

3 Using an instrument that allows you to play more than one part at once (a computer sequencer or percussion instrument), perform a series of solos exploring each of the texture archetypes introduced in this chapter:

- single strand
- parallel strand
- alternating focus
- hierarchical: melody and drone
- hierarchical: chordal
- hierarchical: melody and accompaniment and
- multiple strand

4 Combine all the textures in a single performance.

5 Improvise a work in a group based on a multiple-strand structure. A simple way would be to play or sing melodies or rhythms that form a complex web when performed simultaneously.
Does your listening focus shift as all the parts interact with each other?
Does the texture change?
How do the different strands contribute to the changes?

18 SPATIALISED TEXTURES

> McTaggart first offers us an order of events in which there are no differences of past, present and future, but only differences of earlier and later ... every happening always stays the sort of happening it is...
>
> J.N. Findlay[36]

1 SPATIALISATION

Sound spatialisation is the placement of sounds within a musical environment to create virtual movement. Alternating strands are probably the most useful of the texture archetypes introduced in Chapter 17 for creating a sense of space. Its most basic form is the call-and-response texture in which one voice calls and another responds. Often, for example in a political chant or a religious ceremony, the one calling is physically separated from those who respond. The spatialisation helps to keep the two streams distinct from each other as the focus shifts back and forth between them. However physical separation is not essential to an alternating stream structure; – can also take place in an imaginary or virtual space. The shifting focus between alternating streams is like watching a tennis match from the sidelines. In alternating streams, we hear the sound being 'passed around' between timbres. The same phenomenon is created by stereo panning when a sound is moved from one loudspeaker to another. The sensation of movement within a space is controlled by changing the dynamics of a sound, its timbre and the physical position of its source.

Abrupt shifts in register such as leaps from high to low can also produce a sense of spatialisation. Traditionally this is called disjunct motion and refers to melodic leaps larger than the interval of the third. Disjunct motion causes streaming, resulting in the listener perceiving two or more strands in the melodic writing. (See Figure 38 and Figure 39.)

Special Topic 1
Music Exists in a Space and Antiphony Exploits It

The Greek phon means sound. From this is derived homophony: same sounds; polyphony: many sounds; and antiphony: sounding against or across. Much music, from folk music through to the concerto, involves a dialogue between two groups – the question and the answer. A phrase played by one instrument or group of instruments (ensemble) is responded to by another. In antiphonic music two or more sets of musicians are placed physically in different parts of the listening space. This gives the piece an acoustic spatial perspective in addition to that created by the natural reverberation of the environment. It was particularly popular in early Western music. Canons and fugues could be treated antiphonally. This then gave way to the more homogeneous sound of the orchestra with or without a soloist.

It was not until the twentieth century that the practice was revived in any substantial way. Mahler, in his First Symphony, asks for the distant sound of an offstage trumpet and Respighi, in The Pines of Rome (1924) (a magnificent orchestral extravaganza), calls for double basses to be placed all around the auditorium to envelop the audience in a powerful, low frequency pulse, like being in the midst of marching Roman soldiers. Stockhausen uses the effect in Gruppen (1955-57) which calls for three orchestras to be placed to the left, centre and right of the audience; and even more spectacularly in Carré (1959-60) for four spaced orchestras and choirs.

→

➤ *Today, the PA system has encouraged musicians such as Pink Floyd and Jean-Michel Jarre to develop quite magical antiphonal spectaculars using digital delay lines and echo units. Antiphony was made possible at home with the introduction in 1958 of the stereo record and more recently with domestic or cinematic surround-sound systems.*

Antiphony should not be confused with antiphon which is a term denoting certain categories of Gregorian chant. A.A.

Special Topic 2
Stereo Panning

Stereo panning gives the effect of a moving sound. The sound does not actually move at all but the impression of movement is created by using a volume control called a pan potentiometer ('pan pot'). To make a sound 'move' from the left speaker to the right, the pan pot dial is turned from left to right (See Figure 42). What this does is control the location of the sound source. Turning the dial completely to the left causes the sound to be emitted from the left speaker alone. As the dial is turned to the right, the volume of the left speaker is gradually reduced while the volume of the right speaker is gradually increased. As the listener's perceptual focus becomes weaker on the left and stronger on the right the sound appears to move. When a sound of equal volume is emitted through both speakers it is perceived to emanate from the middle space between the speakers. If the pan pot dial is turned further to the right, the left speaker becomes softer and the listener's focus becomes attuned towards the louder sound coming from the right speaker, causing another perceptual shift. Finally as the dial is turned completely to the right, the sound from the left is cut out and only the sound from the right is heard, creating the impression that the sound has moved in space from left to right. R.V.

a Dial turned to the left only allows the signal to be emitted from left hand speaker

b Dial turned to the centre allows both signals to be emitted from left and right hand speakers

c Dial turned to the right only allows the signal to be emitted from right hand hand speaker

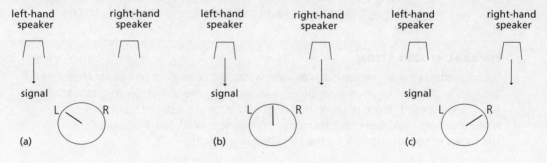

Figure 42: *Stereo panning.*

KLANGFARBEN MELODY

Klangfarben (from the German for 'sound colour'), is a technique which explores or implies sound spatialisation. It is similar to the medieval practice called hocket which explores rapid changes between instrumental sounds within a melodic line. This technique shares a note or group of notes in a melodic line between two or more instruments. Whereas hocket is usually associated with certain rhythmic units, or notes which alternate between the parts, klangfarben is usually identified by the use of timbre and most probably register to distinguish different parts of the melody. There are many examples of this technique in every culture.

Activity 1

1 Sing the first verse of 'Twinkle, Twinkle Little Star' as a solo:

Twinkle, twinkle little star,
How I wonder what you are.

2 Sing 'Twinkle, Twinkle Little Star' with at least one other person using klangfarben technique. Break the verse up into syllables, words or phrases while retaining their sequence and rhythm. For example:

Voice 1:	twin	twinkle	star.		won	what	are
Voice 2:		kle,	little	How I	der	you

Allocating the notes of the melody to different vocal timbres creates an impression of movement from one timbral location to another. In the solo version of the song, rhythm, timbre and melody combine to form a single homogenous unit or stream of information in which all the elements are interdependent. In the klangfarben version, rhythm, melody and sound colour are released as independent elements. The listener starts to perceive the whole as a number of discrete entities and the spatialisation immediately becomes apparent. The song is no longer a smooth surface but a sum of disparate parts which, while they all conform to the same concept of time, emanate from different locations and registers.

Listening Example 79: Demonstration of klangfarben on drums

Drum kit solos are often constructed through klangfarben technique. Each timbre in the kit contributes to the total rhythmic structure of the solo. In this example the snare, tom-toms and bass drums are all combined to form a texture based on implied spatialised timbres and their associated registers.

Listening Example 80: Vocal melody, sung by Monique Eichperger

In this example, the singer rapidly alternates between one timbre and another.
The rhythmic thrust of the piece holds all the timbres together. Notice how the example adopts a foreground, middleground and background structure as the various timbres approach and recede.

TIMBRAL MODULATION

Sound spatialisation techniques such as klangfarben are dependent on timbral modulation. Changes to tone colour in an aural stream are caused by one sound blending into another. This is an important device in orchestration, studio recording and electronic music. A sound stream could begin as a trumpet, continue as a violin and finish as a flute. The choice of sounds depends on the composer or arranger.

Activity 2

Turn on an electric appliance such as an alarm clock or a shaver or some other constantly sounding timbre which you can imitate with your voice in the same register. First turn on the appliance, imitating the sound with your voice, then turn it off while you continue to sing. The modulation of timbre from the sound of an electric appliance to a voice causes an automatic change of focus.

Activity 3

Sing the vowel a (as in 'ah'). Retaining the same pitch, gradually change the sound to e ('ee') then i ('I'), o ('oh') and u ('oo'). In this exercise timbral modulation is caused by each vowel's overtones.

Special Topic 3
Klangfarben Melody

The change from one timbre to another can be subtle or dramatic. Composers often explore timbral change either as a trick (making one instrument sound like another) or contrast. There are many examples of music in which one pitch is played by many different instruments. This gives a sense of metamorphosis as we hear the sound change in time (Figure 43).

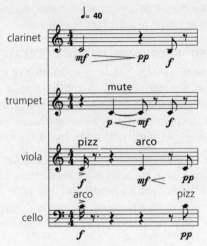

Figure 43: *Klangfarben technique on one note.*

A very famous example of klangfarben melody is Anton Webern's orchestration of J.S. Bach's Ricercare (Figure 44). Webern divides the melody, which originally would have been played by one instrument, into sections. Each section is played by a different instrument. This approach produces some of the most extraordinary nuances. One hears the melody kaleidoscopically as each section is played by a new sound. (The original melody is written out at the bottom of the figure).

R.V.

original version before orchestration

Figure 44: *Anton Webern's arrangement of J.S. Bach's* Ricercare.

Listening Example 81: Op. 10, No. 1 Anton Webern (opening)

In the opening few seconds of this example, the music quickly shifts from one timbre to another. The first seven notes of the melody are virtually sliced up into different colours as different instruments play them. Firstly you will hear a trumpet in unison with a harp in the middle register. The next note consists of three timbres: harp harmonic, cello harmonic and celesta. The third note combines a flute (flutter tongued) with the harp again. The next three notes are played by a high register glockenspiel, which is followed by a tremolo note played in the middle register by the celesta.

HETEROPHONY (SIMILAR SOUNDING STREAMS THAT CREATE A BLURRED FOCUS)

Heterophony is a spatialised homogenous texture in which two or more performers play essentially the same gesture with slight modifications. It is homogenous because the quality of the gesture is agreed, but the exact detail is different. Usually heterophony involves the addition or omission of notes. It has a multiple focus (polyphony) so that the listener perceives a single musical gesture produced by many slightly varied parts.

Heterophony produces a type of shadowing effect or an impression like a cubist painting, in which one part tracks another, or many parts track each other. It can also involve slight adjustments to the rhythmic treatment of a melodic part: the parts are slightly out of synchronisation with each other and time becomes blurred and multi-layered. Sometimes heterophony is used to create more dense structures, called sound masses or blocks (discussed in Chapter 21).

Activity 4

Ask two groups to sing 'Twinkle, Twinkle Little Star' with this slight variation in the second part. The variation causes the timbre to blur.

Group One: Twinkle, twinkle little star, how I wonder what you are.
Group Two: Twinkle, twinkle little star, I wonder how you are.

Special Topic 4
Heterophony and Rhythm

The three rhythms in Figure 45 when played together, produce a heterophonic texture. The criterion is a slight variation in rhythmic values, but there is no hard and fast rule about how this effect is achieved.

Much of the music of the Hungarian composer György Ligeti (b. 1923) explores heterophony. He creates textures through the heterophonic overlaying of instruments playing similar rhythms. Two of his works, Lontano *(1967) and* Chamber Concerto *(1969-70), begin with heterophonic techniques in which the shifting focus on the different timbres creates a kaleidoscopic effect, like a mirror ball reflecting light in many directions at once.*   R.V.

Figure 45: *Heterophony created by slightly different rhythms.*

Listening Example 82: 'Auld Lang Syne' (traditional)
In this example of heterophony the singers make no attempt at synchronisation, creating a subtle interplay that results in a wonderful kaleidoscopic effect.

2 A SENSUOUS MIX

It is a common compositional practice to combine textures, sometimes layering different archetypes to form more complex structures. The next example by Liza Lim is only a small excerpt from a large work full of texture archetypes and combinations.

Listening Example 83: *Garden of Earthly Delights*, Liza Lim (1989-90)
The instruments accompanying the oboe in the opening solo all conform to a similar gestural motif. The structure is essentially a single stream combined with a heterophonic texture. It opens with a rising single-strand sound from the oboe followed by the other instruments descending in the same fashion. While the texture of the rhythms is hetero-phonic, their gestures are unified within the same time continuum. Listen to instruments coalesce or momentarily associate with each other by playing similar rhythmic gestures and timbres. This is an example of a multiple focus in which a solo stream is balanced against clusters of instruments. The unifying device is gesture not beat. The sense of sounds prolonged, the use of up-beats and falling sounds are all gestures. The excerpt is highly contrapuntal and heterophonic. Parts are played in counterpoint but we still recognise a common relationship between them. One part may answer another, one instrument may extend the melody of another.

3 SUMMARY

While textures based on sound spatialisation create virtual movement, they are still homogenous as their unifying feature is a gestural or rhythmic link. The spatialisation can be created by changing dynamics (as exploited in stereo panning) or abrupt shifts in register and timbral modulation (as used in klangfarben technique and heterophony). Many pieces of music explore a multiplicity of textures. Webern's Op. 10 No. 1 is an example of a piece which moves freely through a variety of texture archetypes while retaining temporal continuity.

4 QUESTIONS

1 What defines a spatialised texture?
2 How is stereo panning achieved?
3 Why do alternating strands created a spatialised texture?
4 What is a klangfarben texture?
5 What is timbral modulation?
6 What is heterophony?

FURTHER LISTENING

- Gustav Mahler, Symphony No. 1 (1888).
- Ottorino Respighi, *The Pines of Rome* (1924).
- Karlheinz Stockhausen, *Grüppen* (1955-57) and *Carré* (1959-60).

KLANGFARBEN

- Anton Webern, Opus 10, No. 1 (1913).

- J.S.Bach, *Ricercare* arranged by Anton Webern (1934-35).

- Arnold Schoenberg, Five Orchestral Pieces, Opus 16, Nos 3 *(Farben)* and 5 *(Das obligate Rezitative)* (1908/9).

HETEROPHONY

- Liza Lim, *Garden of Earthly Delights* (1989/90).

- Witold Lutoslawski, *Mi Parti* (1976).

- Stefan Wolpe, Piece in Two Parts (1961).

- Ornette Coleman, 'Lonely Woman', *The Shape of Jazz to Come* (Atlantic 1960).

Special Topic 5
Op. 10 No. 1, Anton Webern (1913)

Anton Webern's (1883-1945) enigmatic Opus 10 No. 1 lasts only about 26 seconds but in that short duration a wide variety of textures are articulated.

The opening three-note melody uses klangfarben technique beginning with a harp in unison with a trumpet. This melody functions as an antecedent phrase. The following delicate glockenspiel melody is a consequent phrase, closing the structure. The next sound, a tremolo of the celeste, creates a background drone over which the clarinet plays a foreground melody accompanied by string instruments. A multiple-streamed texture follows as independent lines are played in counterpoint to each other. The flutter-tongued flute melody comes into the foreground ending this multiple-focus section.

The violin timbre heard at the end of the flutter-tongued flute melody is an example of timbral modulation in which the focus shifts from a flute timbre to a high register violin timbre. This violin sound can also be interpreted as a concluding line to the preceding music. The remaining few seconds function as a recapitulation, reducing the gestures from the previous music to their salient elements as repeated short notes, a melody and a klangfarben texture similar to the opening which passes the same note between a flute, trumpet and celeste.

This piece is a wonderful example of a composer's appreciation of timbre. Each sound is delicately and sensitively handled. The ambiguous musical environment it creates is largely due to the exploitation of similarity between sounds.

R.V.

IMPROVISATIONS

Start and finish the session with a free or structured improvisation.

1 Improvise a voice solo exploring klangfarben. Make each timbre in your solo distinct.

2 With another person, improvise a melody exploring movement between heterophony and unison.

3 On a single note, explore timbral modulation with your voice or instrument.

4 Improvise a heterophonic variation based on a song or rhythm which is also being played at the same time on a tape recorder or by someone in the same room.

COMPOSITION PROJECT 6

1 Using texts from newspapers, books and other printed material, compose
a work for four voices utilising single-strand, parallel, alternating, klangfaben,
hierarchical and multiple-strand textures. Notate the work using signs of your
own invention and standard symbols wherever appropriate. If you need to
introduce a rhythm, write the rhythm out or use a pulse track to show where
the words should be placed.

For example, in Figure 46, two voices read aloud from right to left the texts
and their dynamic indications specified in their boxes.

Texture Type	Single Strand	Parallel strand (together)	Hierarchical Strand
voice 1	This is an example of a single strand *p*	This is an example of a parallel strand *mf*	This is an example of an hierarchical strand *mf*
voice 2		This is an example of a parallel strand *mf*	Thi..................sss *p*

Figure 46: *Creating textures using spoken words.*

or

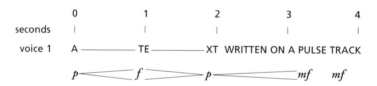

Figure 47: *Text on a pulse track.*

or

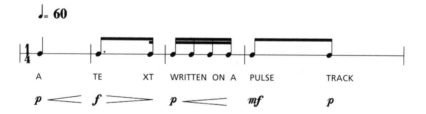

Figure 48: *Text set to rhythm.*

2 Compose a work for sung voices or instruments using as many of the textures
discussed in Chapters 17 and 18 as possible. Use whatever notation is
appropriate.

3 Compose a work incorporating two approaches to time:

a time as something to be divided and perceived that way, and
b time as something which is not divided into perceivable units.

HETEROGENEOUS TEXTURES

The textures discussed in this module are defined as heterogeneous. They rely on disparate information which either tenuously conforms to a common concept of time or to multiple time strata. We do not hear an hierarchical approach to sound organisation but focus on multiple layers or streams. In these textures, sounds exist simultaneously. Sometimes due to the saturation of information, the ears perceive disparate units as a single total.

CHAPTER 19	Ambiguous Textures
Key concepts or themes	Disjunct structure Cut-up, cells and montage
Special Topics	1 Analogue (Tape) and Digital (Computer) Editing 2 Textural and Rhythmic Cells
Improvisations	

CHAPTER 20	Stratified Textures
Key concepts or themes	Simultaneity
Special Topics	1 Multiple Tempi 2 The Autonomous Aural Object 3 Analysis of Anton Webern's Op. 10 No. 3 (1913)
Improvisations	

CHAPTER 21	Clouds of Sounds: The Sound Mass
Key concepts or themes	Sound Mass Modules and mobiles, multiplicity, micropolyphony, minimalism, repetition music and indeterminacy
Special Topics	1 Edgard Varèse (1883-1965) 2 Sound Mass, Register and Dynamics 3 Micropolyphony 4 Modules and Mobiles 5 Repetition Music and Minimalism 6 Indeterminacy
Improvisations	

Composition Project 7

AMBIGUOUS TEXTURES

There is a succession of states [perceptions, memories, motor responses], each of which announces that which follows and contains that which precedes it. They can ... only be said to form multiple states ... In reality, no one of them begins or ends, but all extend into each other.

Henri Bergson[37]

1 IN DELICATE BALANCE

Texture and focus are created by the balance between all the elements of a piece of music. If any one of these elements is manipulated, the texture changes. 'Natural Woman' and Webern's Op. 10 No. 1 both demonstrate types of texture changing without disrupting its continuity: all the textures conform to a common concept of musical time, gesture and space. In the next listening example, the performer achieves continuity in another way. The solo uses a variety of sounds and gestures but while the surface is very active, the skillful placement and transformation of sounds within a single line prevents the piece from fragmenting.

Listening Example 84: Voice solo demonstrating a variety of timbres

This solo displays a wide array of articulations and sounds. While the melody is clearly produced by a solo voice, the detail and use of multiple effects call into question the term single focus. This is a much more complex sound fabric; one which is not as smooth as Listening Example 69 (*Ricercare* by J.S. Bach) in Chapter 17. The juxtaposition of timbres demands an active listening focus and the melody becomes a form within which different types of sounds are placed. The sonic surface becomes a rich tapestry of events held together in a delicate balance.

2 TIME, TEXTURE AND MUSICAL SPACE

All the listening examples in Chapters 17 and 18 were based on the perception of a common concept of space and time from which the performer could deviate. These textures were homogenous due to the use of an agreed metre, pulse or gestural structure. The textures discussed in this and the following chapter are heterogeneous. The word heterogeneous refers to the inclusion of 'foreign' or 'outside' elements. The foreign elements could be stylistic, gestural, timbral, rhythmic or temporal. Their presence creates a sense of multiplicity. They make the listener aware of a more complex surface in which parts do not necessarily have to conform with each other. A heterogeneous texture may be full of disruptions, multi-layered, fragmented or full of disparate entities. It demands active listening to a musical surface in which difference is the norm.

3 TEXTURES CONSISTING OF DISJUNCT UNITS

Textures based on disjunct units consist of discrete events combined to form a whole. Listening Example 84 uses a disjunct texture. Rather than blending sounds into each other, the piece juxtaposes and collides them together. In film this would be called montage. Klangfarben textures can also be perceived as disjunct juxtapositions of textures. In many ways klangfarben represents a borderline or delicate balance between homogenous and heterogenous textures.

Textures based on disjunct units explore spatialisation in a more eruptive way. They use disjunct units which are gesturally unified. Alternating-strand textures (call-and-response) are one example. They divide a common musical space into two alternating foci.

CUT-UP, TEXTURAL CELLS AND MONTAGE

Cut-up is similar to klangfarben. However, where klangfarben slices a melodic passage or chords into separate timbres, cut up slams together disparate melodies or textures in a montaged sequence. The result is a more ambiguous relationship to time in which both uniformity and diversity are simultaneously apparent.

Listening Example 85: '.' Amanda Stewart (1986)
Each phrase in this spoken piece uses a different voice quality or articulation, or quotes a well-known song. This produces a montage of voices within a single voice.

In the next example, each section – and sometimes a part of a section – is given a separate articulation and instrumental colour. Each event is like an organic cell expanding, contracting and combining with other cells to form new entities. Like a biological cell, these events are organic, continually growing, subdividing and re-combining.

Listening Example 86: *Peter's Piece*, Raffaele Marcellino (1996)
This work can be approached as a series of minute cells of texture, rapidly juxtaposing each other and then combining to form a larger structure. The piece begins with a low and high register note on the clarinet. These are interrupted by rapid legato passages in the high register. The piece gradually collides all the low and high registers and the rapid passages. The units re-combine, coalesce and converge.

Special Topic 1
Analogue (Tape) and Digital (Computer) Editing

Recent computer software has made it possible to edit music at a very powerful and sophisticated level. Once a piece of music or sound has been recorded onto a computer hard drive, it is possible, with the appropriate software, to cut, dissect, invert or transform the sound in an unlimited number of ways. Sounds become bits of information. Today a recording engineer can transfer a phrase, note or virtually anything audible, from one performance to another simply by 'cutting' and 'pasting' on the computer. It's as easy as cutting and pasting paragraphs in a word document. Modern digital recordings are rarely records of a single live performance. Generally they are hybrid constructions of many recordings. The engineer selects the best bits from each performance to create an ideal performance. This is called non-liner editing. Before the invention of the computer, editing was done by tape manipulation, whereby parts of a tape were physically cut and stuck back together with special adhesive tape, or by overdubbing, which could record or layer a piece of music using a multi-track recording. Appendix 2, Postcards from History: Electroacoustic Music, discusses the introduction of musique concrète *by composers immediately after World War Two. This involved tape manipulations such as cutting tape into little pieces and recombining them in new sequences, overdubbing, reverberation, playing tape backwards, slowing down or speeding up and looping. The production of this type of music-making was painfully slow and it was often impossible to slice a sound event as accurately as a computer. However, in both tape and computer editing, the end result is similar: the ability to combine disjunct pieces of sound into a new sound world.*

Early famous examples of works using tape editing are 'I am the Walrus' (1967) by the Beatles, Orphée *(1953) by Pierre Henri and* Gesang der Jünglinge *(1956) by Karlheinz Stockhausen.   R.V.*

Listening Example 87: Demonstration of radio improvisation

In this example each little unit is montaged against another creating a bizarre example of multiple focus. Each station represents an independent time span. While we experience a multiplicity of disparate musical events, we also experience a temporal paradox. On the one hand, each sound is heard as individual yet, at the same time, all disparate sounds are unified by the rapidly changing radio dial.

4 SUMMARY

The textures introduced in this chapter explore structures which focus on the unique qualities of the sound unit. In more traditional textures, the melodic part is usually played by one instrument creating a well-balanced, evenly-blended melodic unit. Like klangfarben technique, cut-up and montage violently attack the notion of the self-enclosed musical space by introducing disparate elements. The result is an ambiguous textural form which creates an awareness in the listener of many discrete sounds instead of one unified whole. Focusing on a discrete sound creates a sense of disjunction in time and space. The separate sounds are heard both individually and as a unit. This creates a paradoxical feeling of time struggling to keep in check the incongruous units and fragments that make up the piece. Cut-up creates a sense of rapid movement from place to place like a radio tuner running through the stations. In cut-up whole sound worlds are juxtaposed in a brilliant display.

5 QUESTIONS

1 What constitutes a disjunct texture?

2 What is cut-up?

3 What is montage?

4 What is the difference between klangfarben and cut-up?

Special Topic 2
Textural and Rhythmic Cells

A rhythmic cell is a pattern which can be expanded or contracted by duration and is similiar in function to cut-up. Rhythmic cells are a very powerful means of musical organisation and they can be used as the basis for whole movements. Messiaen used them extensively, most notably in Livre d'orgue (1951). An earlier twentieth-century example is Stravinsky's Le sacre du printemps (1913) in the movements 'Rondes printanières' and later in the 'Danse sacrale'.

The following is an example of the use of two rhythmic cells (A and B). As A gradually expands, B contracts.

Figure 49: *Two rhythmic cells: A expands while B contracts.*

There are many examples of music in which complex cells are created from a combination of simpler ones. These new cells are then contrasted against the originals to form an interplay of rhythmic patterns. R.V.

FURTHER LISTENING

- The Beatles, 'I am the Walrus', *The Magical Mystery Tour* (Capitol 1968).
- Pierre Henri, *Orphée* (1953).
- Olivier Messiaen, *Livre d'orgue* (1951).
- Gunther Schuller, *Transformation* (1957).
- Amanda Stewart, *I/T Selected Poems* (SPLIT Records 1998). *
- Karlheinz Stockhausen, *Gesang der Jünglinge* (1955-56).
- Igor Stravinsky, *Le sacre du printemps* (1913).
- Frank Zappa, 'The Return of the Son of Monster Magnet', *Freak Out* (Verve 1966).

IMPROVISATIONS

Start and finish the session with a free or structured improvisation.

1 Improvise with your voice a melody based on cut-up. Notice what happens to your organisational powers as you have to deal with all the different elements.

2 Rapidly move a radio dial from one station to another. Listen to the cut-up textures created by your dial movements and how the rhythm of the dial changes holds the overall sound together.

3 Improvise a work using cut-up or cellular units of disparate sounds. The units can be stylistically different or belong to a palette of sounds of your choice, such as long notes, high fast notes, descending glissandi, etc. Develop the solo so that the units expand, contract and re-combine to form new units.

4 Improvise a solo based on two different rhythmic cells. Expand one cell while contracting the other.

20 STRATIFIED TEXTURES

Recipe for Simultaneous Ice-Cream: Dairy cream and little squares of raw
onion frozen together.   Giuseppe Steiner[38]

The collision of different musical realities can produce radical changes in the listening
focus. For example, while walking down the street you might hear from one house
someone practising the piano; at the same time, across the road, someone playing a new
pop song on their stereo; in the next house, someone mowing the lawn. All these activities
express different realities; none conforms to any other and the listening focus has not
been directed towards ordering the events in any particular hierarchy. We become aware
of different foci as the musical space divides into distinct layers. The term multiple focus
is appropriate but does not indicate any relationship between the parts. There are many
approaches to multiple-focus organisation which do not depend upon a unified conception
of time, gesture and space. An important technique is stratification.

1 STRATIFICATION

Stratification is the process by which sounds or textures are layered or stacked up to
form a complex structure. The layering techniques discussed in Chapter 11 are based on
metrical organisation and are often hierarchical. Stratification exploits the use of multiple
streaming. The ear hears distinct bands of sounds which retain their independence. These
strata could be defined according to rhythmic pattern, dynamic shape, timbre, tempo or
register.

A stratified texture can be metric or non-metric. The important aspect is the differentiation
of layers. Imagine you are standing at a busy junction. Across the road is a construction
site and to your right a brass band. On your left is someone with a microphone advertising
bargains to be had in his shop. You would probably hear the sounds from the traffic,
the building site, the brass band and the man with the microphone as independent strata.

The opening tutti sections of Stravinsky's *Le sacre du printemps* are good examples of
stratification. In these sections no instrument is more important than any other. The ear
perceives the total sonic landscape.

 **Listening Example 88: Demonstration of non-metric stratification using organ
accelerando and piano decelerando**
This example simultaneously speeds up and slows down, precluding any uniform beat or
time unit. Consequently no architectonic time structure is possible and we hear the two
lines as independent strata. The piano part gradually gets slower (decelerando) and lower,
while the organ voice gradually gets faster (accelerando) and higher. The example has
multiple strands shifting the focus from layer to layer. The stratified layers or strands have
a temporal independence. The listener is aware of two layers of time: one speeding up and
one slowing down.

Listening Example 89: *Convergence* (excerpt), Richard Vella (1995)
This excerpt contains four strata:

1 a melody played in octaves by the violin and cello;
2 fast ascending scalar passages played by clarinet, flute, trumpet and oboe;
3 an ornamental piano figure;

➜

➤ **4** a trill which begins on the flute and is then transferred to the viola.

The four strata are independent, but in combination form a delicate, light texture.

Complementary strata are an important aspect of stratification. When used in combination they can produce dense or intricate sound structures. For example, while the four strata in Listening Example 89, *Convergence*, are perceived as discrete layers, their relationship to each is interdependent. By balancing the layers against each other, it is still possible to listen to the work as a totality of parts. When a piece creates an awareness of separate, unrelated parts, the technique is called simultaneity and it is the logical extension of disjunct textures. The examples used in Chapter 19 created disjunctive time spaces by jumping sequentially from one sound to another.

2 SIMULTANEITY

A piece employing simultaneity is more like a collage, overlaying and juxtaposing different materials. In music it creates an awareness of several concepts of time and space at once. There are two types of simultaneity:

A multi-layered strata using the same time reference but different stylistic references; and

B multi-layered structures in which there is no temporal relationship between the various strata.

Simultaneity is an open system which allows anything to be mixed with anything else. Its essential quality is the mix.

Activity 1
Half the class sings a well-known song while the other half sings something unrelated.

MULTI-LAYERED STRUCTURES USING THE SAME TIME FRAME

In some music employing simultaneity the foreground texture uses the same temporal values as the others within the piece but they are heard together. The distinct textures result in a very mobile listening process. Although this technique uses layering, it is not hierarchical. In hierarchical layering events are stacked up so that the parts support each other. Polyphony, for example, by definition demands a certain level of simultaneity: individual strands have to be heard at the same time. But simultaneity is more than sounds heard together. It involves a different perceptual focus. In simultaneity the listener becomes very much aware of a listening focus that splits. This split can be created by temporal units or a stylistic contrast which may refer to other time spaces. The band Enigma's mixing of medieval Gregorian chant with a drum machine is an example. The most obvious historical precedent can be found in thirteenth and fourteenth century motets in which songs were sung in two or three different languages at once, each part forming an independent layer.

Listening Example 90: Thirteenth century Motet, anonymous, from the period of Petrus de Cruce (instrumental version)
Originally this example would have been sung. Instruments are used here to bring out the three parts. Each part in the vocal version of this motet sings in a different language and has a specific rhythmic structure. The combination of individual language and rhythm creates a stratified structure in which each layer is heard independently and simultaneously. This was a common technique in the thirteenth century.

A more modern example can be found in Malcolm McLaren's arrangement of Puccini's famous aria 'Un bel di vedremo' from *Madama Butterfly* (1984). The use of simultaneity is very similar to the thirteenth-century motet. Although the drum beat ensures that all the parts belong to the same time and space, notice how the choice of different musical styles creates a sense of multiple textures. Each texture, like a quotation, refers to a different time location:

1 Puccini's opera Madama Butterfly (1904)
2 The American occupation of Japan in 1946
3 A 16-year-old female singer from New York in the 1980s.

MULTI-LAYERED STRUCTURES WITH LITTLE OR NO TEMPORAL RELATIONSHIP BETWEEN THE PARTS

Simultaneity can also make use of separate textural time zones. Not only are the textures heard separately, but each texture has its own concept of time. This is what happens in 'In ruhig fliessen der Bewegung', the third movement of Luciano Berio's extraordinary work Sinfonia (1967-71). This example involves four groups of performers: two orchestras, one playing the second movement of Mahler's Second Symphony, the other providing orchestral interjections; a speaker reading from *The Unnameable* by Samuel Beckett, and an eight-voice a cappella group, the Swingle Singers. Sometimes the music converges on a central time space, at others, it fragments into a multi-layered collage of textures, each with its own time and space.

Listening Example 91: 'Impermanence', 2nd movement, Robert Iolini (1996)
In this example two strata are combined. The organ and voice, referring to a liturgical style, are layered over a recorded mix of two soundtracks from films by the French director Jean-Luc Godard. The form of the song is asymmetric and the singer's text is the dialogue from one of the Godard soundtracks. This piece is an enigmatic collision of two very different worlds: the sacred liturgy and the profane film soundtrack.

Listening Example 92: Six Studies on a Trombone Melody, No. 2, Richard Vella (1989)
In this example two tempi are heard simultaneously. The flute, piano and vibraphone combine as a three-part stream in one tempo. At the same time the short staccato punctuations, from the trombone and cor anglais, articulate a slower tempo.

3 SUMMARY

The musical textures introduced in this chapter are created through stratification. This means that the textures are based on many time planes rather than just one. In order to appreciate these structures the ear has to change strategies and listen to sound as a mixture of interdependent planes combined to form a whole unit. This allows the listener to perceive a more complex entity in which the listening strategies are continually active. The focus shifts from place to place as the music articulates various temporal units.

4 QUESTIONS

1 What is a stratified texture?
2 What creates simultaneity?
3 Give some examples of stratified textures from the environment.

Special Topic 1
Multiple Tempi

The incorporation of different tempi in a single piece is a technique used by many cultures. The hemiola is one such approach. A hemiola regroups subdivisions to create different beat patterns. For example:

3 groups of 2 quavers............. ..... 2 groups of 3 quavers..3 groups of 2 quavers...

Figure 50: *Hemiola in which three groups of two change to two groups of three in the third bar.*

Here the tempo of ♩ = 60 is slowed down by regrouping the quavers into two groups of three. The beat becomes slower implying a tempo ♩. = 90.

The regrouping of a subdivision or counting unit can produce intricate tempo changes. In the next example each part accents the semiquaver into different groupings creating a multiplicity of tempi: *R.V.*

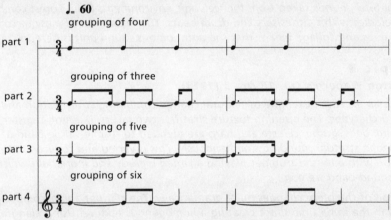

♩ = 60

grouping of four

part 1

grouping of three

part 2

grouping of five

part 3

grouping of six

part 4

Figure 51: *Multiple temporal layers produced by various groupings of the sixteenth note subdivision*

Part 1 ♩ = 60, ♪ = 240 (60x4)
Part 2 accent every 3 semiquavers, 240 ÷ 3 = 80, implied tempo ♪. = 80
Part 3, accent every 5 semiquavers, 240 ÷ 5 = 48, implied tempo ♩♪ = 48
Part 4, accent every 6 semiquavers, 240 ÷ 6 = 40, implied tempo ♩♪ = 40

Special Topic 2
The Autonomous Aural Object

In our aural world there are always sounds which seem to have a function or meaning in relation to other sounds and others which seem to have none. There are many examples of sound environments in which sounds or events exist independently of each other. A car going by has no relationship to the sound of the telephone ringing or a door slamming. Some sounds in the environment have a relationship to each other, such as two birds answering each other or a dog barking at the sound of a footstep. However, we accept most of the sounds as independent events. Any sound which exists in the same environmental space as another but has no temporal relationship to it is an example of an autonomous sound event. Musical structures are no exception. A collage composition might consist solely of autonomous events and its pleasure is the appreciation of the disparate events colliding, combining, mixing or following each other in surprising ways. Each sound can be appreciated for its own unique timbre and shape.   →

➨ *There are many compositions which consciously explore non-hierarchical presentations of sounds. Recordings which mix unrelated natural sounds together, for example. The sound of a dog barking can be played backwards and slowed down to half its speed, or a train whistle repeated in a rhythmic loop. In* musique concrète *the soundscape becomes a rich tapestry of disparate sounds juxtaposed, manipulated, edited and organised according to their timbre, register, shape etc. (See also Special Topic 6, Indeterminacy, in Chapter 21 and Appendix 2, Postcards from History: Electroacoustic Music.)*

The impulse to rationalise an irrational world in which order and chaos exist simultaneously is also apparent in the later works of the American composer Charles Ives. Ives composed a whole corpus of works exploring simultaneous layerings of irreconcilable events. In Stockhausen's Grüppen, *composed between 1955 and 1957, four orchestras are placed around the audience to create simultaneously sounding structures. Similarly Stefan Wolpe (1902-72) developed a musical language around a clearly-controlled harmonic plan within which unrelated incongruous musical events or harmonies would suddenly occur. He called these ruptures to the controlled harmonic scheme 'autonomous fragments'. The 'liberation of sound', as the composer Edgard Varèse once termed it, has resulted in the common acceptance today of any non-instrumental sound in music. The Icelandic pop musician Björk mixed a string ensemble with natural sounds taken from the Icelandic environment, Deep Forest combines African tribal melodies with synthesisers and drum beats. The revolution of* musique concrète, *recording techniques and collage means that the autonomous sound unit is here to stay.   R.V.*

Special Topic 3
Analysis of Anton Webern's Op. 10 No. 3 (1913)

This movement is an excellent example of textural change combining stratification and homogenous textural archetypes. The opening texture stratifies two layers: i) a high-register tremolo in which mandolin, bells, guitar, celeste and harp are blended to form a single band of sound; ii) a lyrical solo violin stratum sounding simultaneously. This is varied and reduced in time in the next section with a muted trumpet playing a varied melody and more bells which refer to the opening sound-band tremolo.

The middle section of the piece changes quite dramatically. The clarinet and accompanying instruments play in the same time space creating a homogenous texture. Using klangfarben technique, the violin picks up from the clarinet melody to conclude this section.

The final section is a variation on the opening texture in which a muted trombone plays another variation of the opening melody while, at the same time, cow bells, mandolin, harp and glockenspiel blend to form another sound stratum. The final two bars of the work establish an alternative stream texture between the last few notes of the previous texture and a snare drum. This is sounded over the ominous drone of a bass drum.   R.V.

FURTHER LISTENING

- Charles Ives, *Three Places in New England*, 'Putnam's Camp' (1914).
- Béla Bartók, *Bagatelle* No. 1 (1908). This piece employs two keys at once and uses multi-layered structures in the same time frame.
- Herbie Hancock, title track of *Sound System* (Columbia 1984). In this piece the kora, balaphone and dusunguni are layered over heavy techno music.
- Richard Vella, *Memory Pieces* Nos 2-5, *Australian Piano Music Vol 1: The Hands, The Dream* (Tall Poppies 1991).

IMPROVISATIONS

Start and finish the session with a free or structured improvisation.

1 Improvise a work with another person in which you each play in a different style.
Were there any points of intersection or were the two parts completely independent?

2 Improvise a work with another person exploring different tempi or changing tempi.

3 If you feel confident enough, create a solo demonstrating multiple time levels.

CLOUDS OF SOUNDS: THE SOUND MASS

Timbre ... would become an agent of delineation like the different colours on a map separating different areas, and an integral part of form.

Edgard Varèse[39]

1 SOUND MASS

Sometimes there is so much happening in a sonic event that all the sounds blur into a massive wall of timbre. The detail is lost and we experience a sense of mass. This is called a sound mass or sometimes a sound block. The roar of a waterfall or the effervescent bubbling of a fizzy drink are examples of sound mass. Sounds in these examples are particles and we listen to them the same way we view something from a distance: small details conglomerating into larger structures. The techniques associated with blending (Chapter 12) and heterophony (Chapter 18) are an important part of creating a sound mass.

The mass or block of sound is heard as a sensory unit in which all the sounds are blended together in a single object. The gestures within a sound mass can contribute to the same time space or act autonomously, referring to a multiple time space. A chorus of cicadas, for example, is a sound mass belonging to a single time space because the individual voices are gesturally similar, whereas a chorus of different birds is an example of a sound mass in which each species' voice is gesturally different, belonging to its own time space. They avoid any sense of accent in favour of duration and density. They can be defined by timbre, register, dynamics and textural activity, including tone or instrumental colour, density, rhythmic activity, speed and type of articulation. A musical work can be made up of a number of distinctive sound masses which the composer may choose to manipulate or simply place in juxtaposition to other sound masses.

'A Day in the Life' from the Beatles' *Sergeant Peppers' Lonely Hearts Club Band* is a famous example of sound mass technique. In this song a massive string sound emerges from the background into the foreground as it gradually gets higher. It gives the impression of weight and mass. This sonic mass occurs three times: an ascending violin mass heard twice at the end of the third verse referring to four thousand holes in Lancashire and later, at the song's end when a massive E major chord is played by a considerable number of pianos. The ascending violin mass is perceived quite separately from the song's harmonic structure and an awareness is built up in the listener of two different time events: the gradually rising violin sound and the 4/4 structure of the song.

As well as being homogenous and heterogeneous textures themselves, sound masses also occur within larger homogenous and heterogeneous textures. The use of heavy distortion by a guitarist in a rock song is an example of a sound mass within a homogenous texture. The combination of disparate sound masses produced by a building site, a jack hammer, passing traffic and an aeroplane, is an example of a heterogeneous texture using sound mass.

Listening Example 93: Example of a homogenous texture: Guitar distortion sound mass

Listening Example 94: Example of a heterogeneous texture: Building site and traffic sounds

Special Topic 1
Edgard Varèse (1883-1965)

The term sound mass is associated with the French-born American composer, Edgard Varèse. Varèse described his sound constructions as unified masses or blocks of sound, similar to blocks of granite, constellations of stars, mounds of gravel, tapestry patterns or schools of fish. In a lecture he gave at Princeton University in 1959, he said: 'There is an idea, the basis of an internal structure, expanded and split into different shapes or groups of sound constantly changing in shape, direction and speed, attracted and repulsed by various forces.'[40] In his work Intégrales *(1925), for winds, brass and percussion, the listener experiences sound masses in collision. Each mass is defined by timbre, dynamics and register. Varèse has been a major influence on both composers and musicians, especially the American rock'n'roll musician Frank Zappa. Varèse's desire to hear sound liberated has only really been fulfilled in the last thirty years. His works are monuments to sound unleashed.* R.V.

Robert Erickson defines sound mass as those sounds that show:

    a precarious balance of forces, where
    b individual instrumental sounds lose their identifiability, and where
    c an unexpected, or striking or otherwise memorable fused sound is in the perceptual foreground.[41]

There are two approaches to forming sound masses or blocks:

1 fusing, in which the sounds are blended to form a unified whole; and

2 multiplicity, in which the sounds multiply themselves to form a large-scale mass.

FUSING

A fused sound mass can be extremely dense, very thin, or rapidly change from one to the other. Composers often create huge walls of sound in which masses collide, are layered or blend with each other. Other examples of fused sound masses can be heard in the course of an ordinary day, such as the roar of a plane overhead or the roar of a crowd at a football match.

Listening Example 95: Concertino (opening), Elena Kats-Chernin (1995) performed by the Sydney Alpha Ensemble
The opening chord played by the piano, percussion and winds is a fused or blended mass. By combining them the composer forms a new sound. The viola is simultaneously stratified against this mass.

MULTIPLICITY

A sound mass based on multiplicity uses the multiplication of a gesture. The gestures multiply to form a larger textural unit or mass of sound. The ear can either perceive the sound mass as a single event or focus on aspects of the mass's structure. In the next two examples polyphonic listening (multiple focus) is automatic. As the ear scans the contrapuntal landscape it can focus on the work as a whole or any part of interest. The instrumental works of Steve Reich are fascinating bands of sounds in which each instrument can be heard as a melodic unit. *Octet* (1979) and *Vermont Counterpoint* (1982) consist of minute repeating melodic units in which the foreground becomes a compound of momentary accents within the mass of sound.

Listening Example 96: Example of a mass of sound produced with drums

Although at times some of the drum-sound combinations in this example move into the foreground, it would be quite pointless to try following just one. The impact of the piece comes from the combination of all the drum sounds at once.

Listening Example 97: Layering of melodies to produce a sound mass

The continual layering of melodic material in this piece produces a complex of melodies. The ear can choose to listen to individual parts or the total texture as a mass of sound.

2 HETEROPHONY REVISITED

Heterophony was introduced in Chapter 18. It is created when two or more instruments or parts play the same material with slight variations. Heterophony can also be used to create a sound mass by overlaying heterophonic parts – be they melodic units or rhythmic motifs – to the point of saturation so that the layers merge into one sound event. This approach is called micropolyphony.

Listening Example 98: A sound mass created by heterophony

In this example each singer sings a slightly different version of the same material. As each new singer enters, the texture transforms from heterophony to a mass of sound.

Activity 1

List any sound mass, such as birds singing, an aeroplane passing overhead, distant traffic, that you can hear in your immediate surroundings. How would you describe each mass of sound?

Special Topic 2
Sound Mass, Register and Dynamics

Register and dynamics are essential parts of sound mass. Some masses are only effective if they are very loud, while others can be incredibly soft and distant. The choice of register plays an important role, not only in creating the structure of the sound mass but also establishing its identity. A work might begin, for example, as a low-register mass of sound covering one octave and finish as a high-register mass but still within the range of one octave.
The following graphic score demonstrates the relationship between register and dynamic: R.V.

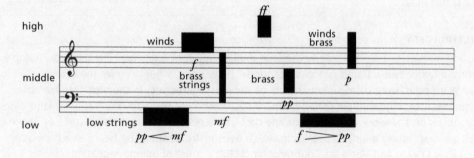

Figure 52: *Sound mass, register and dynamics.*

Special Topic 3
Micropolyphony

The technique of micropolyphony is sometimes used in the same way as multiplicity and often the two terms are used synonymously. In a polyphonic or multiple-strand texture one can hear the independent parts creating a texture unit. In a micropolyphonic texture, the melodic units are not meant to be heard independently. In many ways micropolyphony is an extreme version of heterophony (blurred focus), in which each part plays a slightly different melodic or rhythmic variation on the other. The multiple-blurring creates a micropolyphonic sound mass. Many composers explore this technique to create huge canvases of sound.

Figure 53: *Micropolyphony.*

Lux Aeterna (1966) by György Ligeti is a famous example of micropolyphony. In this work 16 voices fuse together in a single sound unit. Each voice sings a slightly different rhythmic version of the melody. Sometimes a single voice or group of voices moves into the foreground, but most of the time, the composer wants us to listen to the complete texture. R.V.

3 SUMMARY

The textures in this chapter explore sound constructions as independent units or masses of sound. These masses are primarily defined by timbre, register, dynamics and textural activity. They have so much information that all the sounds fuse or multiply to form a larger unit. They can be created through fusing, multiplicity or micropolyphony. Sound masses require the listener's focus to change from the specific to the general. Sound masses are sensory in nature; we experience weight, density and mass. The environment is full of sound masses and blocks such as the roar of a passing jet (fusing), rain on a roof (multiplicity) or cicadas in summer (micropolyphony). Feedback from an electric guitar is an example of a sound mass with a sensuous and plastic shape.

4 QUESTIONS

1 What is a sound mass?
2 What are some everyday examples of sound mass?
3 What are some musical examples of sound mass?
4 What is fusing?
5 What is multiplicity?
6 What is micropolyphony?
7 What is a module?
8 What is indeterminism?

Special Topic 4
Modules and Mobiles

In the 1950s artists started exploring non-linear time structures. Alexander Calder's mobiles are among the most famous visual artworks of the period. In music the concept of the mobile – freely moving elements arranged according to certain parameters – was also new ground for exploration. Fragments of music were composed from which the performer could choose which to play and in what order. Each module had its own distinctiveness. The interest of the piece lay in the juxtaposition of the modules and the order chosen by the performer. The following example is a simple demonstration.

Modules for four players
Play each module ad lib and for as long as you wish.

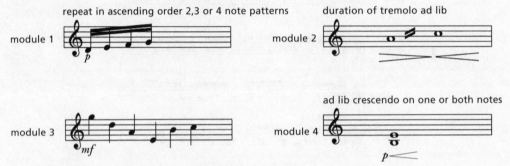

Figure 54: *Modules to be played in any order and by any number of instruments.*

In this piece the players freely choose which module to play and its duration. The result is an intricate overlapping of blocks as modules pass each other. Each of the modules is defined by a particular choice of register and rhythm.

Modules do not have to traditionally notated. They can also be a set of directions:

Module 1: play soft staccato and high
Module 2: middle register crescendo and decrescendo with long duration
Module 3: low register fast repetitive movements
Module 4: glissando either up or down, choice of speed variable
Module 5: wide leaps over two octaves.

Terry Riley's, In C is one of the most famous pieces written for modules.

Techno music in the 1990s is a modern-day example of modular music. DJs layer fixed dance rhythms and synthesiser music to create an ecstatic, shifting wall of sound.   R.V.

Special Topic 5
Repetition Music and Minimalism

Repetition music and minimalism have much in common with sound mass. Both focus on the creation of tableaux of sound through the repetition of limited material. The two terms are often used in the same breath, but they can refer to quite different approaches to making music. Both use minimal resources but repetition music, as its name suggests, means that something has to be repeated. Usually this will be a rhythmic pattern which is why it tends to be associated with minimalism. Minimalism refers to the use of minimal material in the search for maximal variation. The material could be limited by the choice of scales or pitches or the number of gestures or rhythmic values. Minimalism in music was introduced by La Monte Young who composed pieces of one interval played over a long period of time. Minimalism's use of limited material creates a sense of time in suspension or a sense of stasis. One of the

→ *main exponents of repetition music is Steve Reich. In his music, tableaux of sound are created through slowly-evolving repeating rhythms. Shifts are caused by the introduction of new notes or rhythms, exemplified in the piece Violin Phase (1967). Minimalism has had a major influence on composers since the 1960s. The Beatles also experimented with minimalism and repetition music, their most famous example being 'Number 9' on The White Album. The first minimalist popular music hit was Laurie Anderson's 'O Superman' (1981), which is an excellent example of the minimalist use of fixed modules and repeating structures.* R.V.

Special Topic 6
Indeterminacy

The textures discussed in this chapter can often be produced by random processes. Indeterminacy is a common compositional technique whereby a set of known elements are used to produce a set of unknown results which are either set in motion by random procedures or a rule. In constructing an indeterminant structure, although the overall sound can be safely predicted, the exact occurrence of each element cannot.

There are many approaches to indeterminate music. One can establish complex or simple structures. The radio assignment (Composition Project 5) was one example of an indeterminate process. In that exercise, even though the process was controlled, it was impossible to predict exactly what sounds would be played at any given moment because the performer had no control over what sounds were broadcast. Another simple example is the sound made by tearing a piece of paper at different speeds. Indeterminant procedures allow the discovery of new ways of solving problems, thereby opening up new ways of listening and thinking about the world. R.V.

Activity 2
Slowly sing soft, high-pitched staccato sounds, in your own time.

The type of texture this exercise will produce can be roughly predicted but at no point is it possible to say exactly when a sound will take place; nor is it important to the piece. The texture becomes a musical space within which events happen. The sounds collect to form a phenomenon. This is exactly the type of listening we apply when we listen to an environment.

The next exercise represents an indeterminant process based on a rule.

Activity 3
Clap your hands every time you hear the word 'THE' in the following sentence:

The purpose of the exercise is to show how the word 'the' represents a rule where we have to clap our hands upon hearing the said word 'THE'.

As in the previous exercise, the parameters allow one to predict the overall quality of the sound but not its exact shape. There are many examples of music based on these procedures.

FURTHER LISTENING

- Alan Lamb, *Journeys on the Winds of Time* on *Austral Voices: For Telegraph Wires, Tuning Forks, Computer Driven Piano, Psaltery, Whirly, Cello, Synthesizer and Ruined Piano* (New Albion 1990).

- Terry Riley, *In C* (1964).

- Krzysztof Penderecki, *Threnody for the Victims of Hiroshima* (1960).

- György Ligeti, *Lux Aeterna* (1966).
- Edgard Varèse, *Ionisation* (1930-33).
- Steve Reich, *Vermont Counterpoint* (1982).
- Jimi Hendrix, 'Foxy Lady', *Are You Experienced?* (Track 1967).
- Iannis Xenakis, *Metastaseis* (1953-54).
- Karlheinz Stockhausen, *Grüppen* (1955-57).
- Witold Lutoslawski, Concerto for Oboe and Harp (1884). Listen to the string sections.
- Led Zeppelin, 'Immigrant Song', *Led Zeppelin III* (Atlantic 1970).
- John Coltrane, 'Ascension' (1965). The ensemble sections are examples of sound mass.
- La Monte Young, *Death Chant* (1961).
- Alvin Lucier, *Music on a Long Thin Wire* (Lovely Music 1980).
- Sun Ra, *The Heliocentric Worlds Vols I, II & III* (ESP 1965).
- Techno and dance club music.
- Heavy metal recordings.

IMPROVISATIONS

Start and finish the session with a free or structured improvisation.

1 Build up a wall of sound using voices, instruments and sound objects, or a sequencer in which small units are multiplied to form a larger mass of sound.

2 Create your own sound-mass textures using indeterminate procedures

3 Using voices, instruments and sound objects or a sequencer create two sound masses which are registerally separated from each other.

4 Compose a mobile for solo performer or a group. Think about the use of register, timbre and dynamics in each module of the mobile and the overall effect that will be created when they combine.

COMPOSITION PROJECT 7

1 Compose a multi-part vocal or instrumental work, a maximum of four minutes long, exploring as many of the techniques introduced in Chapters 19 and 20 as possible: rhythmic or textural cells, cut-up and simultaneity. Notate the work any way you like for performance by other people. Take into account the topics introduced in earlier chapters such as register, timbre, dynamics and shape.

2 Compose a work of four to ten minutes, exploring the techniques for creating sound mass. The composition may be for voices, instruments, computer sequencer, found objects or a combination. Think about the role of register, dynamics and timbre and the use of these parameters in your composition's form and design. Use any notation appropriate to the context of the performance available to you.

PART 3

APPENDICES: COMPOSITION

COMPOSITION

Various approaches and techniques towards the creation of a composition are discussed. Each appendix deals with a specific issue on representational issues (notation), cognitive, historical or transformative (structure, process and variation).

REPRESENTING SOUNDS

There are many approaches to notating sounds. The level of detail is largely determined by the system the composer has adopted.

Generally notations either use words or symbols to represent actions or the use of objects in the performance. Combinations of both are common, especially in Western music notation.

Any form of musical notation conveys some or all of the following:

- pitch (one or more at the same time)
- loudness
- duration and rhythm
- speed and changes in speed
- expression (the intention of the composer)
- articulation (how to make the sound)
- what sound and when to make it.

Notations can give the most minimal information or the greatest detail. The amount of information determines the level of freedom the performer can exercise. Sometimes a single indication, such as 'swing feel' in jazz music, represents a whole style of playing which would need a treatise to explain. 'Swing feel' asks the player to alter the written rhythms to suit this style. If the rhythms were written out exactly it would be too cumbersome to read. Instead the interpretation is left up to the performer.

PITCH

In traditional notation pitch can be described in very specific terms. In the staff system, for example, each line or space indicates a particular pitch.

Figure 55: *Pitch stave notation.*

In guitar notation a finger position is indicated by an image of a fret board with dots referring finger positions.

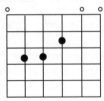

Figure 56: *Example of guitar finger position notation.*

But notation can be more indeterminate. An x on a staff can mean 'play any note in the range indicated'.

Figure 57: *Cross indicating 'play any note in this range'.*

Boxes or blocks can also be used. This means play all the notes between F (bottom line) and E (fourth space):

Figure 58: *Block indicating a black note cluster.*

In piano music 'play the white notes only' can be indicated by a white block. Gestures can also be described by notation. This means play with the palm of the hand in the register shown.

Figure 59: *Notation indicating gesture.*

Pitch notation can be as simple as arranging the words 'high', 'middle' and 'low' on a page to indicate register and occurrence.

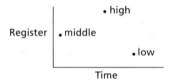

Figure 60: *Graph notation indicating register in relation to time.*

DURATION

In traditional music notation a set of values is combined to represent rhythmic patterns. Each sign equals a length of time in relation to the beat.

1 Another, less precise, approach is to represent duration by the length of a line. This is called 'proportional notation':

Figure 61: *Proportional time lines.*

2 Another version of proportional notation places the lines inside boxes marked with seconds as reference points. Performers place the sounds in the time frame indicated:

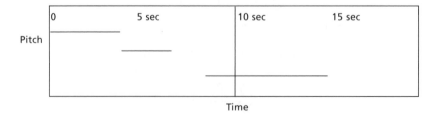

Figure 62: *Duration indicated within time boxes.*

or

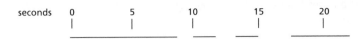

seconds   0   5   10   15   20

Figure 63: *Time line using seconds.*

3 Signs used to indicate brevity include:

Figure 64: *Flagged notes.*

4 Numbers can be used to signify patterns through repetition:

5x means 'play this five times'.

PITCH AND TIME

It is common practice to represent pitch or register by a vertical axis and time by a horizontal axis.

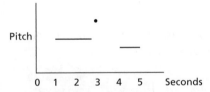

Figure 65: *Pitch time graph.*

Here the middle-register note is articulated at the one-second mark for a duration of two seconds, the high note is articulated at the at three-second mark and the low note is articulated at the at the four-second mark.

GESTURE

Gesture can be indicated by words such as pizzicato, strum or pluck; graphics, such as a picture of the palm of the hand which means to play with this part of the body; or signs like + and -, for which the performer must refer to the composer's notes for the meaning.

A pitch slide can be represented by:

Figure 66: *Pitch slides.*

DYNAMICS

Music notation often uses figures such as *p* *pp* *mf* *f* *ff* etc to indicate loudness. They range from very soft to very loud:

ppp pianississimo – as soft as possible
pp pianissimo – very soft
p piano – soft
mp mezzopiano – a little louder than soft (*mezzo* meaning half)
mf mezzoforte – half loud
f forte – loud
ff fortissimo – very loud
fff fortississimo – extremely loud.

Other approaches use the size of the note to indicate loudness:

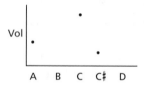

Figure 67: *Indicating loudness by the size of the note.*

Sometimes numbers are used:

    1 – soft
    2 – middle
    3 – loud

A graph can also be used to represent pitch and volume: the vertical axis indicates volume and the horizontal axis indicates pitch.

Figure 68: *Graph showing volume in relation to pitch.*

Notation can take any form so long as it is clear and consistent. Composers often come across situations where they have to devise a new system or symbols to describe their instructions. Whatever approach a composer takes, the best is the one which incorporates the most information with the least explanation.

Moving or changing from one dynamic level to another is indicated by:

crescendo: becoming louder, represented by

Figure 69: *Crescendo.*

decrescendo or *diminuendo*: becoming softer, represented by

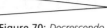

Figure 70: *Decrescendo.*

The attack time of a crescendo is incremental: from soft to loud. Conversely the decay time of a decrescendo is decremental: from loud to soft. Many pieces of music explore combinations of these two simple structures. For example, imagine the following combination of crescendi and descrescendi:

Figure 71: *Overlapping crescendi and decrescendi.*

Or the shape of a graphic can be used to illustrate the amplitude (attack, sustain and decay) envelope of a sound, e.g. a drum or cello-string vibration.

Figure 72: *Amplitude envelopes for a drum and a cello.*

MORE THAN ONE PART

A musical score is the compilation of everything that is meant to be played and heard. If the piece has a lot of parts the score can be very bulky. For this reason the players are only given their own parts and the conductor cues them from the main score.

Parts are usually illustrated in layers to show when and where they sound in relation to each other. In Figure 73, the higher the note is placed in notation, the louder the sound.

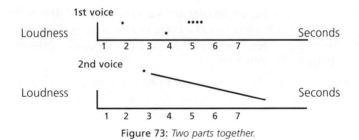

Figure 73: *Two parts together.*

Here, Voice 1 makes a loud sound followed by a quieter sound at three seconds. At four seconds it makes successively softer sounds.

Voice 2 begins loudly and gradually becomes softer.

FURTHER READING

Richard Rastall, *The Notation of Western Music*, London: J.M. Dent & Sons Ltd (1983).

Kurt Stone, *Music Notation in the Twentieth Century, A Practical Approach*, New York: W.W. Norton and Company (1980).

2 | POSTCARDS FROM HISTORY: ELECTROACOUSTIC MUSIC

1 THE EARLY YEARS (1877-1945)

Since the turn of the century, the development of electronic music in particular has been inextricably linked with the exponential expansion of new technology in general. We can only make an intelligent guess about the future. Many inventions fall by the wayside and other, seemingly irrelevant, discoveries grow in significance as time passes. Thomas Edison said of the first telegraph line between New York and London, 'But will we have anything to say to each other?' The original idea of recording machines was to archive events. Music recording was not even considered. So many musical inventions, especially electronic or computer-based, have been by-products of other research.

The quest to make music in new ways and to use new materials is one of the driving forces behind Western music. In 1709 Bartolommeo Cristofori invented the piano in Florence and Mozart seized upon the new palette of timbres it offered. Nearly two hundred years later in 1897 Edwin S. Votley patented the pianola – a programmable instrument using punched paper rolls driven by clockwork. Unlike sound recording, the pianola records performance. Rolls can be punched by hand or as the performer plays. Performances by Anton Rubinstein and Percy Grainger have been captured on paper and subsequently re-recorded digitally from the pianola. This approach has been revived by MIDI (Musical Instrument Digital Interface). MIDI messages can be transmitted in performance which trigger sounds or by being preprogrammed like a piano roll. Early preprogrammed music includes the musical box and later the steam organ played at fairs.

In the 1870s, while Wagner was composing his operas, Edison and Berliner invented the phonograph, a mechanical device for recording sound. The first electronic musical instrument was the telharmonium or dynamophone, a precursor to on-line music, invented by Thaddeus Cahill. It was a music-making machine, almost 20 metres in length and weighing about two hundred tons, linked to a telephone line – not exactly home entertainment. The telharmonium was an electronic dynamo which would produce an alternating current. This AC could be changed via a set of 'gears'. This current, if transformed into an acoustic signal (using a horn, like the early gramophone), would be heard as different frequencies. Several of these frequencies could be played together, creating the first polyphonic synthesiser.

Any good hardware needs a software developer to exploit it properly. The composer Ferruccio Busoni looked like taking on this role and wrote enthusiastically about it in 'Sketch of a New Esthetic of Music' (1907). Sadly, however, he never composed the promised music for it.

In that same year Lee De Forest patented the triode vacuum tube, the basis of the first electronic amplifiers and an inspiration for a new breed of musician. After the First World War, several electronic musical instruments appeared, the best known being the theremin and the ondes martinot, both invented in the 1920s.

The theremin comprises a metal rod antenna mounted on a box attached to radio frequency antennas. The player does not touch the instrument. Volume and pitch are controlled by vertical and horizontal hand movements which move in and out of the antenna's electromagnetic field. The movements cause changes in pitch and volume.

This produces a high-pitched warbling sound. It was a popular novelty in the 1920s and 1930s. In the 1960s the Beach Boys used it in 'Good Vibrations', and an eccentric British group promoted by the Beatles called Bonzo Dog Doodah Band used it as part of their performance disguised as an artificial leg. In recent years the theremin has resurfaced as a legitimate electronic performance instrument.

The ondes martinot, designed by the French musician Maurice Martenot and introduced in 1928, is a monophonic keyboard instrument. While similar to the theremin in sound, its keyboard and internal mechanisms and electronic controls make it easier to use in performance. It has a hauntingly pure tone and has taken up a permanent place in the orchestral repertoire mainly due to the works of Olivier Messiaen (1908-92).

Another survivor is the Hammond organ (1935). This instrument, based on the same principles as Cahill's telharmonium, makes its sound by generating a series of tones. These tones relate to each other by referring to the partials of the harmonic series. Pulling out various draw bars makes the harmonics of the organ richer, giving it a fuller sound. However, an acoustic instrument's harmonic component varies over the life of the note, whereas the tone on a Hammond remains static. Sonic movement was introduced by putting a fan in front of its speaker which gave a swirling sound, known as a 'Leslie'. The Hammond organ combined with the Leslie speaker system can be heard in many popular songs from the 1960s. In 1962, the British group the Tornadoes popularised the sound with their global hit 'Telstar'. However, the most famous example is 'A Whiter Shade of Pale' (1967) by the English pop band Procul Harum. The Hammond organ is still used in rock music today.

2 SOUND BITES: MUSIQUE CONCRÈTE TO SAMPLERS

The definition of music has broadened to incorporate all sound:

> Today, a new music is on the rise, one that can neither be expressed nor understood using the old tools, a music produced elsewhere and otherwise. It is not that music or the world have become incomprehensible: the concept of comprehension itself has changed; there has been a shift in the locus of the perception of things.
>
> Jacques Attali[42]

Technological development is always boosted during wartime and so World War Two was an important catalyst in the advancement of electronic music, including tape recording. Tape recordings became commercially available around 1948 and with their advent came the ability to move sound out of real and linear time: to edit. Development of tape recording continued in many countries on parallel paths. As is so often the case, rivalry ensued. The big battle was between Paris and Cologne.

In France Pierre Schaeffer pioneered *musique concrète* based upon the manipulation of recordings of real sounds. In previous eras musical notation had been the only means of capturing music. The introduction of recording now made it possible to capture live sounds. It could be viewed as the start of post-modernism in music. Tiny fragments of sound (*objets sonores*) could be manipulated or played around with, exploring the nature of the sound itself. In many ways this exploration grew out of the Futurist movement of the 1920s which saw all sound as potential music. Schaeffer attempted to catalogue sounds into groups according to their sonoric characteristics. This allowed composers to give form to their *musique concrète* in similar ways to the serial techniques of Schoenberg. The most fundamental parameters to be documented were pitch, dynamics (sound volume), harmony and timbre against time.

What did this music sound like? Much of it was strange and yet aesthetically prosaic. The pieces were often nearer to sound experiments than musical structures, but a new sonic vocabulary was being developed to add to musical language.

Varèse, who was loosely associated with this movement, was perhaps the leading artist in the move to turn the technology into art. In 1956 he composed *Poème electronique* which was the music component of a sound environment piece exhibited in a pavilion designed by Le Corbusier at the 1958 World Fair in Brussels.

Although the early pioneers of electronic music came from an art music tradition, many of the more recent developments in real-sound manipulation have been most readily accepted and championed by rock and pop musicians. The reason often comes down to money. For instance, a Fairlight digital sampler when it was first launched would have been the price of a small house and rock superstars were perhaps the only musicians who could afford to buy them. Unfortunately, unlike houses, new technology does not hold its value and its resale value is often only enough to buy a dog kennel. Change is also often easier in music from an oral tradition, because the rules are generally less defined than in the formal art-music world, and so musical thought is more fluid and open to new directions.

In the 1960s, the first musical instrument using real-sound manipulation, the Mellotron, appeared in Birmingham. It was a keyboard instrument used extensively by 'progressive' rock bands such as the Moody Blues or Emmerson Lake and Palmer. Playing a key activated a tape loop so that a whole keyboard of loops was available for each bank of sounds. These included acoustic instruments such as flutes or strings. It was also used by film and TV stations as a sound-effects (FX) machine, recording the tape loops with such sounds as footsteps. It was a large instrument but nevertheless technologically delicate. The tape loops broke easily or would stretch, and it was easily superseded by the digital sampler.

3 ELECTRONIC MUSIC

All Sounds Can Be Broken Down To Their Simplest Harmonic Components

Developing concurrently with the *musique concrète* movement was elektronische musik, established by a group of German scientists and musicians who founded a centre for its research. They were led by the composer Herbert Eimert but the best-known member to emerge from this Cologne group was Karlheinz Stockhausen.

What distinguished *elektronische musik* was the desire to work principally in electronically-generated sounds. The group was not interested in manipulating sound recordings. The first machine to capture their imagination was the Voice Coder or Vocoder. This instrument imposed the articulatory characteristics of one sound (usually a voice) onto the timbral characteristics of another (usually a synthesiser). The Electric Light Orchestra used it in 'Mr Blue Sky'. Perhaps the most successful example is 'O Superman' by Laurie Anderson.

They soon moved on to encompass tone and white noise generators. A tone generator sends out a pure pitch with no harmonics, like the purest flute you've never heard. White noise is all the frequencies we can hear emitted at once. It's like the sound of a waterfall or steam from a kettle.

In the 1950s there were two synthesis methods that could be used to shape electronic music. The first was called additive synthesis. This was first postulated by the acoustician Fourier, a contemporary of Beethoven. By adding many pure tones together, he stated that any sound could be resynthesised. This was the principle behind the Hammond organ.

In reality every sound we hear, however short, is like a small piece of music in itself. The timbral structure of these harmonics or partials is forever changing. For instance every eight seconds of stereo CD music uses up one 1.44Mb floppy disk. It would be too time-consuming and complex to create anything but the simplest electronic music piece using additive synthesis.

Subtractive synthesis, on the other hand, is a far more useful tool. It is based on the principle that you start with everything (white noise) and distil it down to what you require. This is achieved primarily through spectral filters, cutting the bass, middle, or treble frequencies or a combination of them. It can be applied to the duration of the whole sound or used to emulate timbral movement through an envelope by changing the filters during the course of the sound.

Through these and several other related processes it became possible to create sounds that had never been heard before, to create microtonal pieces: pieces of sond. This freedom demanded structure. Many mathematical or algorithmic forms, in the tradition of the serialists, were investigated. For others, who were more feeling and subjective in their approach to composition, the sounds themselves became the inspiration for the form.

And so the post-war battle raged between the French and German Schools. There was a solution, however – to use both approaches and more. Stockhausen's *Gesang der Jünglinge* (1955-56) did just that. This hauntingly beautiful and ground-breaking piece combines the sounds of a boy singing with electronically produced tones. The work was also the first to use the antiphonal properties of multi-speaker performance. Originally it was recorded as a five-track composition.

During this time and away from the heat, the United States was developing its own brand of electronic music. Most notable was Milton Babbitt at Princeton University who had access to a monster of an electronic device, the RCA synthesiser.

4 THE SYNTHESISER

A Synthesiser Creates Sound Using Electronics and Microprocessors

A synthesiser creates sound. It is an instrument which developed firstly with the growth of electronics, and secondly with the introduction of microprocessors. Unlike the violin, or any other acoustic instrument, its rate of evolution has grown exponentially.

There have been synthesis experiments throughout the twentieth century. The most famous of the early synthesisers was the Moog, named after its inventor, Robert Moog. The Moog was an analogue 'subtractive' synthesiser which was effectively the only type of synthesis available at that time. This synthesiser consisted of a combination of electronic oscillators and noise generators. Subtractive synthesis enabled the musician to create a new sound by subtracting certain harmonics and frequency bands from the original sound generated. The instruments had knobs, sliders, buttons and dials to make and change the sounds in real time. It was a monophonic (single voice) instrument but, thanks to the introduction around the same time of multitrack recorders, chords and textures could be built up on parallel tracks. As a performance instrument it allowed real-time control but the downside was that it took a long time to program each sound (the instrument had no computer memory) and the oscillators would continually drift out of tune.

It was not until after the 1960s that synthesisers became available to more than a handful of affluent musicians.

The next wave of synthesisers were digital, using FM synthesis, followed closely
by synthesisers using 'wavetables' (wave shapes digitally stored). Incorporating memory
capability, these instruments were able call up the wavetables at the touch of a button.
They were less noisy, much more powerful and polyphonic, holding up to 128 voices.
But real-time manipulation was not usually as easy on these synthesisers as on the earlier
models, and they had become more keyboard-based in order to link with MIDI (Musical
Instrument Digital Interface, developed primarily by Dave Smith who also invented the first
memory-storing synth, the Prophet 5). Later more choice was available with the growth
of synthesiser controllers such as drum triggers and MIDI guitars.

In the 1990s a new breed of more performer-friendly synthesisers were also coming
on-stream which allowed the musician to control the components of sound-making by
responding to the musician's gestures. There are many proprietary versions but the best-
known phrase used to describe this synthesis is 'Physical Modeling' by Yamaha and Korg.

5 ELECTRONIC MUSIC FOR THE MASSES
'A-wop-bob-aloo-bop alop-bam-boom' Little Richard

Rock'n'roll hit the Western world in the 1950s. It was the result not so much of the
technological developments of World War Two as the encapsulation of the spirit
of a liberated youth who could, they thought, put war behind them.

Rock'n'roll is synonymous with the rise of the electric guitar. Although invented in the
1930s the electric guitar came to the fore in the 1950s and to maturity in the 1960s.
Thanks to such innovators as Les Paul, rock also incorporated the development of the PA
system together with the unique echo effects that resulted from messing around with tape
recorders. Apart from its use in a smattering of film scores, rock music provided the first
popular experience of electronic music, both on record and live in the dance halls.
This was no èlite intellectual movement: this was music, people, electronics and sex.
In many ways it became a modern version of ancient initiation rituals.

And then came the Beatles and the 1960s and 1970s, where popular music embraced its
own form of experimentalism. Jimi Hendrix, Eric Clapton and Brian May, among hundreds
of others, took the electric guitar to new heights of expression. The progressive bands
oversaw the explosion of synthesis, from Bob Moog's ubiquitous monophonic Moog
Synthesiser to Dave Smith's Prophet 5 with its microprocessor-controlled preset memories.
The Beatles, who enthusiastically followed Karlheinz Stockhausen and the avant-garde,
even created their own musique concrète piece 'Revolution Number 9' on *The White
Album*. The youth movements themselves seemed entwined in the possibilities of these
new sound-making devices. The mind-bending and hallucinogenic drugs of the hippies
were the psychological simulation of the sounds that were being concocted on record -
the era of psychedelia.

Meanwhile in the world of serious music, Luciano Berio in Milan eschewed what he
termed the 'retarded-futuristic pioneerism' of the early electronic experimenters, preferring
to compose and concentrate on the relationship of nature and sound as music, using
a combination of acoustic and electronic instruments. In the USA, no one was more
involved in this than the composer and twentieth-century music philosopher John Cage.

By the start of the 1970s it was becoming harder to delineate experimental, popular
and art music; and from these cross-currents, creativity flowed. It is interesting to note,
for example, that John Lennon was a friend of John Cage. TV and the media, the great

levellers of the twentieth century, had allowed people to be exposed to all styles and genres of music.

One of the masterpieces of the 1960s was Steve Reich's *Come Out* which employed tape loops to entrance and mesmerise the listener into a re-evaluation of the sonic material. His approach to music was a portent of both the rise of minimalist music at the end of the twentieth century and the digital sequencer.

Contemporary composers will increasingly find themselves equally at home with acoustic and electronic media. The Mexican composer Xavier Alvarez is such a one, having started in orchestral music before discovering electronic music and its immense possibilities.

6 FROM STEP TIME TO REAL TIME TO VIRTUAL REALITY
Knowledge Doesn't Keep Any Better Than Fish

In the technological arts what you know today could well be of little worth tomorrow. If an engineer from the early days of electronic music were to walk into the Institut de Recherche et Coordination Acoustique/Musique (IRCAM) in Paris today, he or she would be at a loss where to begin.

The computer has taken a hold in most areas of life and music too has entered the 'information age'. Since around 1980 the microprocessor in both rock and classical music has been the prime tool for the innovative musician. Initially instructions would have been entered solely via programming language, but increasingly the musician is able to use a sequencing software package. This allows them to compose either by entering the instructions one by one (step time) or in real time, editing afterwards. This process has been abetted by the introduction of the universal synthesiser interface system known as MIDI. For 95 per cent of composers and performers MIDI is adequate; though, to the annoyance of guitarists in particular, it has been predominantly keyboard based. It has opened up electronic music to everyone from the professional to the child in the classroom.

Computer information is stored as numbers. Digital sound recording uses these same digital storage processes. More recent developments have seen the introduction of hard disk recorders. Any music you hear can be stored in a sound file, accessed, copied or even streamed from a computer or via the internet. So on one side there is the digitally-controlled synthesiser with its range of synthesis methods and on the other the digital sound recorder. Hovering in between the two is the sound sampler, technically neither a synthesiser nor a digital recorder. Via MIDI, or other digital interfaces, all these processes can become one. And so there is no longer a clear delineation between digital recording and synthesis.

Digital Signal Processors are just that. It is a process applicable to sound, effects, graphics or moving images – in fact multimedia. And with the increasing amount of processing power, electronic music is now viable in performance. There is ever more room for expression and improvisation, to shape the sound in real time and to respond to the moment.

And the wheel continues to turn. Now electronic music is trying not only to further investigate the nature of sound, but also the sound of nature. Acoustic modelling attempts to faithfully emulate the acoustic properties of real instruments and thus allow the player to create virtual instruments – sounds which seem to be acoustically real and yet don't exist in the physical world.

General MIDI formalises the more reproductive capabilities of synthesis, frequently making the synthesiser sound like a second-rate acoustic instrument. But for a limited budget it provides the opportunity to work with orchestral and other acoustic sounds, which previously was been beyond the means of the average musician.

Compared to acoustic music, electronic music is still in its infancy. But progress takes time and as each year passes the art form become less and less about electronics and more about music.

7 MUSIC WITHIN MULTIMEDIA

Music has always lent itself to other arts including, in the twentieth century, film, television and multimedia. The performance of primitive musics could be seen as live multimedia events in the original sense as they are multi-disciplined rituals. Opera adapts the same integration to high art.

Musicians have always responded to new media and technologies and it was almost inevitable that as digital technology allowed different art forms to converge, music would be enthusiastically represented. This was aided by the fact that music is relatively economical on digital memory and so it has often been at the forefront of new media developments. Non-linear audio recording, for example, was available long before it was an accessible visual device; and streaming information was first adopted to send sound and music across the internet.

These innovations have provided the scope for devising new musical structures and approaches. Perhaps not since the development of the sonata has Western music offered such opportunities to the imaginative musician. It is truly music that exists in another medium, a virtual world with no live counterpart.

But no one could claim that the TV monitor bears any comparison with the power of live performance. The only way that multimedia can exist beyond the confines of the computer is in real-time presentation.

The non-linearity of multimedia gives scope for thinking in forms that do not necessarily start at the beginning and finish at the end. They can jump around in any direction at the behest of the user. For this the term 'interactive' has been coined. But haven't musicians always been interactive in their two-way relationship with the audience? Interactivity is something that has always been taken for granted between humans and, ironically, it is this fundamental limitation of the computer that has led programmers to reintroduce the concept as something radically new.

The means of delivery may change, but non-linearity of form and content is an exciting area of artistic exploration. It is the start of a postmodern approach in which musical material can be reordered and therefore recontextualised.

So multimedia will remain in its infancy for some time to come. But as Michael Brown has remarked 'Few artists are around during the birth of both a new art form and a new industry. Take advantage of the opportunity before somebody else writes all the rules'.[43] Music will continue to change in a heuristic fashion but, as always, sorting out the wheat from the chaff will be up to us all.

8 RAVE AND TECHNO
Rock'n'roll is Dead, Now It's Techno Instead

Much music is made for dancing. When rock'n'roll dominated the 1950s, the electric guitar and drum kit were central. As performance it was in a very masculine world, with big, macho gestures such as Elvis Presley's pelvic thrusts, and the songs were popular both on radio and the dance floor. By the 1970s, the introduction of drum loops and the synthesiser made a huge range of new musical sounds and musical feels available. The regular beat of the drum machine, which created the sound of disco in the late 1970s, emphasised the physicality of the sound and its attraction to dancers.

In the early 1980s scratch music mixed excerpts from any type of music over a drum beat to produce highly energetic sound collages. Malcolm McLaren was perhaps its best-known exponent. The word 'scratch' comes from dragging the needle back and forth across the record. Any music could be used while the drum beat gave it a cohesive structure. The record player essentially became a new musical instrument, a new timbral resource.

By the late 1980s, musical subcultures had mushroomed around Generations X and Y, often referred to as rave culture. Subculture feeds the cutting edge of the mainstream. This happened to rave culture in the early 1990s. It was in many ways a popular embodiment of many of the musical philosophies of the avant-garde movement, and John Cage in particular, where music ceased to be harmonically based, being more defined in terms of organised sound. The music was developed for dance parties rather than home-based mainstream media. The rigid sampled drum beat, the computer functions of cut, copy and paste and the microprocessor-controlled precision of modern synthesiser presets and samplers meant that this music was preoccupied with sound and texture, constructed more by juxtaposing musical cells than constructing a song form. It demanded a new way of listening which had limited appeal on radio.

Its cult nature kept it isolated from the mainstream and it matured into electro, hip hop, house and techno. The word 'techno' refers to its technologically-produced sound, but is equally influenced by the technology of biochemistry in the shape of mind-altering drugs which formed part (but not all) of the culture of its audience. In turn, techno spawned ambient, trance and sundry other movements.

Rap, like techno, exploits sampling technology but superimposes a witty, often political, rhyming spoken lyric which is interspersed with choruses or instrumental passages and sampled sound bites. Sampling however has raised immense confusion over copyright law by its use of sound captured from an enormous range of sources.   A. A.

3 | TIME AND RHYTHM

Music is a temporal art. Without time, there can be no music. Every culture has its own understanding of time and rhythm and a comprehensive study of the two in music is a book in itself.

RHYTHM: The temporal relation between one point in time and another which can be regular, irregular or both.

Between any two sound events a period of time must elapse. The frequency of events can be repetitive or variable. 'Tick, tock, tick, tock' is repetitive whereas the rumble of thunder in a storm is variable.

PULSE: One of a series of regularly recurring, precisely equivalent stimuli. A series of pulses divides time into exactly equal units.

The pulse is the measuring stick of any music based on counting. A good example of a pulse is a metronome. Each new click is exactly the same as the preceding one. Pulses should not be confused with beat (see below).

GROUPING: The organisation of counts into even or uneven collections.

Grouping arranges material into units and is a crucial aspect of any rhythmic organisation. These grouped units can be even (Figure 74), uneven (Figure 75) or combine even and uneven numbers. Clap on each count of 'one' in the following two examples:

```
pulse  |   |   |   |   |   |   |   |   |   |   |

clap   •       •       •       •       •       •
       1   2   1   2   1   2   1   2   1   2   1
```
Figure 74: *Grouping pulses into regular counts of 2.*

```
pulse  |   |   |   |   |   |   |   |   |   |   |

clap   •       •           •   •
       1   2   1   2   3   1   1   2   3   4   5
```
Figure 75: *Grouping pulses into irregular counts of 2, 3, 1, 5.*

BEAT: The regular or irregular organisation of a pulse into a repeating pattern.

It is very common to confuse beat with pulse. In simple parlance, the beat is what the body feels and is the most common main reference for counting time. Generally the beat is regular and manageable because the body has its physiological limits. So long as this is the case, the pulse and the beat can be the same. However, there are many types of music in which the beat is grouped into a repeating irregular count. A typical beat pattern in a lot of Greek music organises the pulse into a repeating seven count: 2 + 2 + 3. This means the pulse is grouped into a cycle of seven in which the beat is even for two counts and uneven for the third. Figure 76 groups the pulse into counts of seven.

```
pulse  •                           •
       |   |   |   |   |   |   |   |   |   |   |   |   |   |
       1   2   3   4   5   6   7   1   2   3   4   5   6   7
```
Figure 76: *Grouping of a pulse into counts of seven.*

Instead of counting 1, 2, 3, 4, 5, 6, 7, it is easier to count as 1, 2, 1, 2, 1, 2, 3:

Figure 77: *Repeating irregular counts of 2 + 2 + 3.*

TEMPO: The speed of the pulse. It is measured in terms of number of pulses per minute.

SUBDIVISION: The division of the beat or pulse into smaller equal units. These units can be any value: two, three, four, five, etc.

The next example shows a beat occurring regularly at ♩ = 60. The subdivisions are evenly spaced within each beat:

Figure 78: *Various subdivisions of a beat.*

In traditional notation this rhythm would written like this:

Figure 79: *Traditional musical notation of Figure 78.*

ACCENT: An action or quality applied to a sound event to create emphasis or draw attention.

Accents can occur on a subdivision or a beat. Dynamic accents are the most common, indicating a sudden change in loudness, and they are sustained for the value of the note to which they are applied. For example, the following pulse is dynamically accented at irregular intervals. The accent indication > means 'articulate louder than the unaccented notes'.

Figure 80: *Groupings created by dynamic accents.*

Accents group rhythmic values together. In the last example the dynamic accents grouped the pulses into counts of 2, 3, 2 and 5, but there are other ways of creating an accent and grouping notes, using a distinctive articulation, rhythm, register, pitch and silence:

Articulation

In this example the small dot •, indicating a staccato attack, creates articulation accent groups of 2, 3, 2 and 5.

Figure 81: *Grouping created by staccato articulation.*

Register

The distinctive register of the high bongo in this example, groups the following pulse into counts of 4 and 3:

Figure 82: *Grouping created with register.*

METRE: The grouping of a specific beat value in which the first beat, indicating the grouping count, has more stress than the other beats. The metre can be regular or irregular.

The metre or bar count is one of the basic building blocks of Western music. It enables performers to keep together by using the first beat of each bar as a common reference point. The metre consists of two components: the number or beats per bar, and the value of the beat to be counted:

4/4 means all counting refers to four quarter-note (crotchet) beats to the bar;

5/8 means all counting refers to five eighth-note (quaver) beats to the bar.

Non-metrical music is music without a metre. In Figure 83 below there is no definable metre. The music is counted according to various subdivisions of the beat.

Figure 83: *Non-metrical music.*

SYMMETRICAL METRE: The sequence of regular metres.

ASYMMETRIC METRE: The sequence of irregular metres.

Asymmetric metres are quite common. An asymmetric bar structure can consist of a completely random sequence of bar counts:

4/4   5/4   5/4   4/4   4/4   3/3   2/4 ...

However, an asymmetric metric pattern such as 3/4 + 2/4 + 4/4 can become symmetrical if it is repeated:

Figure 84: *Repeating asymmetric metres.*

SYNCOPATION: The placement of accents off the beat requiring resolution on the beat.

Syncopation is a type of rhythmic dissonance. The off-beat accents in a pattern create a rhythmic displacement. This produces tension between the accepted beat and the accented off-beat patterns. The tension requires a resolution onto a beat. The combination of a displaced, accented pattern resolving onto a beat creates syncopation. In Figure 86 the shift from accents on the beat to the half-beat creates rhythmic displacement. One hears and feels a sense of rhythmic dissonance which is resolved when the accents occur on the beat again.

displacement causes syncopation ---------------------------------- resolution onto beat

Figure 85: *Syncopation.*

ADDITIVE AND SUBTRACTIVE RHYTHMS: The addition or subtraction of a rhythmic unit from a rhythm.

The expansion and contraction of rhythmic patterns or values create a sense of elasticity as events become unpredictable in their duration. In the following example the basic counting unit, an eighth note, is gradually expanded by the addition of a quaver. It is then reduced to the original rhythm by the gradual subtraction of a quaver.

Figure 86: *Additive and subtractive rhythms: 5 + 6 + 7 + 6 + 5.*

METRICAL TIME: The use of metre for rhythmic organisation.

Music based on metrical time is very common. Popular music, marches and dance music are just some examples. An important aspect of metrical time is the presence of a perceived beat (i) to which all rhythms refer, and (ii) into which the beat is grouped. The metres can be either symmetrical or asymmetric in organisation.

DURATIONAL TIME: The use of a counting unit for rhythmic organisation to destroy any sense of regular beat groupings.

Much of the music of the twentieth-century Western repertoire has no perceptible beat or pulse. The beat or pulse, if present, is an abstract concept whose function is to hold all the parts together. In durational music it is common to see ties, freely accented notes, uneven groupings and a wide variety of temporal subdivisions. The purpose of these is to destroy any feeling of the beat. Its absence makes the music non-metrical. The following examples are two common approaches:

Figure 87: *Durational time with free accentuation in which the beat is abstract.*

Figure 88: *Durational time using the sixteenth-note as a counting unit.*

ORGANIC TIME: The construction of sound durations based not on a pulse or counting unit but other parameters such as physiological determinants (breathing or arm length).

This type of music is measured by some internal clock mechanism which cannot be accurately measured, such as breathing in and out. The Gregorian chant is an early example of this type of rhythmic organisation.

PHRASE RHYTHM: The length of musical phrases measured in beats or bars.

Phrases are present in metrical and much non-metrical music. They can be very short or very long. The sequence of phrases creates a rhythmic structure which can be regular or irregular. The first note determines the length of each phrase. A phrase of two bars in 4/4 has a rhythmic value of a tied semibreve (4 + 4 = 8). Mozart's piano sonatas generally use irregular lengths of phrase. A good improvisation solo uses varying lengths of phrases to avoid predictability.

Figure 89: *Three phrases of regular length (phrase rhythm = ♩ + ♩ + ♩)*

Figure 90: *Three phrases of irregular length (phrase rhythm = ♩ + ♩. + ♩)*

MOVEMENT AND MUSICAL SPACES 4

In Chapter 5 the basic parameters of sound were introduced. These were LOUDNESS, REGISTER, DURATION, ENVELOPE and TIMBRE. A parameter is a variable measured against a constant. The presence of the constant allows us to distinguish the variable. As sound exists in time, the constant it relies on is a timeline using some measure such as seconds or microseconds. The parameters of loudness, register and duration can all be represented graphically in two dimensions:

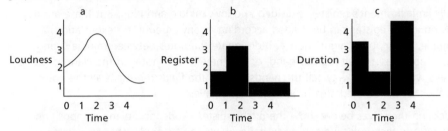

Figure 91: *Two-dimensional graphs for time and (a) loudness, (b) register and (c) duration.*

The parameters of loudness, register and duration are never fixed. They continually move. It is this movement which makes the perception of sound a complex experience. For example, when a CD producer mixes a sound, he or she makes conscious decisions about the placement of the sounds in the mix. Some are softer, others louder. Similarly, we perceptually experience a sense of movement in register. Register is associated with highness and lowness. It is also associated with pitch. A group of pitches, for example between middle C and the octave above, can represent a register or pitch band of an octave.

Expansion and Contraction of Pitch Register Bands

If you sing the opening phrase of 'Three Blind Mice' followed by the opening phrase of 'Somewhere Over the Rainbow' you will find there is a much greater sense of the register broadening out in 'Somewhere over the Rainbow' because the range of notes the song encompasses is much wider than in the first three notes of 'Three Blind Mice'. We can say that 'Somewhere over the Rainbow' has a wider register band than 'Three Blind Mice'. Schematically it could be represented like this:

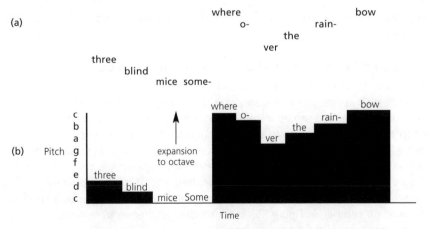

Figure 92: *Expansion of register: (a) schematically; (b) graphically.*

In traditional notation the expansion of register would look like this:

Three   blind   mice   Some - where   o - ver the rain-bow

Figure 93: *Expansion of register in 'Three Blind Mice' and 'Somewhere Over The Rainbow'.*

Generally an instrument's register is divided into low, middle and high. But these are not the only options. Register can be divided according to any criterion for exploration. For example, a composer might choose to designate the notes between middle C and the octave above as a pitch register band; or the three lowest notes of the clarinet. Some composers who work this way call the bands 'fields'; the fields represent all the notes available within the defined area of an octave or octaves.

The blocks on the staves below show the pitch register bands for a piano composition. The squares and rectangles indicate fixed bands while the triangular shapes indicate expanding or contacting bands and therefore increasing or decreasing harmonic options. These are powerful tools for composing.

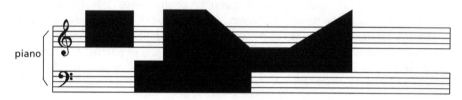

piano

Figure 94: *Expansion and contraction of pitch register spaces.*

The first block encompasses a pitch register band between E above middle C and the E three octaves above. The next block outlines a lower band between A and B, a ninth above. The third block combines both pitch register bands. The fourth band begins with the same pitch register band as the third block but gradually contracts to exclude the higher notes. The middle part of this block is a smaller band between A and D which then expands to include more high notes.

If you have access to a piano, improvise a solo based on these expanding and contracting pitch register bands.

A THREE-DIMENSIONAL MODEL OF MUSICAL SPACE

The graphs in Figure 92 are all examples of sound envelopes. A sound envelope is defined by any parameter such as frequency or loudness which changes in relation to time. While an envelope can be represented in two dimensions, generally more than one sound parameter occurs at once. For example, as a sound gets louder, harmonic or non-harmonic tones might be added or subtracted, changing its tone colour. A three-dimensional model which measures rates of change in all three parameters simultaneously is therefore more useful. In Figure 95 each parameter becomes an axis: frequency, time and loudness. Frequency can be mapped against time on one plane while loudness is mapped against the same timeline on another. In Figure 95, as sound changes frequency in time, its loudness may become softer and then louder.

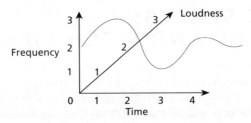

Figure 95: *Three-dimensional model of timbre (frequency versus loudness versus time).*

While sound structure can be discussed purely in terms of frequency and loudness and duration, musical events are discussed in terms of their equivalents of register, pitch, dynamics, rhythm and timbre.

Nothing in music is fixed. It is an endless series of changing parameters. Sounds get louder, higher, shorter, softer, remain stable, become irregular, stop and start. Some sounds feel as if they are expanding while others feel as if they are contracting. The two-dimensional parameters of loudness, register and rhythm are constantly in motion and their movements make a musical environment constantly change.

If you sit in a public place listening to all the sounds around you as objects, you may perceive them as moving in space. For example there might be the high sound of a bird intermittently calling to its mate. At the same time a boy on a bicycle rides by with a radio which causes a dog to bark in the middle range. All of a sudden a small child begins to cry and during all this time a lawn mower goes back and forth in someone's backyard. All these sounds create a listening space or environment and it is the notion of sounds moving in space as well as the appreciation of their structure which forms the basis of Composition Project 2.

Similarly, in music, the movement of register, pitch, dynamics, rhythm and timbre can be represented schematically in three dimensions. A list of timbres can be drawn up based on a unified musical concept of time such as beats or pulses. Each timbre itself is a three-dimensional model in which frequency, loudness, duration and envelope combine. Consequently the following diagram must be understood as a simple representation of a complex process in which the parameters of timbre (loudness, frequency and duration) and music (dynamics, pitch, instrumental colour and rhythm) are in continual movement.

A piece of music for flute, viola and cello can be schematically represented as follows:

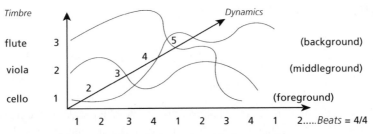

Figure 96: *Three-dimensional model of a musical space.*

As the music progresses, in a series of regular pulses in 4/4 time, the cello, viola and flute move between foreground, middleground and background. The continuous movement of all the parameters and their relation to time forms the basis of Part 2: Sounds in Time.

5 HARMONIC SPACES: SCALES AND PITCH FIELDS

A harmonic space is a two-dimensional space defined by time and interval. An INTERVAL is the distance between any two notes and is measured in semitones, which are the smallest unit in the Western equal-tempered system. There are twelve semitones to an octave, and any interval, either smaller or greater than the octave, can be measured in semitones. Every interval has a technical name which refers to the major or scale. A major second, for example, covers two semitones whereas a minor second is equal to one semitone.

These are the measurements in semitones for all the intervals in the octave. Note that the names don't always follow the order you would expect. A fifth, for example, has seven semitones:

Number of semitones

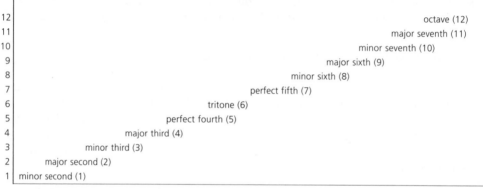

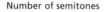

Interval

The space of a minor third encompasses all the other smaller intervals available within it, i.e. minor second, major second and a minor third.

SCALES

SCALES are different patterns of intervals. The major scale uses the following intervallic order measured in semitones:

$$C_2 D_2 E_1 F_2 G_2 A_2 B_1 C$$

Figure 97: *The major scale.*

This will always define a major scale harmonic space. A minor scale harmonic space consists of a different ordering of semitones. The natural harmonic scale is: 2.1.2.2.2.1.2. Notice that this is a permutation of the major scale series.

There are many types of scales ranging from five notes to twelve. Traditional Chinese music uses the five-note scales while jazz improvisers can choose between five, six, seven, eight or nine-note scales.

Note that because interval size take into account the distances between the notes there is always one interval fewer than the number of notes in the scale. The five-note scale only has four intervals, for example.

FIVE-NOTE SCALES: PENTATONICS

Pentatonic scales are commonly used in Irish, Scottish and folk music, blues and rock'n'roll but different five-note patterns can be found in China, Japan and Indonesia. Here are some patterns based on semitone number:

$$2.2.3.2. \text{ (e.g. } C_2 D_2 E_3 G_2 A)$$
$$3.2.2.3 \text{ (e.g. } D_3 F_2 G_2 A_3 C)$$
$$2.1.2.1. \text{ (e.g. } D_2 E_1 F_2 G_1 A\flat)$$

SIX-NOTE SCALES: HEXATONICS

The whole-tone scale which consists solely of major seconds, divides the octave completely symmetrically into equal units and is one of the most famous six-note scales:

$$2.2.2.2.2. \text{ (e.g. } C_2 D_2 E_2 F\sharp_2 G\sharp_2 A\sharp)$$

Other six-note scales are also possible:

$$2.1.2.2.1 \text{ (e.g. } D_2 E_1 F_2 G_2 G\sharp_1 A)$$

SEVEN-NOTE SCALES: HEPTATONICS.

The major and minor scales are both heptatonic patterns. Other seven-note patterns, called modes, formed the basis of the Western musical system before the major and minor scales were introduced. The major and minor scales are actually two modes from the older system. There are many modes but you will notice that they are all permutations of each other. The most common are:

Ionian: 2.2.1.2.2.2.1. (the major scale)
$$C_2 D_2 E_1 F_2 G_2 A_2 B_1 C$$

Dorian: 2.1.2.2.2.1.2.
$$D_2 E_1 F_2 G_2 A_2 B_1 C_2 D$$

Phrygian: 1.2.2.2.1.2.2.
$$E_1 F_2 G_2 A_2 B_1 C_2 D_2 E$$

Lydian: 2.2.2.1.2.2.1.
$$F_2 G_2 A_2 B_1 C_2 D_2 E_1 F$$

Mixolydian: 2.2.1.2.2.1.2.
$$G_2 A_2 B_1 C_2 D_2 E_1 F_2 G$$

Aeolian: 2.1.2.2.1.2.2 (the natural minor scale)
$$A_2 B_1 C_2 D_2 E_1 F_2 G_2 A$$

EIGHT-NOTE SCALES: OCTATONICS

These scales symmetrically divide the octave into alternating tones and semitones and can either begin with a major second or a minor second:

2.1.2.1.2.1.2.1. (Eg. D $_2$ E $_1$ F $_2$ G $_1$ G# $_2$ A# $_1$ B $_2$ C#)   or
1.2.1.2.1.2.1.2.

There are also nine-note scales (nonatonics) and ten-note scales (decatonics). The blues scale is the most famous ten-note scale.

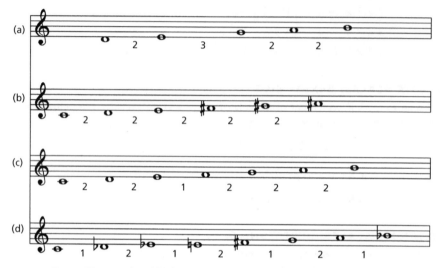

Figure 98: *Examples of (a) five, (b) six, (c) seven, and (d) eight note scales.*

PITCH FIELDS

A pitch field is a specified set of notes. Scales and modes are pitch fields but pitch fields are not necessarily scales. Some composers and theorists call them harmonic fields. It is possible to build a pitch field consisting only of minor thirds. This means the interval order would be 3.3.3.3.

Many composers combine intervals to form complex pitch fields. 3.4.1.3.4.5.1.6.2.7 for example means that after the first note has been defined the intervals are then calculated according to this pattern of semitones in ascending order. On a musical stave, if the first note were a low F, the pitch field 3.4.1.3.4.5.1.6.2.7. would be:

7 Bb-F
2 Ab-Bb
6 D-G#
1 C#-D
5 G#-C#
4 E-G#
3 Db-E
1 C-Db
4 Ab-C
3 F-Ab

Figure 99: *Pitch field based on 3.4.1.3.4.5.1.6.2.7.*

All of the above examples are based on the Western equal-temperament system but the octave can be divided into different intervals according to other systems. There are many composers who have pioneered this work, one of the most famous being the American composer Harry Partch (1901-74). Partch designed and built his own instruments based on different scales. Warren Burt (b. 1949) is an Australian composer who has pioneered alternative pitch systems. He has written pieces for various sized tuning forks tuned to a nineteen-note system, computer programs and voices. *39 Dissonant Etudes* (1993) and *Three Inverse Genera* (1989) are two examples.

6 MELODIC ORGANISATION: A SUMMARY AND CATALOGUE

Chapter 16 showed that a texture consists of strands which may be a sound event or a melody. Melody is the horizontal sequencing of notes which form an identifiable structure. There are many types of melodic structure. Melodies consist of small units which may include all or some of the following: phrases, motifs, repeating or varied patterns, cells or formulas and ornamentation. Melodies can be repetitive, continuously varied, sectional, evolutionary, brief or very long.

There is no single approach to melodic writing. In some traditions, such as the Indian raga or the Gregorian chant, elegant continuous melodic structures are built up from set patterns or motivic formulas which are varied and extended. In many popular songs, melodies consist of sequences of motifs or phrases combined to form a memorable structure. Melodies can be based on harmonic progressions, such as the period form; or organic structures in which phrases expand and contract over a drone within a modal scale.

Register is an important contributor to structural coherence in melodic writing with the use of expansion and contraction of pitch space. Melodies are either conjunct or disjunct. Conjunct melodies use a succession of pitches stepwise whereas disjunct melodies consist of wide intervallic leaps.

There are many devices for developing melodies. Variation, in which some aspect of the melody's structure is changed, usually through continuous variation or varied repetition, is probably the most common. Exact repetition is also common. In many folk cultures melodies are built from a repeating motivic unit or pattern which is extended or reduced. Renaissance vocal music explores structural variations such as inversion (playing the piece upside-down), retrograde (playing it backwards), retrograde inversion; and augmentation and diminution techniques (extending or reducing the rhythmic values based on rhythmic proportions).

Timbre, through the use of klangfarben or articulation, has been recognised as an important contributor to the formal design of melody.

The sections of this book relevant to melodic organisation are listed below.

ACTIVITIES

Compose or improvise a melodic line using articulation to create clarity.

Compose or improvise a melody in which register is important to the structure or phrases.

Compose or improvise a melodic line consisting of regular phase lengths.

Compose or improvise a melodic line consisting of irregular phrase lengths.

Compose a melodic line which expands or contracts a set of melodic formulas or rhythmic cells.

Create a melody in which the phrases create a sense of opening and closure.

7 TRANSFORMATIVE PROCESSES

IT'S ALL IN THE MOVEMENT

In many pieces of music there are moments of stability and instability. Sometimes the unstable periods are extreme and intense; at other times the shifts and transformations are very subtle. There are many processes that cause these changes. These are just a few:

REPETITION

Repetition is one of the most fundamental of musical processes and can be used to develop material in new areas. Repetition can be the exact repetition of a musical idea. However, exact repetition can have surprisingly varied effects. Depending on the context, exact repetition can be disruptive. For example, a continually repeating pattern makes the listener focus more on the pattern than its relationship to previously heard music. The overall continuum of music is suspended and the listener experiences a different concept of time as the music repeats on itself, becoming cyclical. In some music the continual repetition of a motif is used to great advantage, creating a new interest in the way the repetitions are perceived. In nineteenth-century European music, repetition is often treated as subtle variation. This is called VARIED REPETITION. Too much repetition can shorten the life span of a motif. In popular music if a catchy phrase is repeated too often it becomes predictable. In some other styles of music the predictability of a repeated phrase is essential to its meaning. In dance music, the dancers depend on the repeating rhythm.

Exact restatements of musical phrases are fundamental to 1960s repetition music. This is especially apparent in the music of the American minimalist composers. In their music, repetition is a material into which change is gradually introduced.

VARIATION

The process of variation is another fundamental of musical design. In one sense, anything can be made to be a variation of something else: one can always find a relationship between two things, no matter how different they may seem. However, it is the relationship between the variation and the original that makes a piece of music interesting. Variation can be achieved by pitch, rhythm, dynamic, register or structure. In fact nothing is excluded, which is why it is such a powerful technique.

In Renaissance and Baroque music, the main form of variation is melodic, based on contrapuntal principles. Fragments of melodies are played backwards, upside down or repeated and extended. In early classical music, such as the first movement of Mozart's Piano Sonata in A major, K 331 (1778), the style of variation is primarily elaboration. The melody is enriched with ORNAMENTAL additions or rhythmic transformations which, while, changing the surface of the music, preserve the structure of the melody. However, for Beethoven, variation became a powerful weapon upon which a composer could develop FORMAL STRUCTURES. In his *Diabelli Variations* (Op. 120) he built sections of music from one minute idea of the theme. While preserving the harmonic structure of the original melody, he would transform each variation section with incredible inventiveness. The later Romantics developed CONTINUAL VARIATION in which a melodic line undergoes subtle evolutions. In continual variation, a rhythmic pattern is never repeated without subtle variation. Schoenberg, in the early twentieth century, developed continual variation further with INSTANTANEOUS VARIATION. Here a melodic or rhythmic idea is suddenly transformed by some aspect hidden within the original (see for example, his Op. 19 Nos 1 and 4). It may be a pitch, rhythm or melodic fragment. Exact repetition is avoided; everything is variation.

TRANSFORMATION

Transformation is a process by which something changes its form. In music this becomes apparent when the listener perceives a change in his or her awareness. Variation is a common technique for creating transformations. They can be gradual and subtle or eruptive and volatile. An instantaneous transformation takes the least significant aspect of one musical texture to build another out of this minute element, like a quantum leap from one texture to another.

REDUCTION AND EXTENSION

Reduction transforms a musical statement by reducing it to its simpler elements. It can be applied to melody, rhythm or textural blocks. Extension transforms by the addition of material. Instead of making exact repetitions, these techniques contribute to a process of varied repetition process.

Figure 100: *(a) Reduction and (b) extension.*

INTENSIFICATION

Intensification is an important process which is usually the first step in transformation. It can use dissonant harmonies, increased loudness, reduction in register or increased rhythmic values.

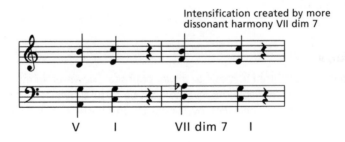

Figure 101: *Intensification.*

SATURATION

The total filling out of a musical space is called saturation. This can be achieved by including all the notes in the octave or the maximum activity possible in a rhythm. Saturation inevitably signifies a change in the musical texture or its perception.

Figure 102: *Saturation.*

EXPANSION AND CONTRACTION

Expansion and contraction are usually associated with register shifts. A melody occupying the space of a major second might suddenly expand to encompass the interval of a tenth.

Figure 103: *Expansion of register.*

Figure 104: *Contraction of register.*

INVERSION

Inversion is the term used in music to mean 'opposite'. However, in music opposites are not always clearly identifiable. An inversion can be textural, registeral, timbral, melodic or rhythmic: a high register becomes low, bright timbres become dark, loud dynamics become soft.

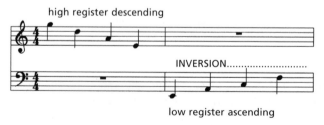

Figure 105: *Inversion.*

SYMMETRY

A symmetrical structure is one that is repeated. It could multiply itself or use a point of reflection. There are many approaches to symmetry in music.

Harmonic symmetry is created when the interval between the first and second notes of a three-note group is the same as the interval between the second and third notes so that the second note becomes in effect a mirror or axis point (Figure 106 a). Melodic symmetry is based on the same principle: each note of the melody is mirrored around an axis point (Figure 106 b).

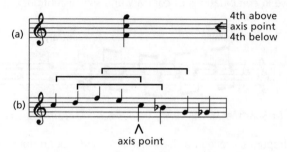

Figure106: *(a) Harmonic and (b) melodic symmetry.*

Rhythmic symmetry is created when a set of rhythmic values is inverted around a central axis point. These are called non-retrogradable rhythms.

Figure 107: *Rhythmic symmetry.*

Symmetry by repetition is created when a pattern is repeated exactly or the length of the pattern is the same as the original. For example, four-bar phrases create symmetry even if the rhythms within the phrases are different.

Figure 108: *Four bars of equal length creating symmetry.*

8 COUNTERPOINT, CONTRAPUNTAL THINKING AND TIME

Traditionally, counterpoint is the craft of placing notes against each other (*counter* – against, *point* – note). Counterpoint is also about the movement of parts. There have been numerous texts written about counterpoint through the ages but they all agree on two fundamentals. In counterpoint,

1 something moves in relation to something else; and
2 the parts move in combinations of contrary and similar motion.

Figure 109: *Movement of parts in similar and contrary direction.*

Numerous contrapuntal procedures have been devised around duration and pattern or combinations of both. Durational techniques involve proportional relationships in which one part moves with a different rhythmic value to another such as 1:2 (Figure 110); a set of fixed rhythmic values used freely (Figure 111) or according to a rule called a canon (Figure 112). In Figure 112, part two follows part one a crotchet later.

Figure 110: *Proportional relationship based on duration (1:2).*

Figure 111: *A set of rhythmic values used freely.*

Figure 112: *Two melodies in canon.*

Pattern techniques can produce very elegant structures using simple transformations such as mirroring (playing the piece upside down), inversion (playing it upside down and transposed) and retrograde (playing it backwards).

Figure 113: *Mirror transposition: part 1 is mirrored around 'e' to produce part 2.*

Figure 114: *Inversion: part 1 is mirrored then transposed down a major third creating part 2.*

Figure 115: *Retrograde: bar 2 plays bar 1 backwards.*

The combination of these fundamental techniques can produce the most elaborate and intricate music and it forms the basis of most of the Western world's written repertoire from the thirteenth to the eighteenth centuries.

However, counterpoint is not limited to notes. Much of the music written in this style since the late eighteenth century has included other parameters such as dynamics and orchestration. Beethoven's music, for example, necessitates an acknowledgment of dynamics even though his use of harmonic language is the more complex aspect. It is the interplay between these various elements that gives the work its structural meaning. See Special Topic One, Chapter Thirteen.

The rise of electronic and computer music in the twentieth century has necessitated a complete review of the meaning of the word counterpoint. No longer is counterpoint defined by notes against notes. Sounds against sounds or sounds with sounds, texture and new timbres are now included in the paradigm; movement is created by the metamorphosis or juxtaposition of events. Counterpoint now means the process of moving sound events within a defined musical space. These processes include transformation, complementation, juxtaposition, simultaneity, expansion and contraction. It is for this reason the term 'contrapuntal thinking' is preferable to counterpoint. The term counterpoint has become synonymous with an historical application of a set of principals involving notes and durations.

9 GENERATIVE PROCESSES

The generation of music based on a process is an important approach to composing. This requires some rule or game plan to which the composer adheres in order to generate new musical ideas, patterns, structures, etc. The aim is to deliberately produce unpredictable outcomes and ways of hearing sound events. Many styles of music have been generated by these procedures, including deterministic methods such as serialism, experimental music and indeterminacy.

DETERMINATE MUSIC

Determinate music is generated from a set of rules. The medieval canon is one such example: each part is derived from a set of rules administered by the leading part (called the *dux*) or a composer's direction such as 'play backwards at the same time' or 'transpose a fifth above the original part'. Serialism is a more recent example of determinate music. In this system a pattern of numbers is applied to pitch, rhythm, dynamics, instruments, etc. Stockhausen's *Kreuzspiel* (1951) and Pierre Boulez's *Structures I* (1952) are two early examples.

If the series C D E B F♯ G♯ D♯ A♯ F C♯ G A were translated into a number series based on semitone distances away from the note C it would become 0 2 4 11 6 8 3 10 5 1 7 9:

0	(0 semitones from C = C)
2	(2 semitones from C = D)
4	(4 semitones from C = E) etc.

This provides harmonic variation and consistency at the same time. Another series could use numbers to represent rhythmic values such as semiquavers rather than pitch. Messiaen adopted this approach in *Quatre Etudes de Rhythme* in the third movement: 'Mode de valeurs et s'intensités' (1949).

Figure 116: *Sixteenth-note values associated with a number sequence.*

Once these numbers have been derived, a composer can generate a wide variety of note patterns such as playing the sequence backwards (Figure 117).

Figure 117: *Rhythmic sequence of Figure 116 reversed.*

Another possibility is rotating the pitches in which the first note becomes the last note of the sequence (Figure 118).

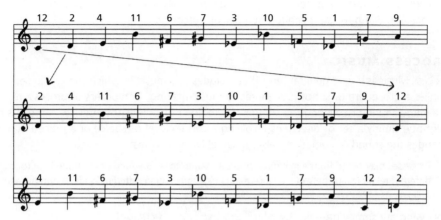

Figure 118: *Pitch rotations.*

TWELVE-TONE MUSIC

Twelve-tone music was a predecessor to Serialism devised by the Austrian composer Arnold Schoenberg (1871-1951). In this system, all the notes of the chromatic scale are used and ordered according to the qualities the composer wants to hear. The pattern of notes is called a row. Once the row has been established it can be played backwards or mirrored, in a similar way to the techniques discussed in counterpoint. The row provides the composer with a set of options which help to create a musically coherent structure (Figure 119)

Figure 119: *Original row and its inversion.*

INDETERMINATE MUSIC

Indeterminacy is a compositional procedure whereby a set of unknown results is created from known elements set in motion by random or chance procedures. In constructing an indeterminant structure, the overall sound can often be safely predicted, but the exact moment when anything happens cannot. For example, we can predict the quality of sound that will be produced by a room full of people whispering, but exactly when each person whispers is not important to the texture.

There are many approaches to indeterminate music, both simple and complex. Indeterminate works can be notated with a series of directions such as 'Play as fast as possible in the highest register of the instrument' or, as in some of John Cage's works, with plastic transparencies marked with various shapes to be stacked randomly by the performer and interpreted according to criteria specified by the composer. Indeterminant procedures open up new ways of listening and thinking about the world. Whereas deterministic music is concerned with detail and formal shape, indeterminacy acknowledges that any composition can have an unlimited number of outcomes.

PROCESS MUSIC

Process Music is a very general term that includes any music in which the composer applies a procedure or set of procedures to music-making. Composers of process music are interested in discovering the sounds created by procedures they devise. A process piece might be simply a set of directions involving a certain level of choice or a procedure which changes the sound of something else. Michael Nyman writes:

> Processes may range from a minimum of organisation to a minimum of arbitrariness, proposing different relationships between chance and choice, presenting different kinds of options and obligations.[44]

Following are some strategies by which process music is created.

CHANCE PROCESSES

The number of ways chance can be introduced into the compositional process is limitless. For example, the wind can be used to activate wind chime instruments. The random gusts of wind produce tinkling notes which the listener appreciates in any order or rhythmic combination. Similarly random numbers from a telephone book can be used to determine vocal actions.

PEOPLE PROCESSES

People Processes allow performers to make musical actions based on their own abilities. It could use instructions such as 'Play as fast as possible' or 'In your own time, sing a certain number of notes' or ask the performer to improvise within a certain context.

CONTEXTUAL PROCESSES

Contextual processes require performers to make decisions based on a specific musical environment, such as to play three high notes when they hear particular sounds.

REPETITION PROCESSES

Repetition processes use repetition as a means of generating musical textures or structures. In these works gradual change is achieved by the subtle shifting of rhythms out of phase, creating a chorus effect or by slightly extending or reducing the length of a repeating rhythmic and melodic pattern (Figure 120).

Two people play the melodic pattern. After ten repeats, one player is to begin playing the same pattern starting on the second note. After ten repetitions of this combination, the other player begins on the third note of the pattern. Continue in similar fashion until both players arrive at the beginning simultaneously.

Figure 120: *Melody repeated to create phasing.*

ELECTRONIC PROCESSES

Electronic Processes depend on the presence of an electronic device such as a computer, synthesiser, tape recorder, microphone etc to transform a natural or found sound into an electronic sound.

ALGORITHMIC MUSIC

Algorithmic Music is a common approach to computer music, which uses a program to create indeterminate music according to a series of conditions such as 'If the sound is above middle C play loudly. If the sound is not above middle C, play with a *decrescendo*.'

FURTHER LISTENING

Twelve Tone Music

- Arnold Schoenberg, Piano Suite Op. 25 (1924).
- Anton Webern, Op. 27, Piano Variations (1936).

Rhythm and Number Sequences

- Olivier Messiaen, *Quatre Etudes de Rhythme*, 'Mode de valeurs et d'intensités' (1949).

Early Serialism

- Karlheinz Stockhausen, *Kreuzspiel* (1951).
- Pierre Boulez, *Structures* I (1952).

Indeterminate Music

- John Cage, *Variations* V (1965).
- Earle Brown, *Available Forms I* (1961) and *Available Forms II* (1962).
- Witold Lutoslawski, String Quartet (1964).
- Karlheinz Stockhausen, *Zyklus* (1959).

Music Based on Processes:

- Brian Eno, *Discreet Music* (1975).
- Terry Riley, *In C* (1964).
- Alvin Lucier, 'I Am Sitting in a Room' (1970).
- Paul Lansky, 'Six Fantasies on a Poem by Thomas Campion' (c.1981).
- Gavin Bryars, *The Sinking of the Titanic* (1975).
- Joel Chadabe, *Rhythms* (1981).
- Warren Burt, *Three Inverse Genera* (1989) on *Austral Voices: For Telegraph Wires, Tuning Forks, Computer-Driven Piano, Psaltery, Whirly, Cello, Synthesizer and Ruined Piano*, New Albion Records (1990).
- Greg Schiemer, 'Monophonic Variations' (1986) on *NMATAPE 6*, NMA Publications (1988).

1   Alan P. Merriam, *The Anthropology of Music*, Illinois: Northwestern University Press, 1964, p.63.

2   Alistair Riddell, Liner Notes, *Black Moon Assails*, NMATAPES 6, Melbourne: NMA Publications, undated.

3   Ian Croft and Donald Fraser, *A Dictionary of Musical Quotations,* New York: Schirmer Books (MacMillan, Inc.) 1985.

4   Quoted in Robert Morgan, *Twentieth Century Music*, New York: Norton, 1991, p.115.

5   J.H. Kwabena Nketia, 'African Music', AMSAC Newsletter 3 (March-April), quoted in Alan P. Merriam, *The Anthropology of Music*.

6   John Cage, Silence: *Lectures and Writings*, London: Marion Boyars, 1980, p.15.

7   John Fire Lame Deer, 'Lame Deer' in John Halifax, *Shamanic Voices: A Survey of Visionary Narratives*, New York: E.P. Dutton, 1979, p.74.

8   Bashō, *Haiku*, R.H. Blyth (trans.), 4 Vols, Tokyo: Hokuseido 1949–1952.

9   R. Murray Schafer, *The Tuning of the World*, New York: Knopf, 1977.

10 Walt Whitman, 'Song of Myself'.

11 John Cage, *Silence*, p.49.

12 John Cage, *Silence*, p.49.

13 Joseph Moran and Michael Morgan, *Meteorology: The Atmosphere and the Science of Weather,* 4th edn, New York: Macmillan College Publishing Company, 1994, p.318.

14 Joseph Moran and Michael Morgan, *Meteorology*, p.312.

15 Quoted in Robert Erickson, *Sound Structure in Music*, Berkeley and Los Angeles, California: University of California Press, 1975, p.23.

16 There are two approaches used in discussing the harmonic series. One treats the fundamental as the first partial with the second partial being twice the frequency of the first. The other system treats the second harmonic as the first overtone to the fundamental.

17 Allen Strange, *Electronic Music: Systems, Techniques, and Controls*, 2nd edn, Dubuque, Iowa: Wm. C. Brown Company Publishers, 1983, p.1.

18 For a more detailed discussion of instrumental classifications and the work of Mahillon, Hornsbostel and Sachs, see Margaret Kartomi, *On the Concepts and Classifications of Musical Instruments,* Chicago: University of Chicago Press, 1990.

19 Alice C. Fletcher and Francis La Flesche, 'The Omaha Tribe: Twenty-Seventh Annual Report of the Bureau of American Ethnology 1905–06', quoted in Alan P. Merriam, *The Anthropology of Music*, p.305.

20 Peter Spencer, *World Beat,* Chicago: A Cappella Books, 1992, p.40.

21 Alan P. Merriam, *The Anthropology of Music*, p.314.

22 Hildegard von Bingen, quoted in Sabina Flanagan, *Hildegard von Bingen: A Visionary Life*, London: Routledge, 1989, p.122.

23 Ros Bandt, *Sounds in Space: Wind Chimes and Sound Sculptures,* Camberwell: Victorian Arts Council of Adult Education, 1985, p.5.

24 Joseph Eger, 'The Audience Revolution: A Profession of Faith' in *Cultures,* Vol I, No. 1 'Music and Society', Paris: Unesco and la Baconnière, 1973, p.99.

25 Gil Evans, quoted in Joachim Berendt, *The Jazz Book*, Frogmore, St Albans, Herts: Paladin, 1976, p.93

26 Columbia CDCBS 62066. Musicians: Miles Davis (tpt), John Coltrane (ten sax), Cannonball Adderley (alto sax), Bill Evans (pf), Wynton Kelly (pf), Paul Chambers (bass), Jimmy Cobb (drums).

27 Margaret Fulton, *Cooking for Family and Friends*, Sydney: Angus and Robertson, 1993, p.52.

28 Margaret Fulton, *Cooking for Family and Friends*, p.187.

29 Robert Erickson, *Sound Structure in Music,* pp.46-7.

30 Fritz Winckel, 'Space, Music and Architecture' in Cultures, Vol 1, No.3, 'Music in a Changing World', Paris: Unesco and la Baconnière, 1977, p.139.

31 Jeanette Winterson, *Art and Lies*, London: Jonathan Cape, 1994 p.92.

32 Robert Erickson, *Sound Structure in Music*, 1975, p.139.

33 Ernest Nagel, 'Space and Geometry' in J.J.C. Smart (ed.), *Problems of Space and Time*, New York: Macmillan, 1964, p.183.

34 John Cage, *Silence*, p.49.

35 The categories of single, hierarchical and multiple strands used in this chapter are an adaptation of the terminology used in Chapter 1 of Jeanne Bamberger and Howard Brofsky's *The Art of Listening*, 5th edn, New York: Harper & Row, 1988, which provides a comprehensive complement to the topics discussed in this chapter.

36 J.N. Findlay, 'Time: A Treatment of Some Puzzles' in J.J.C. Smart (ed.), *Problems of Space and Time*, p.354.

37 Henri Bergson, 'Duration and Intuition' in J.J.C. Smart (ed.), *Problems of Space and Time,* 1964 pp.139–140.

38 Giuseppe Steiner, 'Recipe for Simultaneous Ice-Cream', in Filippo Tommaso Marinetti (ed), *The Futurist Cookbook*, Milano: Longanesi, c. 1986.

39 Edgard Varèse, quoted in Chou Wen-chung, 'The Liberation of Sound: Edgard Varèse' in *Perspectives of New Music*, Vol 5, 1966.

40 Edgard Varèse, quoted in Chou Wen-chung.

41 Robert Erickson, *Sound Structure in Music*, p.47.

42 Jacques Attali, *Noise: The Political Economy of Music,* (trans. Brian Mussumi), Manchester: Manchester University Press, 1985, p.133.

43 Michael Brown, quoted in *Electronic Musician* magazine, 1995.

44 Michael Nyman, *Experimental Music: Cage and Beyond*, New York: Schirmer Books,1974, p.3.

listening examples

1   *Black Moon Assails,* Alistair Riddell
2   *The Sink,* Graeme Leak
3   *The End,* Manrae
4   *M'saddar,* anonymous
5   'Cymbal and Water', Ros Bandt
6   Water Dreams, Paul Dresher
7   *Vltava,* Bedrich Smetana
8   'Sinous', Rik Rue
9   'Postiche', Amanda Stewart
10 *Overlapping Crescendo,* Richard Vella
11 Demonstration of drum registers
12 *Cut to the Chase,* Richard Vella
13 Guitar solo played by Jason Zadkovich
14 Piano Sonata Op. 31, No. 1 in G major, Ludwig van Beethoven
15 Demonstration of changing instrumental timbres
16 Demonstration of a fundamental tone plus overtones
17 Demonstration of prepared piano sounds
18 *The Naked Kiss,* Andy Arthurs
19 'Ecce Dominus', Gregorian Chant
20 *Lascivious Serenade,* Edward Primrose
21 *La Nanete,* François Couperin
22 Demonstration of harpsichord combined with percussion
23 *The Naked Kiss,* Andy Arthurs
24 Drumkit Improvisation
25 *Tango,* Richard Vella
26 *Dark Matter,* Jim Denley
27 *Genesis,* Andy Arthurs
28 Example of a piano played from the inside
29 *Fantasy Island,* Andy Arthurs and Philip Chambon
30 *Orchid,* Greg White
31 *Splinter,* Jon Drummond
32 'Hodie Christus Natus Est', anonymous
33 Church bell from Margherita Piazza, Venice, recorded by Trevor Pearce
34 Wind Chimes recorded by Herb Jercher
35 'Ocean Bells', Ros Bandt
36 *Spectral Dance,* Greg Schiemer
37 Vocal demonstration of staccato
38 Vocal demonstration of legato
39 Sonata in C, K545, Third Movement, Wolfgang Amadeus Mozart
40 Vocal demonstration of pitch bends
41 Trombone melody using pitch slides
42 *Asp 3,* Brigit Burke and Rainer Linz
43 *Isis,* Chris Blackwell
44 'Kyrie', *Missa L'homme arme,* Josquin des Prés
45 *Cadences, Deviations and Scarlatti,* Elena Kats-Chernin, performed by the Sydney Alpha Ensemble
46 'This Old Man', traditional
47 Symphony No. 5 (opening), Ludwig van Beethoven
48 *Charisma,* Iannis Xenakis
49 *Fantasie,* Alistair Riddell

50   *Ave Generosa*, Hildegard von Bingen
51   *More Than Molecules,* Andy Arthurs and Philip Chambon
52   Symphony No. 5, 1st movement, Ludwig van Beethoven
53   Example of white noise
54   Symphony No. 3 *(Eroica)* Op. 55, 2nd movement, Ludwig van Beethoven
55   *Isis,* Chris Blackwell
56   *Ricercare a 6* (opening) J.S. Bach
57   'Eye of the Hurricane', Andy Arthurs and Philip Chambon
58   'Physic', Brigid Burke and Rainer Linz
59   *Allegro,* Concerto Grosso in A minor, Op. 6 No. 4, George Frederic Handel
60   *Icy,* Antoine Olivier
61   *Savannah Flyer,* Dennis Farnon
62   *Iyeya,* Vivien Ellis
63   'Persephone sleeps amidst the blossoms', Andrée Greenwell
64   Sonata in C, K545, 3rd Movement, Wolfgang Amadeus Mozart
65   'Oompah', St Crustacean
66   Demonstration of a common musical space created by metric organisation
67   Demonstration of common musical space created by gesture
68   Demonstration of an architectonic structure
69   *Ricercare a 6* (opening) J.S. Bach
70   Demonstration of unison and octave doubling
71   Demonstration of an alternating focus texture (call and response)
72   An example of a scale as a single line and then in parallel motion
73   'When I Was a Young Boy', Richard Vella
74   'High Up', Richard Vella
75   *If You Want Me,* Niqi Brown
76   *British National Anthem* (excerpt)
77   *Ricercare a 6* (opening) J.S. Bach
78   African Frame Drums
79   Demonstration of klangfarben on drums
80   Demonstration of vocal melody using disparate timbres sung by Monique Eichperger
81   Op.10, No.1, Anton Webern
82   'Auld Lang Syne' (traditional)
83   *Garden of Earthly Delights,* Liza Lim
84   Voice solo demonstrating a variety of timbres
85   '.' Amanda Stewart
86   *Peter's Piece,* Raffaele Marcellino
87   Demonstration of radio improvisation
88   Demonstration of non-metric stratification using organ accelerando and piano decelerando
89   *Convergence* (excerpt), Richard Vella
90   Thirteenth century Motet, anonymous, from the period of Petrus de Cruce
91   'Impermanence', 2nd movement, Robert Iolini, commissioned and produced for the Listening Room, ABC Classic FM
92   Six Studies on a Trombone Melody, No. 2, Richard Vella
93   Example of a homogenous texture: Demonstration of guitar distortion sound mass with backing band
94   Example of a heterogeneous texture: Building site and traffic sounds
95   Concertino, Elena Kats-Chernin (opening) performed by the Sydney Alpha Ensemble
96   Example of a mass of sound produced with drums
97   Layering of melodies to produce a sound mass
98   A sound mass created by heterophony

RICHARD VELLA

Richard Vella is a composer, music theatre maker and tertiary music education adviser. He has composed for a wide range of contexts and styles and his diverse output includes works for orchestra, large ensemble, choir, film, cable television, CD-rom, chamber music, opera and music theatre, dance and popular music genres. His work is performed nationally and internationally and has been included in many festivals. Many of his works are now recognised as set repertoire for specific instruments. He is artistic director of Calculated Risks productions, a music theatre company which has premiered three of his music theatre productions: *Tales of Love, The Last Supper* and *Bodysongs*. Formerly Professor of Music at La Trobe University, Victoria, Vella has held advisory professorial positions with the Tasmanian Conservatorium of Music, Hobart, Queensland Conservatorium of Music and Queensland University of Technology. Between 1992 and 1996 he implemented the innovative Music at Macquarie University Project by establishing undergraduate and postgraduate music courses within the School of Mathematics, Physics, Computing and Electronics. *Sounds in Space, Sounds in Time* is one of the successful outcomes from this program.

ANDY ARTHURS

Born in Cheltenham, England, Andy attended University of Surrey (UK) (1970-74) where he was the first person to gain a recording degree in the UK (BMus tonmeister). His professional career began at AIR studios, London (1971-75) working with the Beatles production team, and in particular producer George Martin. From 1975 he spent 15 years in the UK as a freelance recording producer, sound designer, composer and recording artist through the punk era etc. After working with John Cage and Merce Cunningham on the International Course for Choreographers and Composers in the UK, Andy began composing music for dance, which led to his forming the music, dance and multimedia group La Bouche with Phil Chambon and Lloyd Newson (1984-90). In 1991 with his partner Fiona Cullen he moved to Australia, subsequently having two children, Ella and Julian. He is Head and Professor of Music at Queensland University of Technology.